Wordsworth
and
Coleridge

WORDSWORTH AND COLERIDGE

The Making of the Major Lyrics 1802–1804

Gene W. Ruoff

RUTGERS UNIVERSITY PRESS

NEW BRUNSWICK, NEW JERSEY

Library of Congress Cataloging-in-Publication Data
Ruoff, Gene W.
  Wordsworth and Coleridge : the making of the major lyrics, 1802–1804 / Gene W.
Ruoff.
      p.   cm.
  Bibliography: p.
  Includes index.
  ISBN 0-8135-1398-7   ISBN 0-8135-1399-5 (pbk.)
  1. Wordsworth, William, 1770–1850—Criticism and interpretation.   2. Words-
worth, William, 1770–1850—Influence—Coleridge.   3. Coleridge, Samuel Taylor,
1772–1834—Criticism and interpretation.   4. Coleridge, Samuel Taylor, 1772–
1834—Influence—Wordsworth.   5. English poetry—19th century—History and
criticism.   6. Romanticism—England.   7. Dialogue.   I. Title.
PR5888.R86 1989
821'.7—dc19   88-28292
                                                                     CIP

THIS IS FOR LAVONNE

Contents

a

Acknowledgments

THIS book would not have been possible without the support and assistance of a number of institutions. I should first thank The University of Illinois at Chicago for a range of support that may bear ampler testimony to the length of time my book has taken than to its ultimate value. My time has been freed by a sabbatical leave, by a short research leave underwritten by the Graduate College Research Board, and by a fellowship of the Institute for the Humanities. The Research Board also contributed to travel for research in manuscript collections in both the United States and England and to the cost of reproducing manuscript materials. I am also grateful for a Grant-in-Aid from the American Council of Learned Societies, which assisted materially in defraying my research expenses.

I have had the pleasure of conducting archival research in some of the most welcoming environments imaginable: the Wordsworth Collection, Olin Library, Cornell University; the Pierpont Morgan Library, New York; the Newberry Library, Chicago; the British Library, London; and the Wordsworth Library, Grasmere, which is the spiritual home of all scholars of Wordsworth and Coleridge.

Although I have tried scrupulously to record my use of the labors of other scholars, citation is not enough for some obligations. Every-

one who reads this book will see that I stand on the shoulders of
Mark Reed, for his monumental work in establishing Wordsworth's
chronology, and Kathleen Coburn, for her equally arduous work with
Coleridge's notebooks. I have made copious use of the editions of
Wordsworth correspondence begun by Ernest de Selincourt and carried forward by Allan G. Hill, Mary Moorman, and Chester Shaver,
as well as the edition of Coleridge's letters by Earl Leslie Griggs. My
beginning work on the poetic texts I explore was grounded in the
early research of Jared R. Curtis, and I have been able to profit in the
closing stages of my work from the superb editorial work of both
Curtis and Stephen Maxfield Parrish, which has come into print in
time to save me from many errors.

Wordsworthians and Coleridgeans are a gregarious bunch. I have
profited from both continuing and fugitive conversations with many
of the scholar-critics who have worked this or adjoining patches of
ground. They include Jerome Christensen, Stuart Curran, George
Dekker, Paul Fry, Alan Grob, Michael Jaye, Theresa Kelley, Thomas
McFarland, Paul Magnuson, Lucy Newlyn, Samuel E. Schulman,
Clifford H. Siskin, L. J. Swingle, Robert and Pamela Woof, and
Jonathan Wordsworth.

Other debts are more specific: from its inception, J. Robert Barth,
Kenneth R. Johnston, Karl Kroeber, and Peter Manning helped me
plead the cause of this project before various tribunals (just and unjust). In fact, Karl Kroeber may be to blame for my having under-
taken this study at all, because I wrote my first graduate paper on
the Immortality Ode for him at a time when he was too young and
too kind to discourage me sufficiently. Peter Manning, on the other
hand, may take credit for whatever he finds right about the book,
because he read parts of it piecemeal and then provided an exhaustive
reading for the press when I brought myself to let it go. I have also
profited greatly from full and wise readings of the manuscript by
Don H. Bialostosky and Marshall Brown.

Various colleagues past and present at UIC have listened to me
talk about this project, read and heard snatches of it, and offered so
many suggestions that it may seem to them a departmental rather
than individual publication. They don't all get footnoted, but they
include Michael Anania, Jonathan Arac, Beverly Fields, John Ed-

ward Hardy, Clark Hulse, Howard Kerr, Michael Lieb, Ned Lukacher, Leah Marcus, Lawrence Poston, and Gerald Sorensen. My administrative assistant at the Institute for the Humanities, Linda Vavra, has cheerfully done much of my work as well as her own as I have stolen time in the final stages of preparing my manuscript. The Institute has probably been the better for my mental absences.

Although no sections of this work have been published previously, I have learned much from the discussions following presentations at a number of forums. Sections have been presented at the UIC Institute for the Humanities, at the University of Washington, at Marquette University, at the University of Wisconsin in Madison, and before the Wordsworth-Coleridge Association.

My editor at Rutgers University Press, Leslie Mitchner, has been unfailingly supportive of my work, and she deserves a gold medal for prodding and goading, with a high degree of difficulty. Stuart Mitchner performed miracles as my copyeditor and helped to make the experience of refining the final manuscript into a family project.

I have saved the best for last: my wife and colleague in romanticism, A. LaVonne Brown Ruoff, nurtured me all the while this work was in progress, and her practiced eye for my idiosyncracies has greatly improved my work. My many obligations to her are expressed in my dedication.

Note on Texts

TEXTS of the major works under consideration head my central chapters, and each chapter begins with an account of the difficulties involved in establishing a text. My versions are fair copies, which make no attempt to record internal corrections and revisions. Readers who want more detailed textual information are directed below to the appropriate sources. Where my versions differ slightly from those of Jared R. Curtis and Stephen Maxfield Parrish, who have saved me from countless misreadings, I am probably in error. But like most scholars who have spent time in archives, I am partial to my own mistakes.

Wordsworth's Ode of 1802

A conjectural reconstruction of Wordsworth's work of March 1802, which is lost. Text based upon the earliest surviving manuscript, DC MS. 44 (also known as *Prelude* MS. M), by permission of the Dove Cottage Trust, Grasmere, Cumbria. See Curtis, *Poems, in Two Volumes, and Other Poems, 1800–1807* (Ithaca: Cornell UP, 1983), 360–73, for a facsimile and transcription of the manuscript.

Coleridge's Verse Letter

Text based on "A Letter to ————. April 4, 1802," DC MS. 39, by permission of the Dove Cottage Trust. See Parrish, *Coleridge's Dejection: The Earliest Manuscripts and the Earliest Printings* (Ithaca: Cornell UP, 1988), 77–93, 107–31, for a facsimile and transcription.

Wordsworth's "The Leech-Gatherer"

Text based on DC MS. 41, by permission of the Dove Cottage Trust. See Curtis, *Poems, in Two Volumes*, 316–23, for a facsimile and transcription. Also see Curtis, *Wordsworth's Experiments with Tradition: The Lyric Poems of 1802* (Ithaca: Cornell UP, 1971), 186–94, for conjectural reconstructions of some of the stanzas lost from the manuscript.

Wordsworth's "Resolution and Independence"

Text based on Coleorton Papers, MA 1581, courtesy of the Trustees of The Pierpont Morgan Library, New York, New York. See Curtis, *Wordsworth's Experiments with Tradition*, 187–95, for a transcription.

Coleridge's "Dejection"

Text based on *Morning Post*, 4 October 1802, 2–3. See Parrish, *Coleridge's Dejection*, 98–100, for a facsimile.

Wordsworth's Ode of 1804

Text based on DC MS. 44, by permission of the Dove Cottage Trust. See Curtis, *Poems, in Two Volumes*, 360–73, for a facsimile and transcription.

Abbreviations

BL   *Biographia Literaria.* Ed. James Engell and W. Jackson Bate. 2 vols. Vol. 7 of *The Collected Works of Samuel Taylor Coleridge.* Princeton: Princeton UP, 1983.

CD   *Coleridge's Dejection: The Earliest Manuscripts and the Earliest Printings.* Ed. Stephen Maxfield Parrish. Ithaca: Cornell UP, 1988.

CEY   Mark Reed. *Wordsworth: The Chronology of the Early Years, 1770–1799.* Cambridge: Harvard UP, 1967.

CMY   Mark Reed. *Wordsworth: The Chronology of the Middle Years, 1800–1815.* Cambridge: Harvard UP, 1975.

CNB   *The Notebooks of Samuel Taylor Coleridge.* Ed. Kathleen Coburn. 3 vols. to date. New York: Pantheon Books, 1957–.

CO   Markham Peacock. *The Critical Opinions of William Wordsworth.* Baltimore: Johns Hopkins UP, 1950.

CPW   *The Complete Poetical Works of Samuel Taylor Coleridge.* Ed. Ernest Hartley Coleridge. 2 vols. Oxford: Clarendon P, 1912.

Dekker   George Dekker. *Coleridge and the Literature of Sensibility.* New York: Barnes & Noble, 1978.

DWJ   *Journals of Dorothy Wordsworth.* Ed. Mary Moorman. New York: Oxford UP, 1971.

EY   *The Letters of William and Dorothy Wordsworth: The Early Years, 1787–1805.* Ed. Ernest de Selincourt, rev. Chester Shaver. Oxford: Clarendon P, 1967.

Heath   William Heath. *Wordsworth and Coleridge: A Study of Their Literary Relations in 1801–1802.* Oxford: Clarendon P, 1970.

HG   William Wordsworth. *"Home at Grasmere": Part First, Book First of "The Recluse."* Ed. Beth Darlington. Ithaca: Cornell UP, 1977.

LB   *Wordsworth & Coleridge: Lyrical Ballads.* Ed. R. L. Brett and A. R. Jones. London: Methuen, 1963.

MY   *The Letters of William and Dorothy Wordsworth: The Middle Years.* 2 vols. *Part I, 1806–1811.* Ed. Ernest de Selincourt, rev. Mary Moorman. *Part II, 1812–1820.* Ed. Ernest de Selincourt, rev. Mary Moorman and Alan G. Hill. Oxford: Clarendon P, 1969–1970.

P2V   William Wordsworth. *Poems, in Two Volumes, and Other Poems, 1800–1807.* Ed. Jared R. Curtis. Ithaca: Cornell UP, 1983.

Prelude   William Wordsworth. *The Prelude, 1799, 1805, 1850.* Ed. Jonathan Wordsworth, M. H. Abrams, and Stephen Gill. New York: W. W. Norton, 1979.

Prose   *The Prose Works of William Wordsworth.* Ed. W. J. B. Owen and Jane Worthington Smyser. 3 vols. Oxford: Clarendon P, 1974.

PW   *The Poetical Works of William Wordsworth.* Ed. Ernest de Selincourt and Helen Darbishire. 5 vols. Oxford: Clarendon P, 1940–1949.

RC&P   William Wordsworth. *"The Ruined Cottage" and "The Pedlar."* Ed. James Butler. Ithaca: Cornell UP, 1979.

STCL   *Collected Letters of Samuel Taylor Coleridge.* Ed. Earl Leslie Griggs. 6 vols. Oxford: Clarendon P, 1956–1971.

WET   Jared R. Curtis, *Wordsworth's Experiments with Tradition: The Lyric Poems of 1802.* Ithaca: Cornell UP, 1971.

Wordsworth
and
Coleridge

"*. . . It seemed to me, as I read this page, that I had read some of these words before, and some phrases that are almost the same, which I have seen elsewhere, return to my mind. It seems to me, indeed, that this page speaks of something there has been talk about during these past days. . . . But I cannot recall what. I must think it over. Perhaps I'll have to read other books.*"

"*Why? To know what one book says you must read others?*"

"*At times this can be so. Often books speak of other books. Often a harmless book is like a seed that will blossom into a dangerous book, or it is the other way around: it is the sweet fruit of a bitter stem. In reading Albert, couldn't I learn what Thomas might have said? Or in reading Thomas, know what Avveroës said?*"

"*True,*" *I said, amazed. Until then I had thought each book spoke of the things, human or divine, that lie outside books. Now I realized that not infrequently books speak of books: it is as if they spoke among themselves. In the light of this reflection, the library seemed all the more disturbing to me. It was then the place of a long, centuries-old murmuring, an imperceptible dialogue between one parchment and another, a living thing, a receptacle of powers not to be ruled by a human mind, a treasure of secrets emanated by many minds, surviving the death of those who had produced them or been their conveyors.*

—ADSO, RECALLING A CONVERSATION WITH BROTHER WILLIAM OF BASKERVILLE, IN *The Name of the Rose* BY UMBERTO ECO

1

Introduction

*A*LTHOUGH methodological introductions are obligatory for studies that remap frequently explored literary territory, they risk diminishing their nominal subjects into occasions for the exercise of a critical mode. Because this introduction shares that danger, it is essential to declare immediately the importance of its subjects of study. This work addresses six early texts of three works which have long since become icons of English-speaking culture: William Wordsworth's "Ode: Intimations of Immortality from Recollections of Early Childhood" and "Resolution and Independence" and Samuel Taylor Coleridge's "Dejection: An Ode." Through processes of cultural codification and appropriation now approaching two centuries in length, these three poems are firmly established as canonical works: necessary for an understanding of their authors, necessary for an understanding of their age, necessary for an understanding of poetry in English.

A study which proposes a fresh examination of such works has one advantage. It does not have to establish the significance of its subject in the way that a book of similar length on Wordsworth's "Sonnets on the Punishment of Death" or Coleridge's epitaphs might be expected to do. It suffers from disadvantages as well. One is that all three poems come to us bearing generations of cultural encoding, which began as early as their authors' retrospective accounts of their origins. In the case of Coleridge, only a few months elapsed between his writing of the Verse Letter to Sara Hutchinson and his first revisionary accounts of his intentions in it.[1] As these or any other poems have become canonical, perhaps even as a crucial part of their becoming canonical, they have also become implicated in larger cultural arguments which may once have been only peripheral to them, and they have acquired cultural lives quite apart from their textual lives. For example, it is hard for any of us to separate our renowned works from our great commentaries upon them, and this cycle of poems has attracted more than its fair share of powerful critical voices. Geoffrey H. Hartman has observed this phenomenon, likening those "interpretive solutions stabilized by the gravitational field of a well-known poem" to "a ring of cosmic junk around planets."[2] Finally, and perhaps contradictorily, studies of canonical works face the specter of critical exhaustion, the fear that commentary has at last achieved its dark dream and explored the poems so fully that no one will ever have to look at them again. Unless I misread the tones of Karl Kroeber and Max F. Schulz in their overviews of recent criticism of these poems, there is an undercurrent of concern that, with honorable exceptions, the remarkable critical explosion of the past decade and a half has not radically altered or greatly improved our understanding of them.[3] I am inclined to agree, but I think the cause for the exhaustion may be attributed more to our methods of analysis than to any exhaustibility of the texts themselves.

In what remains of this introductory chapter, I will talk about four intertwined issues: the origins of this book, its evolving intentions, its form and methodology, and its often uneasy relations with current criticism of Wordsworth and Coleridge. My work is located firmly within the romantic paradigm it explores. To borrow Clifford H. Siskin's clinical and less than complimentary diagnosis of the dominant mode of romantic commentary, this is a "developmental tale": fascinated by origins it knows it can never reach, as given to the explanatory mode of analytic narrative as *The Prelude* itself, and fond of psychologization as an explanatory device.[4]

On the other hand, the study contains little except its old-fashioned global procedures—diachronic organization and chapters with titles that do not themselves require explication—to comfort those who are content with mainstream understandings of the writings of the romantic poets. To some it will seem a work written under the sign of suspicion rather than celebration. It is as skeptical about the existence of stable authorial character as it is about the ability of literary biography to recover or recreate it. It traces writing rather than creation, and it views writing as a socially constrained rather than individually autonomous act. It readily grants poetic discourse those obvious rhetorical and formal characteristics which mark its differences from spoken or written prose, without any belief that either the use or end of language within poetic discourse is radically different. Within these pages figurative language is granted its effects but allowed no miracles. The study consequently does not rely for its explanations on such terms as *imagination, organic unity*, or *natural supernaturalism*, and (with apologies to Crazy Jane and the Bishop) it generally avoids the sole/soul/whole/hole complex of academic romantic discourse. While assimilating many basic understandings of post-structuralist discourse, it neither adopts those languages nor attempts to create its own. Neologisms have surely crept in, and where they have passed unremarked or seemed useful or inoffensive, they have been allowed to remain.

The table of contents provides a clear map of the study, which is a cumulative serial commentary on six verse texts, long known to be intimately related:

1. Wordsworth's fragmentary Ode of late March 1802;
2. Coleridge's "A Letter to ———, April 4, 1802.—Sunday Evening";
3. Wordsworth's "The Leech-Gatherer" of early May 1802;
4. Wordsworth's revised poem on the leech-gatherer, later entitled "Resolution and Independence," of June-July 1802;
5. Coleridge's "Dejection. An Ode, Written April 4, 1802," as published in the *Morning Post* on 4 October 1802;
6. Wordsworth's completed Ode, c. March 1804, which we have come to know as the Intimations (or Immortality) Ode.

In each chapter a full text of the poem is followed by commentary. No form of organization could appear simpler or more obvious. But it was not how my work on this poetic cycle began.

All readers of romantic literature should by now have become wary of such genealogies as we find embedded in Wordsworth's advertisement (1798) and prefaces (1800 and 1802) to *Lyrical Ballads* (and confusingly supplemented in Coleridge's alternative account in *Biographia Literaria*). We are also nervously aware of the playful or fictive genealogies which head works as diverse as "Kubla Khan," *Castle Rackrent, Waverley,* and *The Private Memoirs and Confessions of a Justified Sinner.* When romantic writers begin describing the origins of their tales, we check for our wallets, and we have become accustomed to constructing our own counter-tales from the best available textual evidence.[5] Readers of this book, for example, see before them more than a hundred thousand words, bounded at either end by lengthy chapters on the great Ode. They might with some justice assume that this book began as an essay on that poem which ran amok. The reverse is nearly true, because the work started in the middle. It began as an attempt to write a modest article of a stepchild kind, sources and analogues, on the influence of Robert Burns on "Resolution and Independence." It was, I thought with the confidence of relative youth, "a theme / Single and of determined bounds." That attempt, though, almost immmediately led into a consideration of relationships between the two early texts of Wordsworth's poem and, in rapid order, to the surrounding issue of their relationship to his and Coleridge's concurrent writings of the period. Burns began to shade into Coleridge, a phenomenon I found at first unsettling and then exhilarating. Unavoidable intertextual data kept disrupting my single theme, which could be kept single only by a willed exclusion of other resonances.

It became apparent that my task would have to become a more ranging genetic inquiry. Genetic method, Jonathan Arac has offered, is at the heart of Wordsworth's own poetic endeavor in *The Prelude.* In the *Biographia Literaria* it is also at the core of Coleridge's critical mission. Arac adds that genetic method was as much a philosophical project of Wordsworth's as our own historical moment: "In a usage that philosophers took up in the 1830s, to define something by describing the manner of its formation is to offer a 'genetic' definition."[6] Scholarship on Coleridge as well as Wordsworth offers plentiful manifestations of this impulse. Modern textual editing has scrupulously noted and preserved earlier variants of works, on the assumption that drafts and revisions help to explain the nature of the final text, and Ernest de Selincourt's publication in 1926 of a facing-pages edition of the "1805" and 1850 texts of *The Prelude* set commentary on that poem on a developmental track which is expanded to most of the poet's canon in the monumental work of all the editors of the Cornell Wordsworth Edition. Literary biography has always taken as its primary task revealing the origins of a writer's work in his life experience. And of course, that search for sources and analogues in the writings of others on which I originally embarked was, as Morris Dickstein has wittily observed, "a staple of the old historical and philological scholarship, which was gradually routed by the New Criticism but still leads a shadowy half-life in the lower depths of the caves of academe."[7] Its example continues, with less historical constraint and greater conceptual excitement, in the work of Harold Bloom and others on literary influence.

EDITORIAL PRINCIPLES AND TEXTUAL GENETICS

TO A REMARKABLE DEGREE, these ways for studying literary genesis—editorial, biographical, and influence studies—have been followed in isolation from one another. In demonstrating the need for a more capacious understanding of literary genetics, I will comment in order on the strengths and limitations of current study founded on these subdisciplines, beginning with editorial scholarship.[8] As we all realize, editorial procedures embody critical presuppositions, however murkily or subconsciously. Arac has observed the way in which an "industrial revolution in the American academic study of Wordsworth" over the past twenty years has fed upon a "powerful interplay of . . . fresh critical orientation and scholarly documentation," the latter culminating in but by no means limited to the Cornell Wordsworth project. Arac feels, for example, that adding the 1799 text of *The Prelude* to our canon has confirmed a continuing psychologization of critical perspectives on Wordsworth, as a private text has assumed, or been encouraged to assume, aesthetic as well as temporal priority over the vastly enlarged public text of 1850. We remain, he says, "fascinated by the explorations provoked by the interaction of

positivism and nihilism, the resonance of editorial with deconstructive rigor in our new literary genetics."[9]

A brief episode from the ongoing debate about the Cornell Wordsworth should clarify other issues in our current critical situation. It
is a family fight, and as is usual in such struggles, issues of right and
wrong are difficult to resolve. Reviewing in *The Wordsworth Circle*
James Butler's edition of "The Ruined Cottage" and "The Pedlar,"[10]
Jonathan Wordsworth was concerned that insufficient privilege had
been given to what he calls *Pedlar* One, the life story of the title
character as found in Dove Cottage MS. D of 1799. Butler had not
provided an edited "reading text" for the poem, thus denying it the
Cornell edition's equivalent of canonical status. Jonathan Wordsworth observes:

> It is almost as if there has been a conspiracy to deny the right
> of this earliest *Pedlar* to be a poem. Cornell editors are not well
> placed to take the view that a poem is a published text, as the
> edition was started in order to make available early versions which
> for one reason or another the poet decided not to print. It is pos-
> sible of course to fall back on the concept of "completeness"; but
> this is the age of the fragment, and in any case *Pedlar* One is
> formally quite as complete as many a Wordsworth poem. It
> stands—indeed has been standing—extremely well as a single
> unit. I can't myself believe that incompleteness would matter (I
> often prefer sketches to finished pictures) but at some level anxiety
> about the possibility of it seems to be implied in Mr. Butler's
> tendency to describe *Pedlar* One as "surplus passages about the
> Pedlar." The phrase has a sort of inaccurate precision. In copying
> into MS. D the lines her brother had excerpted from *The Ruined
> Cottage*, Dorothy left two gaps in her transcription; why she did so
> we cannot know, but the text reads smoothly on.[11]

James Butler responds in the same issue:

> [Jonathan Wordsworth's] "reservation" about my not presenting
> an edited reading text of early Pedlar passages in MS. D raises
> issues of importance not only to editors but to all teachers of Wil-
> liam Wordsworth. Editorial principles are not graven in stone in

Charlottesville—nor in Grasmere, Oxford, or Ithaca, for that matter—and the disagreement of reasonable editors can help to illuminate the poetry. . . . In thinking about whether there should
be an edited reading text of Pedlar MS. D passages in my volume,
I considered arguments such as those given by Mr. Wordsworth.
After all, another ten pages for a reading text meant little once the
book had grown to nearly five hundred pages. It seems to me,
however, that editors of early Wordsworth manuscripts have a particular responsibility not to "manufacture" works from passages;
that is, not to present something to colleagues and students *as a
poem* when it is a collection of surplus verse paragraphs. . . . If
there is "a conspiracy to deny the right of this earliest *Pedlar* to be
a poem," I am happy to play Cassius. . . . By all means let us
continue to teach those beautiful, important, philosophic Pedlar
MS. D passages. But let us also think about what the differences
are between overflow passages and something that only after extensive revision was thought of (at least for a time) as a poem. My
volume has complete sets of photographs, transcriptions, and variants of the overflow Pedlar passages. I decided not to produce an
edited reading text. I don't want my students or your students to
write on "Architectonics in *The Pedlar 1799*." (246)

This exchange has far-reaching implications, because it helps to illuminate what is happening in Wordsworth studies as a result of the
Cornell project.

Putting the problem as bluntly as possible, the availability of multiple texts has outrun the ability of our critical methods to assimilate
expanded textual data. Both Jonathan Wordsworth and Butler assert
the importance of something they call a *poem*, differentiating that
kind of composition from something they call *surplus* or *overflow* passages of verse. Both clearly agree that initial publication is not the
necessary test for a poem, nor does either argue that "completeness"
is a necessary condition. Jonathan Wordsworth grounds his argument
in custom and use: *Pedlar* One has been shown to be a poem because
it has been "printed, . . . anthologized, quoted, discussed, referred
to, and can hardly be thought not to exist." Because it can be and
has been read as a poem, it is a poem. Butler requires confirmation
by an author rather than his readers, and the MS. D passages reveal

to him no customary authorizing marks: they have "no title, no line numbers, no 'The End'," and there are two gaps in the manuscript. Butler does not deny the possibility that the verse passages may have formal features like internal consistency and at least relative closure. He doubts that these features are sufficiently *intended*, and he therefore feels the passages are inappropriate for certain kinds of critical analysis. He wants no studies of *architectonics*, no arguments from design, of this manuscript.

The debate crisply focuses unavoidable problematics of the Cornell project. On the one hand, its editors are scrupulous about recording the *processes* of Wordsworth's formation of his poetic canon and acknowledging the precise amount of reconstruction and conjecture that has gone into their editorial endeavors. On the other hand, the project feels obligated to bring forth editorial *products*, edited reading texts that are to be both intellectually and economically competitive with the published texts ordinarily incorporated into other scholarly editions. This productive emphasis of the Cornell project may unconsciously reflect both economic and critical pressures. Without the promise of new *poems*, would the edition have been commercially viable? Without the promise of new *poems*, could it have hoped to attract the critical efforts of scholars largely trained either to reproclaim or to subvert the holistic presuppositions of formalist commentary? One phrase rings through Jonathan Wordsworth's review—*a poem*—with modifications like "a finished poem," "one of the most important poems he ever wrote," and "a separate—and indeed, publishable—poem" (244, 245). Butler's response reinforces the importance of this aesthetic category, but denies to the lines in question the honor of presentation *as a poem*. Both positions articulate *a poem* as a stable object inhabiting a category of textual privilege, differentiated in its fixity from mere *verse*. Without their agreement that poems must be distinguished from other writings in verse, there would be no disagreement, which is in fact critical rather than editorial.

Because genetic commentary as I conceive it must be constantly aware of accomplished or impending change, it can have little commerce with understandings of poetic meaning endemic to formalist commentary, even though, ironically, those understandings are themselves strongly indebted to aesthetic principles later elaborated by Coleridge. Genetic commentary can continue to employ formalism's arsenal of analytic tools, the most useful of which were borrowed from rhetoric in any event, but it can never assume that a textual whole is self-enclosed and somehow greater than the sum of the parts, and it must be open to the possibility that parts can be more powerful than some wholes. The texts which head my chapters are not to be understood as *poems* in the sense meant by Butler and Jonathan Wordsworth, and the chapters which follow them do not argue from finite products to implied designs. I have not pursued the expedient of abolishing the word and substituting throughout the neutral *text*, because some linguistic cures strike me as being as bad as our diseases. The purposes of the chapters which follow are not only not evaluative, but not even, strictly speaking, interpretive. They might more accurately be characterized as writings about writings than as readings of works.

Most prior genetic studies of Wordsworth and Coleridge have been implicitly guided by the concept of textual privilege outlined above. They have two common storylines. The older is a story of progress, of early imperfect and fumbling efforts, often characterized as "conventional," which through growing artistic discipline and flowering genius result in a finished work which transcends conventions to become "original," or "great." In this story the verse leads to a poem. That this is our culture's canonical tale can be seen by a glance at the "Poems in Progress" sections from the *Norton Anthology of English Literature*. In volume two drafts and finished versions of romantic poems occupy more than half of the section. Wordsworth is represented by a five-stanza version of one of the Lucy poems, followed by the three-stanza received text derived from it, "She dwelt among th' untrodden ways." The footnote observes: "Simply by deleting two weak stanzas from this draft, and making a few verbal changes, Wordsworth converted a rather conventional poem into one of the great dirges of the language."[12] The summary of changes is accurate, but the dialectic of conventionality and greatness is a cultural construction. Just how a brief elegy which gestures both to vegetative assimilation ("A violet by a mossy stone / Half-hidden from the eye!") and to apotheosis ("Fair as a star when only one / Is shining in the sky!") has become less "conventional" remains a mystery.

Our more recent tale of textual change is a story of decay, in which brilliant original inspirations are subverted by fading imagination, messy personal problems, changing social allegiances, or failed nerve. Here a poem comes first, sadly to be followed by verse. The *Norton Anthology* seems more nervous about this tale. "The Two-Part Prelude of 1799" has disappeared from the most recent edition, and only substantial extracts from the 1850 *Prelude* now represent that work. But "The Ruined Cottage," taken from Dove Cottage MS. D (1799), continues to displace Book I of *The Excursion*. Here from the headnote is the core of the argument for that editorial decision: "The version in the first book of *The Excursion* . . . attempts to mitigate the impact of Margaret's sufferings . . . by attributing to her a Christian piety which is conventional rather than deeply realized. In the version reprinted here, we confront the bleak facts of 'a tale of silent suffering'—suffering which is undeserved, unrationalized, and irremissive" (Norton 2 : 178−79). Cultural assumptions present themselves plainly enough here, and we might note that "convention" is a weapon wielded by both parties. What would stand discussion is the willingness of the editors to eliminate, in favor of a manuscript which may have been seen by a couple of dozen readers in Wordsworth's lifetime, an extract from the sole long poem for which he was known. In recent years the tragic or pathetic version of the tale of textual change has been prevalent. I have tried to keep my discussions free of either inherited plot, artistic triumph or artistic decline, because they play no necessary or even valuable part in the study of textual genesis.[13]

LITERARY BIOGRAPHY

LITERARY biography has both fed and fed upon critical studies of textual change, providing their motivations and presuppositions as it incorporates its new data. Any sketch of Wordsworth's great decade, for example, now has to engage the relationship between the 1799 and 1805 texts of *The Prelude*, finding a way to incorporate those shifts into the larger arc it is tracing of the poet's career. The more literary a biographical study becomes—the more it bases its analyses on its readings of literary texts, instead of using them as roadsigns or decorative embellishments—the trickier its project becomes.

My examples here are from philosophical and psychological biography, two dominant modes in romantic studies. They are directly relevant because they turn upon attempts by Alan Grob and William Heath to use Wordsworth's and Coleridge's poetry of the period to reveal shifting metaphysical positions or psychological situations. Both are works which I admire greatly and from which I have learned directly as well as reflexively, although my present rhetorical occasion places an emphasis on the latter.

The first example is Alan Grob's outstanding study, *The Philosophic Mind*.[14] Grob follows the path charted by such scholars of Wordsworth's thought as Arthur Beatty, Melvin M. Rader, and Newton P. Stallknecht.[15] Actually, Grob seeks to reconcile an impasse between empirical and transcendental understandings of Wordsworth's thought by providing a historical framework for the poet's intellectual development. According to Grob, Wordsworth moved in his major works from an empirical phase, 1797–1800, through a transitional phase, centered in 1802, into a transcendental phase, beginning in 1804. Grob's chronological schema is not so rigidly enforced as it sounds in summary, and possibilities for overlap are subtly and appropriately noted. At or near the core of each section is a full exemplary reading of a central major lyric, "Tintern Abbey," "Resolution and Independence," and the great Ode, the last two of which are derived from important articles Grob had published in *ELH* in 1961 and 1965.

Grob's compositional history uncannily reflects Wordsworth's in *The Prelude*: two crucial "spots of time" are composed early, becoming retroactively key episodes in the overview of the growth of a poet's mind. The open question is the degree to which these readings and these poems, in addition to illustrating the pattern of Wordsworth's thought, have constructed it. Grob's opening sentence of his first chapter reveals the core of the biographical problem: "Of the poems of the initial phase, none seems more truly paradigmatic than *Tintern Abbey*." His *seems* is refreshingly honest, but it does not address the problem of the origins of our paradigms. Do we perceive or create them, or perhaps half-perceive and half-create? The issue is crucial to biographical study, because the selection of paradigms generates in turn the selection of supporting texts. To pick at the problem for just a moment, we might note that the second volume of *Lyrical Ballads* (1800) is represented in Grob's study by extensive (and superb) discussions of the Lucy and Matthew poems, while "The Brothers" and "Michael," which begin and end the volume, receive a sentence each. Would different rhetorical emphases have revealed or created different patterns? I am unable to offer a way out of this intertextual expansion of the hermeneutic circle, but historical study must begin to face the problematic it poses. My heuristic solution, perhaps my evasion or separate peace, is not to offer any texts as paradigmatic or characteristic representations of stable patterns of thought, but to select within the narrow temporal band of my study a broad range of utterances as points of reference, and to be at least as scrupulous of difference as I am of likeness.

My second example is also a work that is among the best of its kind, William Heath's *Wordsworth and Coleridge*.[16] Working without the enormous benefit of Mark Reed's *Wordsworth: A Chronology of the Middle Years, 1800–1815*, Heath produced a fine-grained study of two poets working in close creative tension in a period of their lives as rich in personal as in literary events. Wordsworth was coming to his decision to formalize his break with Annette Vallon so that he could marry Mary Hutchinson; his sister Dorothy was coming to terms with any changes her brother's marriage would bring about in their relationship; and Coleridge's ever-fragile marriage was suffering under the strains of his problems with his health, his addiction, and his desperate infatuation with Sara Hutchinson.

Heath saw the texts my work will be engaging as crisis lyrics, rather directly expressive reflections of two writers in psychic turmoil. In a phrase which has endured, he called the spring of 1802 an "elegiac spring," and was the first critic to pay extended attention to Wordsworth's and Coleridge's indebtedness to the conventions of the "spring elegy." In the case of Coleridge, Heath's claim has solid grounds: work toward "Dejection" was virtually all Coleridge accomplished in verse during that spring and even into late summer. In the case of Wordsworth, though, the fragmentary Ode and the poems on the leech-gatherer were virtually all Wordsworth wrote during the time that was clearly elegiac in tone. To a large degree, Heath also works back from the major poems of the period, determines over-arching anxieties within them, and conceives those anxieties as normative indices of the authors' psyches. He explains the poems in terms of a psychological crisis he has extracted from them. As my work will demonstrate, I am dubious of the reality of this "elegiac spring" and trace Wordsworth's work on these poems to other, less intensely personal sources.[17]

STUDIES OF INFLUENCE

HEATH'S work stands near the head of a growing phenomenon in romantic studies, the Wordsworth/Coleridge industry, which has increasingly devoted more attention to questions of mutual influence than to biography. Indeed, questions of influence problematize both Grob's philosophical and Heath's psychological projects, because they undermine fundamental assumptions of expressive poetics. Appearing in *Studies in Romanticism* in 1972, Thomas McFarland's classic essay, "The Symbiosis of Wordsworth and Coleridge," established a strongly influential pattern for understanding the simultaneously fructifying and debilitating relationship between the two poets. McFarland sketches a deep mutual interchange which inevitably generated extreme emotional and characterological tensions: the intellectual relationship of Wordsworth and Coleridge, he says, "was nothing less than a symbiosis, a development of attitude so dialogical and intertwined that in some instances not even the participants themselves could discern their respective contributions."[18]

Since Heath's book and McFarland's essay, the most valuable work appearing on any of the poems I am discussing has dealt increasingly with both writers. One splendid work somewhat outside the mainstream of romantic studies, George Dekker's *Coleridge and the Literature of Sensibility* includes an extremely important chapter on Wordsworth and Coleridge as "Blue Coat Boys," fellow-travelers in the 1790s of the cult of sensibility, in which he sees both "Dejection" and "Resolution and Independence" rooted.[19] Dekker's example is important, because more recent studies have, like McFarland's, concentrated intensely on waves of influence passing between Wordsworth and Coleridge without recording in detail the literary milieu in which they were both immersed. The degree to which Dekker's work remains unassimilated in the growing critical literature on the two writers' relationship suggests its resistance to more traditional forms of influence study.

Three recent studies include one or more chapters dealing with the interplay between Wordsworth and Coleridge in the Ode, "Resolution and Independence," and "Dejection." Jonathan Wordsworth's *William Wordsworth: The Borders of Vision* is perhaps the least elaborate and programmatic of the three, and to my mind suffers by an idiosyncratic concentration on what is either a dubious Wordsworth poem or a wonderful Wordsworthian parody, "The Barberry-Tree." But it does recast the spring of 1802 freshly and sanely, and my study shares its skepticism about the common understanding of this period as a time of crisis for Wordsworth.[20] Lucy Newlyn's treatment of the two poets' work in the spring of 1802 and Wordsworth's Ode of 1804 occupies nearly half of *Coleridge, Wordsworth, and the Language of Allusion*.[21] My study coincides with Newlyn's in a number of details, especially in its selection of significant illustrative texts. It differs markedly in its construction of the terms of the exchange between the poets and in its ultimate constructions of the central texts themselves.

My engagement with Paul Magnuson's *Coleridge and Wordsworth: A Lyrical Dialogue* is necessarily more extensive, because Magnuson proposes "a new methodology of reading their poetry as an intricately connected whole, of reading their works as a joint canon, and of understanding the generation of their greatest poetry."[22] Magnuson bases his conception of the interchange between the verse of the two poets in the growingly influential study of literary dialogics stemming from the work of Mikhail Bakhtin. While sharing Magnuson's admiration for Bakhtin's work, I do not see it as a way around Harold Bloom's view of the struggle of poetic generation. Magnuson offers a model founded on "turns of lyrical dialogue" as a replacement for Bloom's model of intense, anxious parody. While agreeing with Magnuson that many of the materials of poetic composition lie nearer at hand than the writings of titanic precursors, my reading of the lyric sequence sees parody as a fundamental device. Magnuson and I are engaging many of the same materials, but we are telling different stories. My greatest problem with Bloom's model for poetic generation, for which I have great respect, lies less in its psychodynamics than in its insistent elision of the present. To read Wordsworth's Ode as a strenuous contest with Milton's "Lycidas," as Bloom does in *A Map of Misreading* (1975), is to ignore both the fruitful tumult of events and texts of 1802–1804 and other resonances, perhaps equally or more meaningful, from other powerful writers of the past, including Spenser and Jonson. The extent to which Bloom's project disregards the accumulated offerings of more traditional scholarship on sources and influences ultimately reduces the value of his powerful intuitions.

I have tried to be generous with the patient, erudite historical scholarship which has helped us to situate the literary heritages of these texts. In the writings of both Bloom and the students of the Wordsworth-Coleridge relationship I have just discussed, secondary and tertiary resonances play little part, though more in Newlyn than in Jonathan Wordsworth, McFarland, and Magnuson. In some sections they are crucial to me, because they serve as a means of poetic triangulation, the most obvious example of which is Wordsworth's attempt in both "The Leech-Gatherer" and "Resolution and Independence" to address Coleridge through the figures of Burns and Chatterton. I have not incorporated all of the offerings of source scholarship because stories of genesis must finally be based upon critical selection. If my conjectures on influence are not monolithic, neither are they infinitely multiple.

Finally, my work on the lyric sequence differs from that of McFarland, Magnuson, Newlyn, and Jonathan Wordsworth in its more detailed attention to yet another important dimension of intertextuality—poetic genre. I have profited especially from the work of Dekker, already discussed in another context, from Jared R. Curtis's *Wordsworth's Experiments with Tradition* and Stephen Parrish's *The Art of "Lyrical Ballads,"* and from three recent works which have greatly expanded our perception of the importance of genre in poetry of the romantic period: Paul Fry's *The Poet's Calling in the English Ode*, Jeffrey C. Robinson's *Radical Literary Education*, and Stuart Curran's *Poetic Form and British Romanticism*.[23]

INTERTEXTUAL GENETICS

AS EVEN my brief survey has suggested, an adequate genetic criticism would have to understand a text as a confluence of diverse waves of influence. Any text has strong connections to its immediately preceding versions and to the prior body of a writer's work. It also has connections to a surrounding literary climate, which in the case of Wordsworth and Coleridge is embodied especially strongly but not totally in their mutual influence upon one another. A text's origins also must be seen in its relation to several different, often overlapping canons: a canon of relatively recent writing, against which a text will often attempt to demonstrate its individuality; a canon of classic writers and texts, in relation to which it can display a complete Bloomian repertoire of reflexive attitudes, as well as the non-Bloomian attitude of piety; and a canon of forms or kinds, which it will, often simultaneously, incorporate and transcend, or even repudiate. The complexity of intertextual genesis suggests why the individual strands of genetic commentary are so frequently carried out in isolation from one another. Critical awareness of this complexity is by no means of modern origin; as Peter Manning has reminded me, Shelley shows an awareness of all these elements of generative influence in his preface to *Prometheus Unbound*.

If I could offer a theoretical model for encountering these complexities, I would cheerfully patent it and license its use at nominal rates. I suspect, though, that the critical demands of intertextual study point finally to the inadequacy of theory. There can be no unified field theory of intertextual genetics, only examples of its practice, of which this book is one. Intertextual commentary has to operate by constructing narratives of influence, while never forgetting that they are constructions. A book which attempts to tell of the interconnected geneses of a number of texts is faced with further problems, because its understanding of one text, say the Ode of

1802, will condition its understanding of the texts of the remainder of the series. An eccentric construction can consequently be magnified a number of times in the course of the study. If I have placed a disproportionate emphasis upon the 1802 Ode's roots in erotic pastoral, my comments on the subsequent texts in the sequence will suffer as well. My commentary on each text involves a number of choices—in selection, in omission, in proportion—each of which in its turn generates the possibilities from which subsequent readings flow.

A sequential method, though, is not necessarily a topically or thematically consistent method. My lengthy discussions of the groundings of Wordsworth's Ode and Coleridge's Verse Letter in erotic tradition do not presage erotic readings of the first published "Dejection" or the Ode of 1804. My subject is precisely the ways in which the interrelations of the cycle of poems redirect them, so that topics which may have been primary in the poems' origins are submerged in later incarnations. My study of Wordsworth's hypothesized Ode of 1802, to cite the extreme example, is utterly devoid of philosophical or theological dimensions, while my study of the Ode of 1804 is as deeply immersed in these topics as most books specifically on Wordsworth's religion or metaphysics. In the process of completing it, Wordsworth tore his Ode free from the intertextual dialogue which generated it it, engaging instead a far different body of intertextual discourse. I make no argument that Wordsworth's philosophy changed, only that his poem changed radically. I have tried to suggest how and why it changed, but I have inferred no corresponding changes in the patterns of his thought.

Let me close this introduction with reflections on one final question about intertextual genetics. I have argued that I am involved in a constructive process which is at best highly problematical. While I have tried to honor historical evidence, my study makes no claims for the truth of its historical reconstruction. Mine is only one of a number of viable stories which have been or could be made from this sequence of texts. To put the question as baldly as possible, what then is the point of such a project?

The question cannot begin to be answered without some reconsideration of the function of poetry or literature generally, indeed of writing itself. My study is skeptical of all claims that literature provides access to some higher order of reality, that it presents truths unapproachable through other modes of discourse. It is equally skeptical of claims that literature is an expression of the unique personality, providing access to an authentic being. All literary expression is heavily mediated: by language itself, by intertextual filiations, by formal constraints, by cultural conventions, and by historical contingencies. It is less than reasonable to work from an assumption that such a contingent process can result in either formal or personal transcendence. I can understand why many writers have wanted to believe that it *can*, but I cannot understand why anyone who has ever written could believe that it *does*.

If we eliminate appeals to transcendent or subjective truth, literary expression loses much of its distinctiveness from other forms of verbal expression. This loss seems to me a gain. The central work of literature may finally be the construction of character, the presentation of a self rather than the representation of inner or outer reality. Its stories of the self are of course idealizations or fictions. The self which is made by a literary work is profoundly intersubjective, which is to say intertextual. Its relationship to prior textual selves is governed by the same kinds of forces which govern human growth, those which urge on the one hand total assimilation and conformity to a social community, and on the other complete individuation. In any psychological system, balancing these urges is at the heart of living, and this reconciliation is as much the ongoing work of adulthood as it is the formative work of childhood and adolescence. Wordsworth's Ode is as fully aware of this elemental issue as any poem in our language, and its central tableau, juxtaposing the socially imitative child against the heaven-born child, is so viscerally difficult to read that criticism has seemed to approach it wearing blinders. The purpose of literature suggested here is clearly anticipated by Bloom, whose work is self-limited by only two factors: its almost compulsive interest in poets rather than texts and its consequent inattention to or impatience with the more subtle, attenuated, heavily mediated strategies of adjustment that characterize adult discourse.

The work of criticism is an extension of the work of literature, existing in relation to the literary text much as that text exists in relation to prior and surrounding writings. Its social urge is for identity with the text, a kind of merging into its creation of a self which would result finally in simple identity and repetition. Its autonomous urge is to differentiate itself as fully as possible from the text, turning it into an object of study. This tension is very near the core of our present controversies about the study of romanticism. Ranged on one side are the powerful forces of assimilationist criticism, urging a surrender to the power of the self created through the literary text; on the other are variously grounded forces of resistance, arguing that eternal vigilance is the price of criticism's autonomy. In romantic studies this dialectic is complicated by a wonderful irony: assimilationist critics are apostles of the text as a manifestation of individual creative genius, while autonomist critics argue that the literary text is a product of psychological, social, and historical contingencies.

The challenge of criticism is to assist the literary text in fulfilling its constructive mission while not blinding itself to the consequences of those constructions. Of all the emerging critical modes, intertextual genetics is best placed to meet this challenge. Forming hypotheses about the making of texts requires wholesale immersion in them, a giving in to their often obscure and necessarily inferred motives which results in a full reimagining of the circumstances of their formation. Attending to the intertextual dimensions of literary emergence, though, keeps one deeply aware of the historically contingent aspects of literary creation, including all the psychological and cultural messiness of revisionism, about which Bloom writes so persuasively.

Accepting literature as a human construction entails accepting criticism as a human construction, driven by parallel motives. Critical writing is continuous with literature because, after allowances are made for its benevolent wishes to educate its readers and illuminate its subjects, its end is also the construction of an idealized, fictive self. Even the most basic rhetorical analysis of this introduction could establish the terms on which it establishes its ethical appeal. It wishes to present a self that is serious without being somber, intellectual without pretensions, knowledgeable without parading its erudition, judicious but not judgmental, critical but not ungenerous. Those who know its author will be as deeply aware as he of the distance between such an ideal and the reality. Like all other writing, this introduction has covertly gone about its less sublime human purposes as well. While scholarly documentation is a generic requirement, it also honors friendships, acknowledges and evades indebtedness, repays favors, and settles affronts, real or imagined. This human unseemliness critical constructions also share with literary constructions.

My central point is that constructions of the self matter, whether they are carried on in poetic or critical discourse. Practicing therapists know that our stories of the self are never neutral, and the power of psychotherapy may lie less in its ability to reveal truth than in its ability to assist dialogically in the revision of stories. Literary criticism has recently begun to credit and engage fully the power and prevalence of human fictions, those reductive scenarios of authority and dependence, of autonomy and influence, which shape human behavior. My study tracks an intricate poetic dialogue turning upon these very issues. The poems are a part of the central and permanent work of literature, which is the making of human being. My study aspires to share in some small way in that task.

2

Wordsworth's Ode of 1802

There was a time when meadow grove and stream
The earth and every common sight
    To me did seem
    Apparel'd in celestial light
The glory and the freshness of a dream   [5]
It is not now as it has been of yore
Turn wheresoe'er I may
    By night or day
The things which I have seen I see them now no more

    The Rainbow comes and goes   [10]
And lovely is the rose
The Moon doth with delight
Look round her when the heavens are bare
    Waters on a starry night
Are beautiful and fair   [15]
    The sunshine is a glorious birth
But yet I know where'er I go
That there hath pass'd away a glory from the earth

Now while the Birds thus sing a joyous song
   And while the young lambs bound   [20]
   As to the tabor's sound
To me alone there came a thought of grief
A timely utterance gave that thought relief
   And I again am strong
The cataracts blow their trumpets from the steep   [25]
No more shall grief of mine the season wrong
I hear the echoes through the mountains throng
The winds come to me from the fields of sleep
   And all the earth is gay
      Land and sea   [30]
   Give themselves up to jollity
   And with the heart of May
Doth every Beast keep holiday
   Thou Child of joy
Shout round me, let me hear thy shouts thou happy
             Shepherd boy   [35]

Ye blessed Creatures I have heard the call
Ye to each other make: I see
The heavens laugh with you in your jubilee
   My heart is at your festival
   My head hath its coronal   [40]
Even yet more gladness I can hold it all
   O evil day if I were sullen
While the earth herself is adorning
   This sweet May morning
And the Children are pulling   [45]
    On every side
In a thousand Vallies far and wide
   Fresh flowers: while the sun shines warm
And the Babe leaps up in his Mother's arm
   I hear I hear with joy I hear——   [50]
But there's a tree of many one
A single field which I have look'd upon

Both of them speak of something that is gone
    The pansy at my feet
    Doth the same tale repeat   [55]
Whither is fled the visionary gleam
Where is it gone the glory and the dream

HARD task to analyse a soul, in which
Not only general habits and desires,
But each most obvious and particular thought—
Not in a mystical and idle sense,
But in the words of reason deeply weighed—
Hath no beginning.
              PRELUDE (1798–99), 2.262–67

---

*T*HESE LINES, which well up in the midst of Wordsworth's first extended attempt to trace the development of his poetic character, might usefully preface every critical attempt to rediscover or recreate the genesis of a poem. Beginnings are invariably problematical. If the first words of a new poem obviously constitute a fresh start, they just as inarguably reach back into the personal and cultural past, intersecting a tangle of sources. Any definitive effort to separate and clarify such origins must seem, as Wordsworth had suggested a few lines earlier in this poem on his own life, the work of necromancy: "Who that shall point as with a wand, and say / 'This portion of the river of my mind / Came from yon fountain'?" (2.247–49).

My study has to face immediately the obscurity of origins. The text which precedes this chapter should be entirely in brackets, because it does not exist, even though critics have come to speak with some authority about what Wordsworth actually wrote in the spring of 1802. A work rash enough to venture a hypothetical text and examine it at length, though, would do well to explain its editorial reasonings. Dorothy Wordsworth records in her journal of 27 March 1802 that "At Breakfast Wm wrote part of an ode" (*DWJ* 106). A series of circumstances confirms the probability that the poem begun on this date is the one we have come to call the Immortality Ode: Wordsworth cannot be shown to have been working on any other ode around this time; he had begun working on "To the Cuckoo," which bears a strong thematic relationship to the Ode, during the same week (*DWJ* 105–6); he had begun "My Heart Leaps Up," with which he was to associate the Ode in his collected edition of 1815, on the preceding day; and the fair copy of Coleridge's first version of "Dejection," "A Letter to ———," containing what are unquestionably direct responses to lines from the early stanzas of the Ode, bears the date 4 April 1802. (See *CMY* 156, for a concise survey of the evidence on the dating of the Ode.) Neither this evidence nor Dorothy's only other reference to the poem, 17 June 1802, stating that "William added a little to the Ode he is writing" (*DWJ* 137), can pin down just what or how much of the poem Wordsworth wrote in late March. No manuscript has been discovered which can be dated before March 1804, *Prelude* MS. M (Dove Cottage MS. 44), which is the basis of the text presented.

Nevertheless, a plausible text for the beginning stages of the Ode can be constructed on the basis of external as well as internal evidence. The most important external evidence is found in Wordsworth's comments about the poem to Miss Isabella Fenwick in 1843: "This was composed during my residence in Town-End, Grasmere; two years at least passed between the writing of the first four stanzas and the remaining part" (*PW* 4:463). Although the Fenwick notes are occasionally compromised by misrecollections on Wordsworth's part, and indeed in this case his dating of the poem as 1803–6 is clearly in error, his memory of the stages in which the poem developed is not at all hesitant; he does not offer the first few stanzas or early parts of the poem as work of an earlier period but rather a concrete number—the first *four* stanzas. Perhaps emboldened by Wordsworth's misdating of the poem, textual scholars have not accepted his statements about its evolution unequivocally. Jared Curtis finds it "still problematical whether any more stanzas were added at this time" (*WET* 164), and Mark L. Reed, less cautiously than is his wont, remarks of Dorothy's notation of continuing work on the Ode (17 June 1802) that the "amount is uncertain, but possibly includes some or all of stanzas V–VIII" (*CMY* 180).

Curtis wants more of the Ode to have been composed in 1802 than he can demonstrate, partially because he wants to confute those simplistic notions about the Ode's thematic and structural disjunctions which have been the scarcely legitimate progeny of the Fenwick note. He points out rightly, for example, that the crisis of the poem, the "lowest ebb from which the poet must turn himself," comes not at the end of the fourth but the eighth stanza, and that stanzas I–IV and V–VIII consequently have more in common with one another thematically than with the rest of the work (*WET* 114–15). However infrequently realized, this observation can tell us no more of the compositional history of the poem than Curtis's ensuing stylistic analysis, interesting and valuable in itself, which attempts covertly to establish the first eight stanzas as the work of one period.

Nowhere does Curtis or any other commentator until Paul Magnuson properly engage the one piece of external evidence which can delimit Wordsworth's efforts on the poem in the spring of 1802, Coleridge's verse letter to Sara Hutchinson.[1] On the day after Wordsworth began the Ode, he and Dorothy left to spend several days with Coleridge (*CMY* 156–58). Coleridge's first reading or hearing of Wordsworth's fragmentary poem resulted directly in his extended lamentations to Sara, which exist in two fair copies, both probably roughly contemporary and differing only slightly. Although an extended study of the ways in which Coleridge's poem engages Wordsworth's is matter for the next chapter, the extent of its engagement is relevant now. Coleridge's text speaks directly to Wordsworth's six times. I follow here the order in which the allusions appear. Reviewing the heavenly vista he has been observing, the western sky, clouds, stars and crescent moon, Coleridge writes: "—I see them all, so excellently fair! / I see, not feel how beautiful they are" (42–43). If his attempt to find meaning in this catalogue of objects reprises the second stanza of Wordsworth's Ode, the lines I have cited take up Wordsworth's renewed emotional response to the idyllic spring scene of stanza IV, "Even yet more gladness I can hold it all" (41). Indeed, Wordsworth's later revision of this line into "The fullness of your bliss I feel it all"² may acknowledge the sharpened distinction Coleridge had drawn between seeing and feeling. Coleridge's second allusion is more direct. Anticipating Wordsworth's marriage to Mary and Sara Hutchinson's joining the Wordsworths in "one happy Home, / One House, the dear *abiding* Home of All" (134–35), Coleridge says that on that occasion "I too will crown me with a Coronal" (136). Here the reference is once again to Wordsworth's expression of joy in the springtime frolicking of birds, lambs, and children: "My heart is at your festival / My head hath its coronal" (39–40). Coleridge's next allusion takes up the line from Wordsworth's first stanza which had signaled the change in his perceptions, "It is not now as it has been of yore": "I am not the buoyant Thing, I was of yore" (227). Coleridge's fourth allusion echoes the beginning of Wordsworth's poem:

> Yes, dearest Sara! Yes!
> There *was* a time when tho' my path was rough,
> The Joy within me dallied with [?Di]stress;
> And all Misfortunes were but as the Stuff
> Whence Fancy made me Dreams of Happiness.
>   (231–35)

Here Coleridge's engagement with Wordsworth's text is complex and ambiguous; if he is implying that Wordsworth is himself dallying with distress in the opening of his Ode, Coleridge's golden time becomes nearly identical to the present which Wordsworth is lamenting. In Mary's fair copy of the verse letter the lines read "E'er I was wedded, tho' my path was rough, / The joy within me dallied with Distress" (*CD* 122; 231–32), and the allusion is lost. Speaking at lines 290–91 of his diminished emotional response to "These Mountains . . . , these Vales, these Woods, these Lakes, / Scenes full of Beauty & of Loftiness / Where all my Life I fondly hop'd to live," Coleridge concludes his verse paragraph by echoing the line which ends Wordsworth's first stanza: "They are not to me now the Things, which once they were" (295). Coleridge's final allusion is an extended rereading of the beginning of Wordsworth's fragment: he intensifies the garment metaphor underlying Wordsworth's "apparel'd in celestial light" (4), treating dress as an extension of the self ("Our's is her Wedding Garment, our's her Shroud" [298]), thus suggesting a source for the light which has vanished: "Ah, from the Soul itself must issue forth / A Light, a Glory, and a luminous Cloud / Enveloping the Earth!" (302–4).

All of Coleridge's echoes are of Wordsworth's first four stanzas. Coleridge makes nothing of the heaven-born child or his pre-existence, nothing of the journey from God to earth, nothing of the self's journey westward and inland, and nothing of the stages of human existence through which Wordsworth depicts the way the celestial light is lost. In order to believe that Wordsworth had composed any of stanzas V–VIII of the Ode in the spring of 1802, during which he was in such frequent contact with Coleridge, we would have to believe in a Coleridge who had heard or read these lines without reflecting them in any way—not in his verse letter, not in his revised versions of "Dejection," not in his journals, and not in his correspondence. Because such a Coleridge is a simple impossibility, we can safely conclude that none of these stanzas is the work of 1802, and that the history of the composition of the Ode was much as the poet remembered it in 1843.

Delimiting the extent of the Ode in 1802 still does not justify using the four stanzas as they appear in 1804 as the work of the earlier period. This decision is based on the nature of the stanzas themselves and the way they have behaved in subsequent textual revisions. Stanzas III and IV of the Ode have produced the most extensive body of ingenious commentary to be found anywhere in studies of the poet. The "thought of grief" (22) has been variously conjectured, as has the "timely utterance" which "gave that thought relief" (23). The lines seem so elliptical as to cry out for elaboration: what kind of grief? When did it come? What was the utterance? A poem? A proverb? The simple act of articulating the grief? The sounds of the springtime scene? Such puzzles are rare in Wordsworth, who does not often indulge in the perverse delight of making bewildered readers guess his referent. This problem of reference, as Geoffrey Hartman has called it, also afflicts the most notorious crux of the stanza, the line "The winds come to me from the fields of sleep" (28). It seems, as Hartman says, "a periphrasis that should yield a

proper name, perhaps of a place as mythic as the Elysian fields."[3]
The problem here is that performing a substitution, replacing the
vague phrase with "the Elysian fields" or any other which has been
conjectured, does not cause the line to have any more definite meaning within its immediate rhetorical context. The problems created
by the vagueness of the references in stanza III have their counterpart
in the conclusion of stanza IV, which suffers from an over-specificity,
or perhaps more properly, an unearned specificity. The turn from the
gaiety of the spring landscape which dominated the first two-thirds
of the stanzas is brought about by messages conveyed in some way
by "a tree of many one, / A single field which I have look'd upon"
(51–52) and "The pansy at my feet" (54), all of which remind the
poet of his earlier sense of loss. But why these singular things, and
what, particularly, is the "tree of many one?" The first four stanzas
of the Ode make up fifty-seven lines in MS. M, six of which constitute
interpretive cruces. Such a proportion cannot be matched anywhere
else in the poet's work.

As a fair copy compiled to provide the departing Coleridge with
the bulk of the verse Wordsworth had written since *Lyrical Ballads*,
MS. M preserves very few earlier readings. Although it was designed
to be authoritative and at least semi-public, as anything given to
Coleridge would invariably be, the manuscript was hardly set for
publication. Poems in it would be expected to be subject to further
revision, and they were. The Ode of MS. M is succeeded by the version in the printer's copy for the 1807 *Poems in Two Volumes* (MS. L),
by the first printing composed from that manuscript, by the revised
version in the first collected edition of 1815, and by the versions of
the successive collected editions. The text of the poem as a whole
does not reach the state in which we commonly encounter it until
1837. The most striking feature of the textual history of the poem is
what happens to its problem-laden first four stanzas—almost nothing. Certain phrasings will change: the "I see them now no more" of
MS. M (9) will become "I now can see no more" in MS. L; the "Even
yet more gladness I can hold it all" of MS. M (41) will be deleted in
MS. L, which adds "The fullness of your bliss, I feel it all," expanded
into "I feel—I feel it all" in 1807; and the children "pulling" (45)
flowers in MS. M will begin "culling" them in 1807.

While Wordsworth is making only minor changes in the first four stanzas of the Ode, none of which addresses any of their most troubling obscurities, stanzas V—XI undergo considerable and substantial revision. The text of stanzas I—IV seems privileged in a way that the text of V—XI is not. Indeed, strong textual privilege in the works of Wordsworth, a chronic reviser, is rare in itself. My best guess is that the first four stanzas became, for all practical purposes, frozen in the very early stages of the development of the poem, probably because of their complicity in the poetic dialogue I am tracing. Having generated Coleridge's anguished response in the verse letter, they could not in good faith be retracted or greatly altered, whatever their obscurities. They became a given upon which the poet had to build, and we may take them as work of 1802 with reasonable security.

The questions at the end of Wordsworth's fragment of 1802— "Whither is fled the visionary gleam / Where is it gone the glory and the dream" (56—57)—may by their very open-endedness have diverted attention from the pervasive indeterminacies which mark all four stanzas. The work of this phase falls into two unequal and only obliquely related segments. The first two stanzas are extremely general. They trace a change in perception which is apparently both chronic and universal, stressing alternately an indeterminate time when the material world seemed "Apparel'd in celestial light" (4) and a present which is marked only by its absence of vaguely delineated perceptual qualities: "The things which I have seen I see them now no more" (9) and "there hath pass'd away a glory from the earth" (18). Considering how closely the Ode will come to be associated with the lore of childhood, it is striking that nothing in these stanzas establishes childhood as that time which possessed "The glory and the freshness of a dream" (5).[4] Because the stanzas do not name the deep past which they reverence and lament, they could stand for any preceding age, and the break which separates them from the present could have resulted from almost any kind of crisis. In both their generality and in the polar distinction which they draw between states of being, the two stanzas recall one of Wordsworth's most richly problematical earlier lyrics, "A slumber did my spirit seal." I invoke "A slumber" not as a source but only to stress that the change lamented in the Ode could be the result of any number of things, including the death of a loved one or the frustrations of a broken love affair, and that the time separating its states of bliss and loss could as easily be one year as thirty. The closest we come to identifying the blessed time is in the line, "It is not now as it has been of yore" (6). This archaic locution, grafted from legendary or primordial history onto the life of an individual, suggests intensity of alienation as much as chronology. Before following one of the preoccupations of modern commentary, attempting to decide whether the completed Ode is about growing up or growing old, we should note that in 1802 it was not demonstrably about either.[5]

The uneasy generality of the first two stanzas is compounded by the absence of scenic specificity. If we follow M. H. Abrams in viewing a fixed place and time, a locale and an occasion, as the ordinary starting points for what he calls the greater Romantic lyric, the Ode hardly qualifies for the genre.[6] The reader is given nothing like the landscape which becomes the occasion for the meditations of "Tintern Abbey" or the locales which generate Coleridge's remarkable conversation poems. Because Wordsworth's first two stanzas lack the locale and occasion so prevalent in his and Coleridge's extended lyrics, they also lack the sense of conditionality common to their works. We are not led to believe that we are following the fluxes and refluxes of a singular mind on a certain occasion, meditating upon life as the scene before it suggests. The stanzas announce the operations of a mind that has gone beyond its situation and observed carefully and repeatedly ("Turn wheresoe'er I may / By night or day" [7–8], "But yet I know where'er I go" [17]) a change in the way in which it experiences the outer world. Readers attentive to the persistent conditionality of Wordsworth's lyric voice will find little in the first two stanzas of the Ode to suggest that things are not precisely as they appear.[7] The first two stanzas appear to describe a general syndrome, rather than a specific and perhaps reversible crisis. Their abstract and objective quality is enhanced by the rhetorical security with which they move. Identical in length, the stanzas progress without hesitation toward the bleak alexandrines which conclude them. If the loss which the opening stanzas trace has not been assuaged, it is at least rhetorically ordered and formally contained.

The remainder of the Ode of 1802 provides an occasion and setting absent in the introductory stanzas. The "Now" which introduces stanza III beckons specific events rather than describing a state of the spirit:

> Now while the Birds thus sing a joyous song
>   And while the young lambs bound
>   As to the tabor's sound
> To me alone there came a thought of grief
> A timely utterance gave that thought relief
>   And I again am strong.
>
> $(19-24)$

The relationship of these events to the state of being previously described is unclear. Is the thought of grief to be taken as the substance of the first two stanzas? Perhaps, but the very generality of those stanzas would seem to argue against their having been the result of a momentary vacillation of the spirit. Or is the thought of grief a sudden and acute accession of sorrow which somehow descends beneath the understanding of chronic loss presented earlier? The poem offers us no more help in understanding these questions than it does in determining the timely utterance which brings the speaker relief. What is clear is that the rapid cycling from a joyous landscape through depression to relief and strength jars oddly against the careful control and distance of the then-and-now structure of the poem's beginning. We cannot know whether we are dealing with two manifestations of a single phenomenon, with two discrete phenomena linked only by similarly depressing emotional effects, or with a phenomenon within a phenomenon.

As the poet draws strength from his surroundings, its extended sensory description coincides with his growing recovery:

> The cataracts blow their trumpets from the steep
> No more shall grief of mine the season wrong
> I hear the echoes through the mountains throng
> The winds come to me from the field of sleep
>   And all the earth is gay
>   Land and sea
>   Give themselves up to jollity
>   And with the heart of May

Doth every beast keep holiday
  Thou Child of joy
Shout round me, let me hear thy shouts thou happy
  Shepherd boy.

                              (25–35)

This catalogue, for it is more list than scene, develops interestingly.
The rigidly end-stopped pentameters of the first four lines, each of
which is syntactically complete, give way to the enjambments within
the couplets which conclude the stanzas (30–35). The rhymes occur
in lines of unequal measure, and the verse seems to grow in freedom
and suppleness as the thought of grief is overcome. The pattern of
figuration in the passage is similarly transformed. We move from
vigorous personifications of the inanimate cataracts and echoes,
through that orphic and all but unreadable locution, "The winds
come to me from the fields of sleep" (28), in order to return to the
mild and overarching personification—nature as festival—with
which the stanza had begun before the thought of grief intervened.

Where stanzas I and II move toward concluding formulations,
stanza III does little more than recover from a diversion. Its opening
line, "Now while the Birds thus sing a joyous song" (19), could lead
directly into the concluding address of the poet, "Shout round me,
let me hear thy shouts thou happy shepherd boy" (35). The stanza is
largely improgressive and its termination arbitrary. The poet's address to the fellow celebrants of the "Child of joy" is enjambed into
and dominates the first two-thirds of the concluding stanza of 1802.
An address to a specific child might promise to lend itself to a movement toward a more firmly delineated landscape than the poem has
given us to this point. Instead, the joyous aspects of nature are por-
trayed ever more expansively. The land and sea which had earlier
given "themselves up to jollity" (31) are joined in the next stanza by
the laughing heavens (38). The concluding description of "This
sweet May Morning" (44) has "children . . . pulling"

    On every side
  In a thousand vallies far and wide
    Fresh flowers: while the sun shines warm
  And the Babe leaps up in his Mother's arm.

                              (46–49)

The "Shepherd boy" (35) is multiplied into the children at play in a thousand valleys, who themselves merge into the even more capacious generic figures of Babe and Mother.

You can find your way from Dove Cottage to Michael's fields, to the site of the Wishing Gate, or even to the location of the four fraternal yews of Borrowdale. But you will not find the festive valleys of the Ode marked in your walking guides, however imaginative they sometimes are. Nor will local historians offer to identify for you the child-children-babe of stanzas III and IV. The locale and its characters are clearly the stuff of literature alone, inherited from converging traditions discussed later in this chapter. It is tempting to surmise that the center of Wordsworth's ecstatic mood cannot hold precisely because it is so conventional in conception and expression, borrowed from generations of creations which either ignored perception or honored it but fleetingly. Unfortunately for such analysis, the elements which interrupt the poet's joyous address seem equally literary in their origins:

> But there's a tree of many one
> A single field which I have look'd upon
> Both of them speak of something that is gone
> > The pansy at my feet
> > Doth the same tale repeat
> Whither is fled the visionary gleam
> Where is it gone the glory and the dream.
> > > (51–57)

The "tree of many one" derives its power from invoking the fatal tree of Eden (Genesis 2:9, 16–17) and imparts a sense of Edenic loss to the tale told by itself, the "single field" and "pansy at my feet." The objects which speak of loss point back toward the first two stanzas, marking the first return to their topics since their conclusion. And even here the return is indirect. Tree, field, and pansy may surely be subsumed under "every common sight" (2), but then what could not be? The "glory and the dream" repeat directly the locutions of stanza I, while "visionary," which qualifies "gleam," lends an individualized mystical or prophetic edge to the "celestial light" of the beginning of the poem.

In rhetorical development stanza IV is even more fragmented than stanza III, which had been broken early and repaired by its end. Wordsworth's address to the creatures of the fields contains little hint of its subsequent inadequacy. It builds to a pitch of frenzied repetition—"I hear I hear with joy I hear" (50)—only to collapse abruptly under the pressure of remembered perceptions which have not previously figured in the poem. The stanzaic logic established early on has been destroyed by the end of Wordsworth's efforts of 1802. In form as well as theme, the Ode of this period may best be described as a fragment of enormous latent power. Its inability or refusal to specify the time of vanished glory, to reconcile expressions of chronic and acute depression, to justify its adoption of inherited pastoral and Edenic topoi, to make meaningful its obscure locutions, and to make functional formal irregularities which are striking even within the licensed freedoms of the higher ode, all conspire to endow it with a compelling sense of fecundity. The stanzas appear to open out in all directions, suggesting more than they can possibly articulate. Further, they have a fecundity quite different from that of other germinal passages in Wordsworth.

In reading the early drafts of *Prelude* materials, we are most frequently struck by the power of their singularity and specificity. In the first extant version of "There was a boy" in MS. JJ, we are led to wonder what general observations about human life and perception may radiate from this strongly remembered scene. The power of such fragments resides in images and scenes so strongly realized that they need—indeed allow—only the most rudimentary kind of incorporation into a larger thematic or narrative structure. The power of the Ode of 1802 resides instead in its topics. Its grandeur of generality leads the mind in two directions: we are of course concerned with its tendency, where it is going, and what it is doing; but because it remains so steadfastly an exercise in symptomatology, we are led even more strongly to question the sources of its affective power, literary as well as experiential.

Of the immediate origins of the Ode in Wordsworth's canon there is little dispute. The stanzas of 1802 appear to spring from a series of short lyrics, "To a Butterfly," ("Stay near me!"), "To a Cuckoo," and "Extempore" ("My heart leaps up"), all begun within a fortnight and all treating of relationships between adult and earlier experience.

The last of these, composed the day before Wordsworth began work on the Ode (*DWJ* 106), has virtually become absorbed into the larger poem by virtue of the poet's decision in 1815 to use its three concluding lines as the Ode's epigraph in his first collected edition.[8] Conflation of the two works had distorted our responses to both of them. When the lines "The Child is father of the Man; / And I could wish my days to be / Bound each to each by natural piety" (*PW* 4:279) precede the Ode, they identify its time of lamented glory as the period of childhood more strongly than anything within its first four stanzas ever does. They also furnish a conceptual label, "natural piety," in itself problematical, under which the Ode's descriptions of symptoms of loss may be filed. The Ode's effect on the poem on the rainbow has been even more severe. The extensive explorations of the continuity of the self found in the completed Ode have been so firmly associated with this brief lyric that William Heath has been able to read its "very desperation" as a sign of Wordsworth's radical doubt in the connection between man and nature (Heath 104). Separated from the Ode and its aftermath, and seen in its earliest recoverable version, the poem hardly invites such commentary:

> My heart leaps up when I behold
> A Rainbow in the sky:
> So was it when my life began;
> So is it, now I am a man,
> So be it, when I shall grow old
> Or let me die!
> The Child is Father of the man;
> And I should wish that all my days may be
> Bound each to each by natural Piety.[9]

The poem says that the relationship between perception and the affections has remained intact in one particular from the beginnings of life to the present. If its fear of discontinuity seems excessive ("Or let me die!"), its statement of desire ("And I *should* wish that all my days *may* be" [emphasis added]) is restrained.

Read as a direct consequence of "Extempore," the first four stanzas of the Ode can only seem the thematic antithesis of that brief work. A direct expression of continuity, experienced as well as desired, has

somehow led to an exploration of discontinuities which are indeterminate both in source and in ultimate importance. The significance
of "Extempore" for the Ode is clearer aesthetically than thematically.
The short poem names rather than describes its phenomenon, depending entirely upon the traditional associations of the rainbow to underpin the value of the heart's response; without God's covenant with
Noah, the wish to die would become merely extravagant and foolish,
and the identification of exultation in its presence as "natural Piety"
would become almost meaningless. If Wordsworth is not trading in
the family language of poets, he is surely trafficking in their stock
figures more obviously than he has previously wished or dared. The
Ode of 1802 continues his exploration of inherited figural motifs,
including the rainbow. The versification of "Extempore" is also continuous with that of the Ode. Its rhyme scheme is created for the
occasion, and its lineation, basically tetrameter, shrinks to dimeter
before its concluding pentameter couplets. Curtis has discussed admirably Wordsworth's experiments in metrical and stanzaic patterns
in the short lyrics of 1802, pointing to his readings in Herrick,
Herbert, Jonson, and other Jacobean and Elizabethan poets that winter and spring (*WET* 80–96). Wordsworth's newfound willingness
to exploit the affective potential of traditional figuration stems from
similar sources.

The two lyrics which anticipate "Extempore" also show as many
differences from as similarities to the Ode. In "To a Cuckoo" (23–26
March) the topic is once more the relationship between past and
present, but change rather than continuity drives the poem. The
song of a "Cuckoo in the vale" brings a tale "Of visionary hours"
(11–12) in which the creature was "No Bird, but an invisible thing,
/ a voice, a mystery" (15–16). Wordsworth's play between "visionary
hours" and the "invisible thing" may foreshadow his distinction between celestial and ordinary light in the Ode, but here his use of
paradox is at once sharper and more secure. As a schoolboy the poet
looked for the unseen cuckoo "a thousand thousand ways / In bush,
and tree, & sky" (19–20). The poem claims that his altered response
as an adult has not resulted in loss:

>   And I can listen to thee yet
>   Can lie upon the plain

And listen till I do beget
That golden time again.

O blessed Bird! the earth we pace
Again appears to be
An unsubstantial fairy place
That is fit home for thee.

(25–32)

The differences between this poem and "Extempore" help to explain
some of the indeterminacies of the Ode. Both poems exploit golden
age motifs, one assigning this time to schoolboy days, the other to
an implied age of Biblical infancy. Both times recur in the Ode, one
through the extended descriptions of children at play in the valleys,
the other through the brief but significant mention of the "Babe
[who] leaps up in his Mother's arm" (49). But in the Ode Wordsworth does not attribute to either of these ages any particular visionary glory.

"To a Butterfly," which seems to have set in motion the sequence
of poems in which Wordsworth explores past and present experience
in the spring of 1802, muddies thematic issues even more thoroughly. There the "dead times" which are revived by the butterfly—"Thou Bible of my infancy!" (4)—are from an age in which
childhood experience was itself divided:

O! pleasant, pleasant, were the days
The time when in our childish plays,
My sister Dorothy and I
Together chased the Butterfly.
A very hunter I did rush
Upon the prey:—with leaps and springs
I followed on from brake to bush:
—But she, God love her! fear'd to brush
The dust from off his wings.

(10–18)

The poem celebrates a time of varied pleasures rather than certain
qualities of that time, embracing glad animal movements as eagerly
as it does a sort of natural piety.

Begun March 14, "To a Butterfly" is the earliest lyric of spring
1802 in anything like the manner of the Ode. When we think of the
Ode as a part of Wordsworth's lyrical work of that period, consequently, we must always keep in mind how very early in the cycle he
began it. It is as much the cause of the poet's subsequent efforts as
the product of his earlier ones. Putting together the thematic variations on childhood experience found in "To a Butterfly," "To a
Cuckoo," "Extempore," and the first four stanzas of the Ode, we
cannot possibly reconstruct a coherent Wordsworthian way of thinking about the relationship between childhood and maturity at this
time. His writing is exploratory in nature, and as exploratory in form
and expression as it is in content. Other poems touching upon childhood, such as "Alice Fell," "Beggars," and "The Emigrant Mother,"
all composed between March 12 and 17 (*DWJ* 100–102), point out
the diversity of his efforts at this time. The first two of these recall
the encounter poems of *Lyrical Ballads*, while the last is a monologue
in the manner of, if less forceful and complex than, "The Mad
Mother" of 1798.[10] Whatever triggered Wordsworth's nostalgic writings of the spring of 1802, it did not long keep him involved in
rehashing old forms. If the past was to be his subject, it was not to
command his manner. "The Emigrant Mother" is the last work of
this period which would fit smoothly into his and Coleridge's volume
of 1798.

Wordsworth's interest in the continuity of human experience
stemmed most immediately at this time from his strenuous and, by
Dorothy's testimony, exhausting efforts to write a life story in verse,
the history of Patrick Drummond, the newly-named Pedlar whose
life the poet was extricating from previous work on "The Ruined
Cottage." James Butler has recovered much of this nearly lost poem
of 1802, references to which haunt Dorothy's journals from 21 December 1801 through 10 March 1802 (*RC&P* 327–63). Wordsworth
was to describe the Pedlar of *The Excursion* to Miss Fenwick as a
possible version of himself, differently situated: " . . . had I been
born in a class which would have deprived me of what is called a
liberal education, it is not unlikely that, being strong in body, I
should have taken to a way of life such as that in which my Pedlar
passed the greater part of his days. At all events, I am here called

upon freely to acknowledge that the character I have represented in his person is chiefly an idea of what I fancied my own character might have become in his circumstances" (*PW* 5 : 373). As Butler has reconstructed the narrative of 1802, differences between Drummond and Wordsworth in class and education are relatively minor when compared to differences in their emotional experience.

Drummond's life is austere, relatively smooth, and continuous. Upon reaching manhood, he first follows his mother's suggestion that he become a teacher. Finding that a task not suited to his nature, he decides to take up the path of an elder brother and become a pedlar. In this long itinerant vocation,

> From day to day had his affections breathed
> The wholesome air of nature, there he kept
> In solitude and solitary thought
> So pleasant were these comprehensive views
> His mind in a just equipoise of love
> Serene it was, unclouded by the cares
> Of ordinary life unvexed unwarped
> By partial bondage. In his steady course
> No piteous revolutions had he felt
> No wild varieties of joy or grief
> Unoccupied by sorrow of its own
> His heart lay open.
>
> (*RC&P* 361; 205 – 16)

Drummond moves from boy to man with scarcely a disturbance, his days surely, as Wordsworth was to put it in "Extempore," "Bound each to each by natural Piety." If we set his life against Wordsworth's, we have to subtract more than a Cambridge education: he has no London, no France, no Grasmere, no Annette, no Caroline, no Dorothy, no Coleridge, no Mary.

While Wordsworth was assembling this narrative in MS. D of "The Ruined Cottage," sketching out a life which had moved easily from an early love of nature to a capacious and abiding love of mankind, he could hardly have avoided referring its course to his own unsettled state, in which he was busily taking on "the cares / Of ordinary life" and "partial bondage." While engrossed in its composition, he was coming to his decision to marry, writing to Annette Vallon and his daughter Caroline, and finally deciding to visit them in France before his marriage. "The Pedlar" suggests that Drummond's life has about it a melancholia of its own, seen most vividly when the old man is remembered crying over a sprightly ten-year-old girl who comes to listen to his stories when he returns from his rounds. (Wordsworth's daughter Caroline would be ten in December of 1802.) Although this life barren of "piteous revolutions" and "wild varieties of joy or grief" has clearly extracted a price, it must at times in these months have seemed to Wordsworth a mild one compared to that exacted by his own past and present emotional attachments. In any event, Wordsworth's putting together the story of Drummond must have led him to wonder again about the relationship between his desire for the sort of psychic continuity embodied in Drummond and his own more obviously turbulent existence. The series of lyrics which comes in the wake of his intense work on "The Pedlar," tracing variously the continuities and disjunctions between childhood and adulthood, flows naturally from work on the longer poem. Magnuson has found in Wordsworth's turn to shorter forms a possible loss of "faith in a poetic structure based on narrative form" and has speculated that the poet could not bring the Ode to completion until he could once again resume work on *The Prelude* in 1804.[11] Such an insight seems useful because the relationship between Wordsworth's work on the Ode in 1804 and his progress on *The Prelude* is both rich and relatively unexplored. However, any attempt to locate the non-completion of the Ode in narrational anxieties would have to account, as Magnuson does not, for the poet's mastery of these problems a few months later in the two poems on the leech-gatherer, works which anticipate by nearly two years his return to the Ode and the poem on his life.

If "The Pedlar" shaped in an obscure way the thematic emphases of the lyrics which lead to the Ode, it clearly had nothing to do with their aesthetic shaping. That seems to have come from Wordsworth's reading in Anderson's *British Poets*, the extent and impact of which are summarized admirably by Heath (22–24). Wordsworth's readings appear to have been directed not by his work on "The Pedlar," because *Paradise Lost* is virtually the only blank verse narrative figuring prominently in the letters and journals of the period, but by his other major project of these months, the expansion and elaboration of the preface to *Lyrical Ballads* and composition of the appendix on poetic diction for the 1802 edition, which he presumably undertook early in the year (*CMY* 139, 158). Wordsworth's reading, which gives no signs of having been programmatic, probably took two directions, the more evident of which was his search for additional confirmation of the nature and abuses of poetic diction in the preceding century. In the appendix he juxtaposes Proverbs 6:6–11 from the King James Bible against Samuel Johnson's inflated adaptation of the passage in "The Vanity of Human Wishes," referring as well to other metrical paraphrases of biblical material by Alexander Pope and Matthew Prior. He adduces a passage from even "so chaste a writer as" William Cowper to demonstrate the vicious pervasiveness of the artificial poetic language of the last age, and refers the reader once more to Thomas Gray's sonnet on Richard West, found in the preface (*Prose* 1:162–65).

Reading to aggravate old grievances and settle old scores could hardly be expected to have much positive effect on Wordsworth's current poetic practice. In only one instance has the work of his proscribed writers contributed materially to the Ode. Gray's "Ode on a Distant Prospect of Eton College" must have come to Wordsworth's attention as he looked once more at the "curiously elaborate" structure of the poet's diction (*Prose* 1:132). It is a poem Wordsworth never singles out for either praise or blame, and of course one which is especially apposite to the thematic concerns of his lyrics of 1802. In his second stanza Gray speaks of the rejuvenating effects of the landscape before him:

> Ah happy hills, ah pleasing shade,
> Ah fields belov'd in vain,
> Where once my careless childhood stray'd,
> A stranger yet to pain!
> I feel the gales, that from ye blow,
> A momentary bliss bestow,
> As waving fresh their gladsome wing,
> My weary soul they seem to sooth[e],

And redolent of joy and youth,
To breathe a second spring.[12]

The most perplexing single line in Wordsworth's Ode, "The winds
come to me from the fields of sleep" (28), is perhaps a fiercely com-
pressed echo of Gray's stanza. Gray's "gales" blow toward him from
the "fields" where he played as a schoolboy, momentarily renewing
his spirit, anticipating the role played by the winds in the Ode. Such
an echo could hardly be anything but inadvertent and it could hardly
be expected to be functional. It does suggest, however, the extent to
which the Ode is rich in the topical matter of eighteenth-century
verse which Wordsworth held in public disdain.

Wordsworth's positive readings of this period are predominantly
in English poets writing before the eighteenth century. Such writers
had presumably kept intact the honorable trait attributed in the appendix to the "earliest poets of all nations," who "generally wrote
from passion excited by real events; they wrote naturally, and as men:
feeling powerfully as they did, their language was daring, and figurative." These writers were distinguished from the "Poets, and men
ambitious of the fame of Poets," of "succeeding times, . . . [who],
perceiving the influence of such language, and desirous of producing
the same effect without having the same animating passion, set
themselves to a mechanical adoption of these figures of speech, and
made use of them, sometimes with propriety, but much more frequently applied them to feelings and ideas with which they had no
natural connection whatsoever. A language was thus insensibly produced, differing materially from the real language of men in *any
situation*" (*Prose* 1 : 160). Although Wordsworth does not name his
antediluvian giants in the appendix, his readings in late 1801 and
early 1802 suggest that he had added Chaucer, Spenser, and Jonson
to Shakespeare and Milton, both of whom he had mentioned glanc-
ingly in the preface of 1800. As we know, Shakespeare and Milton
can be adopted by almost any aesthetic party, and statements honor-
ing them can consequently mean anything or nothing. But Wordsworth's turn at this time to self-conscious professional poets like
Chaucer, Spenser, and Jonson suggests how much his interests have
broadened since the *Lyrical Ballads* of 1798.

Wordsworth's concern for Chaucer is documented in a series of modernizations which he undertook in early December 1801. He translated at this time "The Manciple's Tale," "The Prioress's Tale," portions of *Troilus and Cressida*, and "The Cuckoo and the Nightingale," by Sir Thomas Clanvowe, which was then attributed to Chaucer. [13] Heath has suggested how important working with Chaucer's rhyme royal was for Wordsworth's versification in his lyrics of the following spring (28–29). However, the poem most influential on his later verse was that bit of pseudo-Chaucerianism, "The Cuckoo and the Nightingale." This poem about the pains of love is specifically about the perils of the month of May:

> For every true heart, gentle heart and free
> That with him is, or thinketh so to be,
> Now against May shall have some stirring—whether
> To joy, or it be to some mourning; never
> At other time so much, as thinketh me.
>
> For now when they may hear the small birds' song,
> And see the leaves spring green and plentiful,
> This unto their rememberance doth bring
> All kinds of pleasure mix'd with sorrowing;
> And lusty thoughts of mighty longing full. [14]

"The Cuckoo and the Nightingale" anticipates the pattern of emotional disturbances in the present scene of the Ode, the pain mixed in with the joy of the season, thus placing its first four stanzas, and especially III and IV, in an erotic tradition which never arises directly in the poem itself.

The disturbance of a sleepless night leads the poet of "The Cuckoo and the Nightingale" to go into nature in search of a comforting timely utterance, "to hear the Nightingale, / Before the sorry Cuckoo silence breaking" (49–50). The landscape he enters is presented with an idealized abstractness perfectly commensurate with that of stanzas III–IV of the Ode:

> Till to a lawn I came all white and green,
> I in so fair a one had never been.

The ground was green, with daisy powdered over;
Tall were the flowers, the grove a lofty cover,
All green and white; and nothing else was seen.
There sate I down among the fair fresh flowers,
And saw the birds come tripping from their bowers,
Where they had rested them all night; and they,
Who were so joyful at the light of day,
Began to do the honours of the May.

(61–70)

The sounds of nature blend into a perfect unity:

Meanwhile the stream, whose bank I sate upon,
Was making such a noise as it ran on
Accordant to the sweet Birds' harmony;
Methought that it was the best melody
Which ever to man's ear a passage won.

(81–85)

If we sprinkle in a few thousand lambs and children, the scene becomes a fitting companion for the generalized pastoral of the Ode.[15]
Wordsworth's readings in Spenser can be traced back to mid-
November 1801 (*CMY*, 129, 130), although no individual titles are
mentioned in Dorothy's journal, aside from Mary Hutchinson's reading of the first canto of *The Faerie Queene* (*DWJ* 66), until after the
Ode had been begun. The readings in Spenser's visionary epic will
become important to Wordsworth's work in transforming "The Leech-
Gatherer" into "Resolution and Independence." For the Ode itself,
"Prothalamion," which Dorothy mentions on April 25, is of extraordinary importance. Abbie Findlay Potts pointed out in 1932 that "in
stanzas I, II, III, IV, X, and XI . . . only eleven rhymes out of forty-
two are not found in Spenser's *Prothalamion*; and from the fifteen
rhymes of the *Prothalamion* not used as rhymes in the *Ode*, seven
words are found in Wordsworth's lines." She moves from this stunning verbal coincidence to note that the poems share a kinship of
mood as well: "Wordsworth's regret for something gone accords with
the feelings of Spenser's discontented poet, whose brain was likewise

afflicted by 'sullen care' . . . and who, walking forth by a silver stream through meads of violets, daisies, primroses, and roses, became one of a wedding-party on its way to London."[16] Turning to the "Epithalamion," a poem not documented in the Wordsworths' reading during the winter and spring of 1801–1802, Potts suggests that from it "Wordsworth borrowed for his *Ode* certain Spenserian properties—the 'pipe' and the 'tabor,' and the boys who shout, and the cheerful birds who chant their lays, singing of joy and pleasance" (608).

Potts's demonstration is convincing, even if "The Cuckoo and the Nightingale" suggests that Spenser held no patent on birds and flowers. Indeed, while the possible individual influences on the Ode are fascinating, what is most intriguing is the class of poems from which they come. Wordsworth had had very little use in the past for erotic pastoral. However fresh it may have seemed in the writings of Spenser, or in the poet Wordsworth took to be Chaucer, the form had worn itself out in a weary procession of shepherds and shepherdesses, sporting in the shade. Wordsworth's earlier feelings about the more conventional figures and themes of pastoral can be seen through a series of poems in the second volume of *Lyrical Ballads* (1800). Five poems there are identified either in their subtitles or notes as pastorals: "The Idle Shepherd-Boys," "The Pet-Lamb," "The Oak and the Broom," "The Brothers," and "Michael," four of which are gently parodic.[17] The first of these is extremely close in spirit and locution to stanzas III and IV of the Ode. Two young shepherds are sitting in the grass:

> It seems they have no work to do
> Or that their work is done.
> On pipes of sycamore they play
> The fragments of a Christmas Hymn,
> Or with that plant which in our dale
> We call Stag-horn, or Fox's Tail
> Their rusty Hats they trim:
> And thus as happy as the Day,
> Those Shepherds wear the time away.
>
> (*LB* 164; 14–22)

The point of the poem is that while the boys are indulging in the pastimes of those carefree shepherds of literary tradition, they are ignoring their genuine pastoral duties. The next stanza moves abruptly from an idyllic spring scene (once more, it is May) to the very real hazards which confront real sheep:

> The thrush is busy in the Wood,
> And carols loud and strong.
> A thousand lambs are on the rocks,
> All newly born! both earth and sky
> Keep jubilee, and more than all,
> Those Boys with their green Coronal,
> They never hear the cry,
> That plaintive cry! which up the hill
> Comes from the depth of Dungeon-Gill.
>
> (25−33)

The poet has to rescue a baby lamb from a pool beneath the torrent into which it has slipped. He thus performs the proper task of the shepherds, who are absorbed in their literary pursuits. The "Poet, one who loves the brooks / Far better than the sages' books" (84−85), is saving life from faulty art.

"The Pet-Lamb" centers on "little Barbara Lewthwaite, a Child of beauty rare" (*LB* 200; 13) and her "snow-white mountain Lamb" (4), an orphan which now lives tethered to a stone. After she has fed and watered her pet, the child walks away but then stops and looks back, seeming to perceive that the animal is not happy. The narrator imagines from "the workings of her face" (18) the song the child might sing to her pet. The lamb, she observes, has soft grass, beautiful surroundings, and shade nearby, and is brought fresh food and water three times a day. It does not have to fear the "rain and mountain storms" (31) which would be its ordinary fate. Further, it has a friend in the little girl, who promises to "yoke thee to my cart like a pony in the plough" (46) when it is older and stronger. Wordsworth imagines that Barbara understands something of the lamb's unease: "Things that I know not of belike to thee are dear, / And dreams of things which thou can'st neither see nor hear" (51−52). Still, her concluding question is "what is't that aileth thee?" (60). The creature is trapped in the role of literary lamb, happy playmate of children, and the girl apprehends only vaguely its desire to be free, even if freedom would mean enduring the hardships of its kind. Both "The Idle Shepherd-Boys" and "The Pet-Lamb" explore the tensions between life and conventional pastoral, finding convention wanting.

In "The Brothers" and "Michael" literary pastoral exists largely as an implicit countertext, against which the lives of genuine shepherds may be seen and appreciated. The subtitle to "Michael, a Pastoral Poem," is an indirect challenge to the reader's expectations of the form. As I have argued elsewhere, in "Michael" Wordsworth is radically revising pastoral, returning it through cadences and echoes to something like a reenactment of the lives of the patriarchs in the Old Testament.[18] In the first four stanzas of the Ode, perhaps encouraged by his readings in Chaucer and Spenser, Wordsworth has relaxed temporarily his scrutiny of pastoral convention in favor of exploring the power of its traditional motifs.

Wordsworth's readings in Ben Jonson were probably to another end entirely. Dorothy reports on February 11 that she and William "were much delighted with the Poem of Penshurt" (*DWJ* 88), to which they returned on February 14 (90). Although Jonson's poem has in its idyllic landscape some vague affinities with conventional pastoral, Wordsworth was probably more interested in discovering a source for the topological, locodescriptive tradition in English poetry in which he had been working in such poems as "Tintern Abbey," the early drafts of *Prelude* materials, and "The Ruined Cottage." His work of the spring of 1802 was probably more directly affected by his readings in Jonson's shorter poems, which Dorothy remarked on February 11 "were too *interesting* for him, and would not let him go to sleep" (*DWJ* 88). Dorothy cites only one specific example, and quotes four lines from "On My First Daughter":

> Here lies to each her Parents ruth,
> *Mary the Daughter of their youth*
> At six months end she parted hence
> In safety of her Innocence.
>
> (88)

Faint echoes of Jonson's epitaphic terseness abound in Wordsworth's plainsongs of the succeeding months, especially in such resolutely non-figurative poems as "Extempore."

What Wordsworth found most interesting in Jonson, though, may have been his versification. While reading his predecessor, Wordsworth was in the midst of his labored revisions of "The Ruined Cottage." Jonson's intricately varied rhymes would have furnished a respite from what had become the tediousness of composition in blank verse. The strophic inventiveness of *Under-wood* is especially striking, and a poem such as "My Picture Left in Scotland" is a plausible candidate for the "beautiful poem on Love" which Wordsworth read to Dorothy on March 9 (*DWJ* 99). It anticipates in lineation and rhyme many of the characteristics of both "Extempore" and the opening stanzas of the Ode:

> I Now thinke, Love is rather deafe, then blind,
>   For else it could not be,
>   That she,
> Whom I adore so much, should so slight me,
>   And cast my love behind:
> I'm sure my language to her, was as sweet,
>   And every close did meet
>   In sentence, of as subtile feet,
>   As hath the youngest Hee,
>   That sits in shadow of *Apollo's* tree.
> Oh, but my conscious feares,
>   That flie my thoughts betweene,
>   Tell me that she hath seene
> My hundreds of gray haires,
> Told seven and fortie yeares.
> Read so much wast, as she cannot imbrace
> My mountaine belly, and my rockie face,
> And all these through her eyes, have stopt her eares. [19]

Like Jonson, Wordsworth freely rhymes on lines of irregular quantity, suspends and weaves his rhymes across several lines of verse, and creates stanzaic forms which have no direct traditional antecedents.

Wordsworth does not appear to have been copying the strophic practices in the poems Jonson calls odes. Characteristically, Jonson composed his odes monostrophically, establishing in his opening stanza a model of rhymes and lineation which he followed throughout the remainder of a poem (see, for example, the "Ode, to Sir William Sydney, on His Birth-Day," from *The Forrest*, or "An Ode, to Himselfe," from *Under-wood*). His most distinguished exception to this practice is in "To the Immortal Memorie, and Friendship of That Noble Paire, Sir Lucius Cary, and Sir H. Morison," in *Under-wood*, where Jonson astonishingly reinvents, without benefit of the later philological discoveries which should have made it possible, the triadic structure of Pindar's odes. Even here Jonson is more regular in his practice than Wordsworth, having created one verse form for his "Turne" and "Counterturne" and another different but equally consistent form for his "Stand," so that the poem consists of four triads identical in versification.

The odic sources of Wordsworth's fragment of 1802 have always been obscure, and with good reason. Although it could be loosely classified as an irregular, higher ode, it is not easily assimilable to this uneven class within English verse. It is much freer in its versification than the other great odes in the language, Jonson's Cary-Morison Ode and Milton's "On the Morning of Christ's Nativity," and it exhibits greater strophic irregularity than the pindarics of Gray or even the odes of Collins. When Collins varies the lengths of his lines most strikingly, as in "Ode to Simplicity," where a trimeter base is mixed with pentameters, he composes in regular six-line stanzas, and the rhymes fall on lines of equal measure. Where the stanzas of Collins are irregular, as in "Ode on the Poetical Character" and "Ode on Fear," the poems depart infrequently from the dominant principles of lineation established in each stanza. "Poetical Character" is largely composed in iambic tetrameter, varied with rhymed pentameters, and with alexandrines closing stanzas I and III. In "Fear," perhaps Collins' most strikingly irregular ode, a strophe and antistrophe based in iambic tetrameter couplets, varied with trimeter and pentameter couplets, surround an epode consisting of five iambic pentameter quatrains. Wordsworth's admiration and sympathy for

Collins are well known, and he certainly responded to him more enthusiastically than to any other writer of odes in the eighteenth century (see *CO* 230–31), but he did not adopt his work as a poetic model. The earlier poem closest to Wordsworth's Ode in its metrical versatility and free strophic invention is Dryden's "Alexander's Feast," a work about which Wordsworth is silent. And Dryden's poem, of course, as befits a poem created specifically for musical performance, contains many formalized repetitions which are either absent from or wholly naturalized in the work of the later poet.

The odist with whom Wordsworth was most intimate was Coleridge. Unlike his friend, Coleridge had used the form several times before. The closest Wordsworth had come was to add a note to "Tintern Abbey" in 1800, stating that he had not "ventured to call this Poem an Ode; but it was written with a hope that in the transitions, and the impassioned music of the versification, would be found the principal requisites of that species of composition" (*LB* 296). Wordsworth's Ode of 1802 is least like Coleridge's well known "France: An Ode," which is thoroughly public in its voice and homiletic in its intention. Coleridge there adopts without substantial variation the formal characteristics of the higher ode of the eighteenth century, including an elaborate invocation, ringing of *O*s and *ye*s, and a weight of personification almost worthy of Gray. In keeping with the formality of public utterance, Coleridge adopts a complexly rhymed twenty-one-line stanzaic structure which he keeps consistent throughout the poem. His basic line is iambic pentameter, with a few tetrameters interspersed, swollen less frequently to alexandrines. Wordsworth's Ode is nearer in its formal characteristics to "Ode to the Departing Year" (1796) and "Ode to Georgiana, Duchess of Devonshire" (1799). The earlier of these smacks as much of neoclassical *allegoria* as "France," but it does exhibit in its irregularities a strophic and metrical virtuosity closer to Wordsworth's Ode than any other familiar predecessor except "Alexander's Feast." Further, its most readable stanza works upon an Edenic/pastoral motif commensurate with that used much more elaborately in Wordsworth's stanzas III and IV:

> Not yet enslaved, not wholly vile,
> O Albion! O my mother Isle!

> Thy valleys, fair as Eden's bowers
> Glitter green with sunny showers;
> Thy grassy uplands' gentle swells
>   Echo to the bleat of flocks.
>   (*CPW* 1:166; 121–26)

Here, as in Wordsworth's poem, pastoral bliss is set against a disruption, which in Coleridge's case proceeds not from personal melancholy but from depraved political policies which portend the downfall of England, and hence the loss of its paradise.

Any attempt to measure the influence of Coleridge on Wordsworth's Ode must eventually deal with the most troubled poem in either writer's canon, "The Voice from the side of Etna; or, The Mad Monk: An Ode in Mrs. Ratcliff's Manner," published 13 October 1800 in the *Morning Post* over the signature "CASSIANI, jun." In 1960 Stephen M. Parrish and David V. Erdman noted that "About every twenty years someone . . . notices that there is a remarkable resemblance between the first stanza of Wordsworth's . . . [Ode] and the second stanza" of this poem.[20] The stanza in question is innocent enough in itself:

> There was a time when earth, and sea, and skies,
>   The bright green vale and forest's dark recess,
> When all things lay before my eyes
>   In steady loveliness.
> But now I feel on earth's uneasy scene
>   Such motions as will never cease!
>   I only ask for peace—
> Then, wherefore must I know, that such a time has been?
>   (9–16)

In both rhetorical development and versification the Ode reflects this stanza from "The Mad Monk." The first four lines include an opening catalogue of objects which recall an earlier and higher general state of perception. The similar turns at line five (the Ode has "It is not now . . .") lead to statements of pain and loss. The rhyme schemes of the stanzas are close (ababcddc in "The Mad Monk" and ababacddc in the Ode), both stanzas rhyme on unequal lines, and both conclude with alexandrines. The Ode's appropriation of "The Mad Monk" could not be clearer; what is muddy is the question of *whose* work Wordsworth is appropriating, and to what end.

Parrish and Erdman vigorously debate the authorship of "The Mad Monk." For Parrish it seems clearly a poem of Wordsworth's which Coleridge, frantic to provide material for which *The Morning Post* had already paid him, sent to its publisher under a pseudonym. Referring to lines slightly later in the poem, Parrish asks, "if we were to meet these four lines 'running wild in the deserts of Arabia,' as Coleridge put it, would we not scream out, 'Wordsworth!'?" (221).

> Last night as o'er the sloping turf I trod,
> The smooth green turf to me a vision gave:
> Beneath my eyes I saw the sod,
> The roof of ROSA's grave.
>
> (21–24)

For Erdman the poem is clearly Coleridge's, its Wordsworthian resonances the result of Coleridge's conscious burlesquing of his friend's periodic descents into the Gothic sublime. Both arguments are convincing, and the debate is a model for textual argumentation.

Whoever wrote the poem, its relationship to the Ode remains the same, and in either case it is perplexing. The stanza Wordsworth echoes is unexceptionable. Problems arise when we identify the crisis which has generated the change in the speaker's perception of nature. The speaker is an unseen "Hermit, or a Monk" (5), lamenting his fate on "Etna's side" (1), where his complaint, "In melody most like an old Sicilian song" (8), is overheard and reported by a goat-herd. The cause of the Monk's unhappiness is his having murdered his beloved Rosa, apparently in a fit of jealous rage:

> I struck the wound—this hand of mine!
> For, oh! thou Maid divine,
>   I lov'd to agony!
> The youth, whom thou call'dst thine,
>   Did never love like me.
>
> (33–37)

The Ode's echo of this absurdly trite poem is unsettling, and it points to some of the dangers Wordsworth has faced in engaging conventions of erotic pastoral. While the use of such a tradition awakens memories of superb medieval and renaissance writers, it calls forth equally the recent and nearly fatal debasement of such conventions in Gothic sensationalism. Frederick L. Beaty has courageously attempted to trace the sources of Wordsworth's Ode past "The Mad Monk" to the writings of Ann Radcliffe, which—the reader may take his choice—that poem had imitated or parodied. Beaty finds in *The Mysteries of Udolpho* two depictions of "ideal fathers who associated the process of growing old with the fading of an illusion that once enveloped the beauties of nature, and in one instance . . . clearly identified this fleeting vision with 'that high enthusiasm, which wakes the poet's dream.' "[21] If this particular influence seems questionable, the analogue at least helps to show the prevalence of such motifs in sensationalist literature of sensibility. When the Ode energizes the conventions of erotic pastoral, it throws itself open to a vast array of its tawdry progeny of the late eighteenth century.

Thanks to James H. Averill's *Wordsworth and Human Suffering*, it is not necessary to document Wordsworth's early enthrallment by Gothicism, which was extensive and intense, and which helped to shape both the formal and thematic qualities of his work.[22] As early as "Lines left upon a Seat in a Yew-Tree," however, composed by July 1797 (*CEY* 192), Wordsworth had clearly distanced himself from the kind of morbid introspection later depicted in the Solitary of *The Excursion*, whom Geoffrey Hartman has called "the Hamletian man in black, and a dangerous part of the poet's mind."[23] This early poem, which could be a fragment from a Gothic melodrama, tells the cautionary history of one who nourished his sorrow, "tracing here / An emblem of his own unfruitful life" (*LB* 39; 28–29). To such a mind the beauty of nature is of a piece with its bleakness. Despair may be fed equally by an immediate barren environment or by a beautiful "distant scene" (31). The anguish of the character is intensified by thoughts of those to whom,

> Warm from the labours of benevolence,
> The world, and man himself, appeared a scene

Of kindred loveliness: then he would sigh
With mournful joy, to think that others felt
What he must never feel: and so, lost man!
On visionary views would fancy feed,
Till his eye streamed with tears.

(36–42)

"Visionary views": "the visionary gleam"; "To me alone there came
a thought of grief." Because no one would bother to exorcise a demon
that does not plague him, we can easily agree with Hartman that
what Wordsworth has dramatized in "Lines left upon a Seat in a Yew-
Tree" and *The Excursion* is a strong tendency in his own personality.
Although he recognized its dangers early, he comes very close in the
first four stanzas of the Ode to re-enacting the role of the proto-
Solitary of "Lines left"—"The man, whose eye / Is ever on himself"
(51–52). The enticements of the self-pitying Gothic sensibility, so
clearly presented in "Lines left" and "The Mad Monk," lurk only a
short distance behind the Ode.

In strong contrast to its Gothic echoes, the final influence on the
Ode illustrates the qualitative range of the poem's literary resonances.
Dorothy reports that after tea on 2 February 1802 she "read aloud
the 11th Book of Paradise Lost. We were much impressed and also
melted into tears" (*DWJ* 84). Book XI ends with God's covenant
never again to destroy the earth by water, with the rainbow as a token
of that pledge. Consequently, it is easy to see, with Abbie Findlay
Potts, the effects of this reading of Milton on Wordsworth's "Extempore."[24] Because Potts considers the influence of *Paradise Lost* on the
completed Ode, her analysis is less helpful than it might be on the
work begun in 1802. The marks of Wordsworth's reading of Milton's
epic are found primarily in those locutions which suggest that the
loss recorded in the poem is comparable to the loss of paradise. Some
of the most affecting moments of Book XI trace Adam and Eve's
fearful anticipations of their expulsion from Eden. Eve asks Michael,
who has come bearing God's judgment,

How shall I part, and whither wander down
Into a lower World, to this obscure

And wild, how shall we breathe in other Air
Less pure, accustom'd to immortal Fruits?[25]

Adam, more concerned with his spiritual than material comfort, asks
whether their removal portends an utter alienation from God:

In yonder nether World where shall I seek
His bright appearances, or footstep trace?
For though I fled him angry, yet recall'd
To life prolong'd and promis'd Race, I now
Gladly behold though but his utmost skirts
Of glory, and far off his steps adore.

(11.328–33)

Wordsworth's phrase, "Apparel'd in celestial light," reverberates
strongly off Milton's text. The "nether World" of the Ode is diminished without similar "bright appearances." Further, Michael's description of the course of mortal life hits forcefully the sensory
deprivation which is to be man's lot:

thou must outlive
Thy youth, thy strength, thy beauty, which will change
To wither'd weak and gray; thy Senses then
Obtuse, all taste of pleasure must forgo,
To what thou hast, and for the Air of youth
Hopeful and cheerful, in thy blood will reign
A melancholy damp of cold and dry
To weigh thy Spirits down, and last consume
The Balm of Life.

(11.538–46)

And finally, as I suggested earlier, Wordsworth's "tree of many one"
flourished in only one setting, the groves of Eden.

My discussion of the backgrounds of stanzas I–IV of the Ode
presents them more as an anthology than as a poem, or even part of
a poem. Such an effect is not altogether unfortunate. Wordsworth's
fragment is a confluence of many tributaries, not all of which blend
smoothly and easily. Certainly it shows few signs of any inscrutable

workmanship which would reconcile their discordant elements. Wordsworth's dominant thematic and figural influences have come from the early English pastoral tradition, especially as he found it in Clanvowe and Spenser, overlain with paradisal implications stemming from his readings in Milton. His stanzaic invention shows evidence of his newfound interest in Jonson, as well as a recollection, conscious or unconscious, of lines which he or Coleridge had written a year and a half earlier in "The Mad Monk." The poem gestures toward a great tradition in English poetry which Wordsworth has been assembling in his criticism, into which he will place himself. But it does so in ways reminiscent of movements in eighteenth-century writing against which he has long been reacting. Although the poem is heavily conventional—even derivative—it does not seem in its first four stanzas to know what it is making of its conventions or where it stands in relation to them.

The power of these stanzas, which has been confirmed by most readers since Coleridge, is precarious. At the first touch of a specifying motivation—at the suggestion, for example, that we are hearing the complaint of a frustrated lover or neglected poet—the affective force of the stanzas could shrivel pathetically into the kind of mawkish self-pity found in "The Mad Monk." Wordsworth's allusions work by invoking signs of deep feeling and loss from the traditions of English poetry, without attaching them to the particular psychological situations and emotional states which have become hackneyed set pieces of the literature of sensibility. When Coleridge develops from Wordsworth's fragment a lament issuing from a despondent poet-lover, he will of course be directly engaging the recent convention above which his friend's poem flutters.

Criticism of the Ode has often followed Coleridge in trying to name the poet's grief, reading through its verbal obscurities and conventional expressions to discover an underlying emotional motivation for the work. For philosophical commentators the Ode springs from an epistemological crisis, an anxiety that nature alone may no longer be enough.[26] For psychobiographers, the poem may come from displacements of Wordsworth's anxieties about his impending marriage, about his betrayal of Annette and abandonment of Caroline, about coming changes and potential strains in his relationship with Dorothy, or about his future as a poet. Heath gives a most balanced and coherent overview of Wordsworth's psychological concerns around the time of his composition of the Ode. He goes on, however, to classify the poem, as well as the poems on the leech-gatherer and the forerunners of "Dejection," as the work of what he calls an "Elegiac Spring." Such an argument has much to recommend it, but it risks circularity, because these poems stand virtually alone in this period in their direct treatment of cycles of emotional depression and recovery. What happens in Heath's study, as in many others less distinguished, is that other contemporaneous poems are drawn reluctantly into the orbit of the Ode and its aftermath, taking from this more powerful body of work a somber or at least ambiguous emotional coloration. Thus we find dark readings of even Wordsworth's most playful, nostalgic, or emotionally secure work of the spring of 1802. Recall Heath's remark on the "desperation" of the poem on the rainbow.

When critics attempt to provide a direct emotional occasion for the Ode's expressions of grief and loss, they very nearly undo what Wordsworth has accomplished in its first four stanzas. They turn them into a version of "The Mad Monk." This chapter has tried to demonstrate that reduction through specification is not necessary. Before they represent anything else, the stanzas show a fascinating turn in Wordsworth's poetic experimentation. Their relationship to his recent writings and their intersections with his earlier canon alike suggest that he is searching for a new direction in his verse, characterized by a more confident and positive engagement with inherited themes and motifs. Wordsworth's decision to write an ode at all is evidence of such a movement. Our language has no more stylized, grandiloquent lyric form, and none more prone to the excesses of that artificial poetic diction against which he was concurrently writing. If Wordsworth could think of "Tintern Abbey" as an ode, it was because he had retained the abrupt transitions and impassioned music of the form while stripping it of its particular formal locutionary traditions, using instead the naturalized conventions of locodescriptive discourse. While Wordsworth's Ode of 1802 avoids the claptrap

of Apollo and the Nine, it makes no other major formal compro-
mises. Even the "elegiac" tone of its stanzas is consistent with the
dominant thematic emphasis of the English ode.

The Ode of 1802 suggests that a highly conventional poem, the
consequence of numerous converging lines of influence, can become
a new beginning. At the time he wrote it, Wordsworth probably had
little idea where this beginning would lead him, including how he
would manage to bring his fragment to completion. He never had
the opportunity to finish it as he might have intended. After Coleridge's Verse Letter, Wordsworth's stanzas are themselves never the
same. Their power has set in motion a dialogue in which they, while
remaining unchanged, will come to mean progressively more and
different things.

3

Coleridge's Verse Letter to Sara Hutchinson

A LETTER TO ——
APRIL 4, 1802. — SUNDAY EVENING

Well! if the Bard was weatherwise, who made
The grand old Ballad of Sir Patrick Spence,
This Night, so tranquil now, will not go hence
Unrous'd by winds, that ply a busier trade
Than that, which moulds yon clouds in lazy flakes,   [5]
Or the dull sobbing Draft, that drones & rakes
Upon the Strings of this Eolian Lute,
   Which better far were mute.
For, lo! the New Moon, winter-bright!
And overspread with phantom Light,   [10]
(With swimming phantom Light o'erspread
But rimm'd & circled with a silver Thread)
I see the Old Moon in her Lap, foretelling
The coming-on of Rain & squally Blast—
O! Sara! that the Gust ev'n now were swelling,   [15]
And the slant Night-shower driving loud & fast!

A Grief without a pang, void, dark, & drear,
A stifling, drowsy, unimpassion'd Grief

That finds no natural Outlet, no Relief
   In word, or sigh, or tear—   [20]
This, Sara! well thou know'st
Is that sore Evil, which I dread the most,
And oft'nest suffer! In this heartless Mood,
To other thoughts by yonder Throstle woo'd,
That pipes within the Larch-tree, not unseen,   [25]
(The Larch, which pushes out in tassels green
It's bundled Leafits) woo'd to mild Delights
By all the tender Sounds & gentle Sights
Of this sweet Primrose-month—& *vainly* woo'd
O dearest Sara! in this heartless Mood   [30]
All this long Eve, so balmy & serene,
Have I been gazing on the western Sky
And it's peculiar Tint of Yellow Green—
And still I gaze—& with how blank an eye!
And those thin Clouds above, in flakes & bars,   [35]
That give away their Motion to the Stars;
Those Stars, that glide behind them, or between,
Now Sparkling, now bedimm'd, but always seen;
Yon crescent Moon, as fix'd as if it grew
In it's own cloudless, starless Lake of Blue—   [40]
A Boat becalm'd! dear William's Sky Canoe!
—I see them all, so excellently fair!
I see, not feel, how beautiful they are.

   My genial Spirits fail—
   And what can these avail   [45]
To lift the smoth'ring Weight from off my Breast?
   It were a vain Endeavour,
   Tho' I should gaze for ever
On that Green Light, which lingers in the West!
I may not hope from outward Forms to win   [50]
The Passion & the Life, whose Fountains are within!
These lifeless Shapes, around, below, Above,
   O what can they impart?
When ev'n the gentle Thought, that thou, my Love!

Art gazing now, like me,   [55]
  And see'st the Heaven, I see—
Sweet Thought it is—yet feebly stirs my Heart!

  Feebly! O feebly!—Yet
    (I well remember it)
In my first Dawn of Youth that Fancy stole   [60]
With many secret Yearnings on my Soul.
At eve, sky-gazing in "ecstatic fit"
(Alas! for cloister'd in a city School
The Sky was all, I knew, of Beautiful)
At the barr'd window often did I sit,   [65]
And oft upon the leaded School-roof lay,
  And to myself would say—
There does not live the Man so stripp'd of good affections
As not to love to see a Maiden's quiet Eyes
Uprais'd, and linking on sweet Dreams by dim Connections   [70]
To Moon, or Evening Star, or glorious western Skies—
While yet a Boy, this Thought would so pursue me
That often it became a kind of Vision to me!

  Sweet Thought! and dear of old
    To Hearts of finer Mould!   [75]
Ten thousand times by Friends & Lovers blest!
  I spake with rash Despair,
  And ere I was aware,
The Weight was somewhat lifted from my Breast!
O Sara! in the weather-fended Wood,   [80]
Thy lov'd haunt! where the Stock-doves coo at Noon,
  I guess, that thou hast stood
And watch'd yon Crescent, & it's ghost-like Moon.
And yet, far rather in my present mood
I would, that thou'dst been sitting all this while   [85]
Upon the sod-built Seat of Camomile—
And tho' thy Robin may have ceas'd to sing,
Yet needs for *my* sake must thou love to hear
The Bee-hive murmuring near,

That ever-busy & most quiet Thing   [90]
Which I have heard at Midnight murmuring.

   I feel my spirit moved—
   And wheresoe'er thou be,
   O Sister! O Beloved!
   Those dear mild Eyes, that see   [95]
   Even now the Heaven, *I* see—
There is a Prayer in them! It is for *me*—
And I, dear Sara—*I* am blessing *thee*!

It was as calm as this, that happy night
When Mary, thou, & I together were,   [100]
The low decaying Fire our only Light,
And listen'd to the Stillness of the Air!
O that affectionate & blameless Maid,
Dear Mary! on her Lap my head she lay'd—
   Her Hand was on my Brow,   [105]
   Even as my own is now;
And on my Cheek I felt thy eye-lash play.
Such Joy I had, that I may truly say,
My Spirit was awe-stricken with the Excess
And trance-like Depth of it's brief Happiness.   [110]

Ah fair Remembrances, that so revive
The Heart, & fill it with a living Power,
Where were they, Sara?—or did I not strive
To win them to me?—on the fretting Hour
Then when I wrote thee that complaining Scroll   [115]
Which even to bodily Sickness bruis'd thy Soul!
And yet thou blam'st thyself alone! And yet
   Forbidd'st me all Regret!

And must I not regret, that I distress'd
Thee, best belov'd! who lovest me the best?   [120]
My better mind had fled, I know not whither,

For O! was this an Absent Friend's Employ
To send from far both Pain & Sorrow thither
    Where still his Blessings should have call'd down Joy!
I read thy guileless Letter o'er again— [125]
I hear thee of thy blameless Self complain—
And only this I learn—& this, alas! I know—
That thou art weak & pale with Sickness, Grief, & Pain—
    And *I*—*I* made thee so!

O for my own sake I regret perforce [130]
Whatever turns thee, Sara! from the Course
Of calm Well-being & a Heart at rest!
When thou, & with thee those, whom thou lov'st best,
Shall dwell together in one happy Home,
One House, the dear *abiding* Home of All, [135]
I too will crown me with a Coronal—
Nor shall this Heart in idle Wishes roam
    Morbidly soft!
No! let me trust, that I shall wear away
In no inglorious Toils the manly Day, [140]
And only now & then, & not too oft,
Some dear & memorable Eve will bless
Dreaming of all your Loves & Quietness.
Be happy, & I need thee not in sight.
Peace in thy Heart, & Quiet in thy Dwelling, [145]
Health in thy Limbs, & in thine Eyes the Light
Of Love, & Hope, & honorable Feeling—
Where e'er I am, I shall be well content!
Not near thee, haply shall be more content!
To all things I prefer the Permanent. [150]
And better seems it for a heart, like mine,
Always to *know*, than sometimes to behold,
    Their Happiness & thine—
For Change doth trouble me with pangs untold!
To see thee, hear thee, feel thee—then to part [155]
    Oh! it weighs down the Heart!

To *visit* those I love, as I love thee,
Mary, & William, & dear Dorothy,
It is but a temptation to repine—
The transientness is Poison in the Wine,   [160]
Eats out the Pith of Joy, makes all Joy hollow,
All Pleasure a dim Dream of Pain to follow!
My own peculiar Lot, my house-hold Life
It is, & will remain, Indifference or Strife—
While *ye* are *well* & *happy*, twould but wrong you—   [165]
If I should fondly yearn to be among you—
Wherefore, O wherefore! should I wish to be
A wither'd branch upon a blossoming Tree?

    But (let me say it! for I vainly strive
To beat away the Thought) but if thou pin'd,   [170]
Whate'er the Cause, in body or in mind,
I were the miserablest Man alive
To know it & be absent! Thy Delights
Far off, or near, alike I may partake—
But O! to mourn for thee, & to forsake   [175]
All power, all hope of giving comfort to thee—
To know that thou art weak & worn with pain,
And not to hear thee, Sara! not to view thee—
    Not sit beside thy Bed,
    Not press thy aching Head,   [180]
    Not bring thee Health again—
    At least to hope, to try—
By this Voice, which thou lov'st, and by this earnest Eye—

Nay, wherefore did I let it haunt my Mind
    The dark distressful Dream!   [185]
I turn from it, & listen to the Wind
Which long has rav'd unnotic'd! What a Scream
Of agony by Torture lengthen'd out
That Lute sent forth! O thou wild Storm without!
Jagg'd Rock, or mountain Pond, or blasted Tree,   [190]
Or Pine-grove, Whither Woodman never clomb,

Or lonely House, long held the Witches' Home,
Methinks were fitter Instruments for Thee,
Mad Lutanist! that in this month of Showers,
Of dark brown Gardens, & of peeping Flowers,   [195]
Mak'st Devil's Yule, with worse than wintry Song
The Blossoms, Buds, and timorous Leaves among!
Thou Actor, perfect in all tragic Sounds!
Thou mighty Poet, even to frenzy bold!
    What tell'st thou now about?   [200]
'Tis of the Rushing of a Host in Rout—
And many Groans from men with smarting Wounds—
At once they groan with smart, and shudder with the Cold!
Tis hush'd! there is a Trance of deepest Silence,
Again! but all that Sound, as of a rushing Crow'd,   [205]
And Groans & tremulous Shudderings, all are over—
And it has other Sounds, and all less deep, less loud!
    A Tale of less Affright,
    And temper'd with Delight,
As William's Self had made the tender Lay—   [210]
    Tis of a little Child
    Upon a heathy Wild,
Not far from home—but it has lost it's way—
And now moans low in utter grief & fear—
And now screams loud, & hopes to make it's Mother hear! [215]

Tis Midnight! and small Thoughts have I of Sleep—
Full seldom may my Friend such Vigils keep—
O breathe She softly in her gentle Sleep!
Cover her, gentle Sleep! with wings of Healing.
And be this Tempest but a Mountain Birth!   [220]
May all the Stars hang bright above her Dwelling,
Silent, as tho' they *watch'd* the sleeping Earth!
Healthful & light, my Darling! may'st thou rise
    With clear & cheerful Eyes—
And of the same good Tidings to me send!   [225]
    For, oh! beloved Friend!
I am not the buoyant Thing, I was of yore—

When like an own Child, I to *Joy* belong'd;
For others mourning oft, myself oft sorely wrong'd,
Yet bearing all things then, as if I nothing bore!   [230]

   Yes, dearest Sara! Yes!
There *was* a time when tho' my path was rough,
The Joy within me dallied with [?Di]stress;
And all Misfortunes were but as the Stuff
Whence Fancy made me Dreams of Happiness: [235]
For Hope grew round me, like the climbing Vine,
And Leaves & Fruitage, not my own, seem'd mine!
But now Ill Tidings bow me down to earth—
Nor care I, that they rob me of my Mirth—
   But oh! each Visitation   [240]
Suspends what Nature gave me at my Birth,
   My shaping Spirit of Imagination!
I speak not now of those habitual Ills
That wear out Life, when two unequal Minds
Meet in one House, & two discordant Wills—   [245]
   This leaves me, where it finds,
Past cure, & past Complaint—a fate austere
Too fix'd & hopeless to partake of Fear!
But thou, dear Sara! (dear indeed thou art,
My Comforter! A Heart within my Heart!)   [250]
Thou, & the Few, we love, tho' few ye be,
Make up a world of Hopes & Fears for me.
And if Affliction, or distemp'ring Pain,
Or wayward Chance befall you, I complain
Not that I mourn—O Friends, most dear! most true!   [255]
   Methinks to weep with you
Were better far than to rejoice alone—
But that my coarse domestic Life has known
No Habits of heart-nursing Sympathy,
No Griefs, but such as dull and deaden me,   [260]
No Hopes of it's own Vintage, None, O! none—
Whence when I mourn'd for you, my Heart might Borrow
Fair forms & living Motions for it's Sorrow.

For not to think of what I needs must feel,
But to be still & patient all I can;   [265]
And haply by abstruse Research to steal
From my own Nature all the Natural Man—
This was my sole Resource, my wisest plan!
And that, which suits a part, infects the whole,
And now is almost grown the Temper of my Soul.   [270]

   My little Children are a Joy, a Love,
      A good Gift from above!
But what is Bliss, that still calls up a Woe,
      And makes it doubly keen
Compelling me to *feel*, as well as *know*,   [275]
What a most blessed Lot mine might have been.
Those little Angel Children (woe is me!)
There have been hours, when feeling how they bind
And pluck out the wing-feathers of my Mind,
Turning my Error to Necessity,   [280]
I have half-wish'd, they never had been born!
That seldom! But sad Thoughts they always bring,
And like the Poet's Philomel, I sing
My Love-song, with my breast against a Thorn.

With no unthankful Spirit I confess,   [285]
This clinging Grief too, in it's turn, awakes
That Love, and Father's Joy; but O! it makes
The Love the greater, & the Joy far less.
These Mountains too, these Vales, these Woods, these Lakes, [290]
Scenes full of Beauty & of Loftiness
Where all my Life I fondly hop'd to live—
I were sunk low indeed, did they *no* solace give;
But oft I seem to feel, & evermore I fear,
They are not to me now the Things, which once they were. [295]

O Sara! we receive but what we give,
And in *our* Life alone does Nature live.
Our's is her Wedding Garment, our's her Shroud—

And would we aught behold of higher Worth
Than that inanimate cold World allow'd
To the poor loveless ever-anxious Crowd,   [300]
Ah! from the Soul itself must issue forth
A Light, a Glory, and a luminous Cloud
   Enveloping the Earth!
And from the Soul itself there must be sen[?t]
A sweet & potent Voice, of it's own Birth,   [305]
Of all sweet Sounds the Life & Element.
O pure of Heart! thou need'st not ask of me
What this strong music in the Soul may be,
   What, & wherein it doth exist,
This Light, this Glory, this fair luminous Mist,   [310]
This beautiful & beauty-making Power!
Joy, innocent Sara! Joy, that ne'er was given
Save to the Pure, & in their purest Hour,
Joy, Sara! is the Spirit & the Power
That wedding Nature to us gives in Dower   [315]
   A new Earth & new Heaven
Undreamt of by the Sensual & the Proud!
Joy is that strong Voice, Joy that luminous Cloud—
   We, we ourselves rejoice!
And thence flows all that charms or ear or sight,   [320]
All melodies the Echoes of that Voice,
All Colors a Suffusion of that Light.

Sister & Friend of my devoutest Choice!
Thou being innocent & full of love,
And nested with the Darlings of thy Love,   [325]
And feeling in thy Soul, Heart, Lips, & Arms
Even what the conjugal & mother Dove
That Borrows genial Warmth from those, she warms,
Feels in her thrill'd wings, blessedly outspread—
Thou free'd awhile from Cares & human Dread   [330]
By the Immenseness of the Good & Fair
   Which thou see'st every where—
Thus, thus should'st thou rejoice!

To thee would all Things live from Pole to Pole,
Their Life the Eddying of thy living Soul.   [335]
O dear! O Innocent! O full of Love!
A very Friend! A Sister of my Choice—
O dear, as Light & Impulse from above,
Thus may'st thou ever, evermore rejoice!   [339]

S.T.C.

*I*T IS DIFFICULT to imagine a more frustrating record of a turning point in literary history than Dorothy's journal entries of
28 March–5 April 1802. On the day after Wordsworth began his Ode,
he and his sister left Grasmere for Keswick to visit Coleridge. In the
entries of succeeding days we read impatiently of a visit to Miss
Crossthwaite, of dinner at Greta Hall with William Calvert and the
Rev. and Mrs. Thomas Wilkinson, of tea with the Miss Cockins, of
jaunts up Seat How and onto Skiddaw (*DWJ* 106–07). Ordinarily,
such matters might divert us, giving as they do glimpses of the daily
textures of lives so far away in time and space. Our attention is
caught by the entry of 4 April, in which Dorothy records having
repeated her brother's verses for a group which included Wordsworth,
Coleridge, and his wife; but we want, perhaps unreasonably, to
know so much more, especially about the nature and magnitude of
Coleridge's response to Wordsworth's recent work, including the
Ode, on which Dorothy is wholly silent.

What we have of that response is a fair copy, in his own hand, of
a 339-line poem entitled "A Letter to ———, April 4, 1802.—Sunday Evening." After our sleight-of-hand with the nonexistent text of
Wordsworth's Ode of 1802, it is reassuring to be in the presence of a
manuscript, particularly one bearing a firm date. In studying Coleridge, though, nothing is easy. Norman Fruman expresses grave
doubts about whether the text presented here was composed on the
evening of 4 April, and even graver doubts about the exact status of
the only extant holograph manuscript:

The holograph manuscript of this "letter" is in Dove Cottage. Apart from its title, . . . surely a common bit of poetic license, there is no reason whatever for including it among Coleridge's collected *correspondence*. The "letter" proves to be a carefully written *fair copy* of an earlier, unknown manuscript. Can one be sure of this? First, in 340 lines there are just ten words canceled and replaced. The poem is carefully divided and spaced into stanzas, which are in turn indented at various points to clarify rhyme patterns. . . . the poem is neatly written on one side of the page into the center leaves of a string-sewn notebook from which the outer leaves, front and rear, may have been removed so that the notebook's covers serve as a binding for the poem. If Coleridge wrote a 340-line poem in one night, he might finally have had several score worksheets, from which at last he made a fair copy. If the poem was finished on 4 April he seems not to have said a word about it to anyone until 17 days later, when he read it to the Wordsworths. [1]

Fruman is surely correct that in Dove Cottage MS. 39 we are dealing not with the letter Coleridge sent to Sara Hutchinson (if indeed he ever sent it as a letter rather than a poem) but with a carefully prepared poetic manuscript. Its version of the Verse Letter appears to antedate the recently discovered transcription in the hand of Mary Hutchinson, called the Cornell MS., which now also resides at Dove Cottage, but unfortunately that manuscript cannot be dated securely either. For Coleridge the date which heads the manuscript was probably a memorial date, commemorating an evening which held great symbolic value for him, a variation on the kind of dates we put on checks we have neglected to mail. George Dekker has offered several such symbolic datings in Coleridge's work. [2]

Fruman and Dekker reasonably argue that the Verse Letter, in this or any other full version, is unlikely to have been composed in any single evening. However, Dekker's suggestion that the Verse Letter "is, in effect, an intermediate and in many ways deviant draft of *Dejection: An Ode*" (54), is dubious. Dekker argues that Coleridge took sections of a poem which already existed in substantial form, improvised new material to suit it to its occasion by adding private gestures of love and friendship, and sent it to Sara Hutchinson. He buttresses his argument by comparing the quality of verse found in sections which survive through the received text of "Dejection" to the quality of those which do not. Although what Coleridge kept was ultimately better than most of what he threw away, Dekker's argumentative method recalls the bad old days of attribution analysis in Renaissance drama: if you run across a clinker in Shakespeare, reassign it to Beaumont and Fletcher.

Dekker's elaborate textual speculations about the Verse Letter ultimately serve only one end. They preserve 4 April 1802 as a possible literal date for the Verse Letter to have been "assembled" out of already existing *ur-Dejection* lines and hasty improvisations. And why is it important to preserve this date, about which Dekker himself confesses "radical scepticism?" If Coleridge can be thought to have started an *ur-Dejection* a month before the date and occasion of the Verse Letter, Dekker can accept the notion that he could be, "for fifty lines here and sixty lines there, one of the greatest and most polished poets in the language, and for stretches of a hundred or seventy lines at a time, no better than a clumsy off-the-top-of-the-head versifier" (48). In fact, it is not necessary to believe that Coleridge actually finished any version of the verse Letter before 20 April, the day on which he arrived at Grasmere for a visit and the day before his memorable reading of the poem to Wordsworth and Dorothy (*DWJ* 113–14). Coleridge has a month to have written the poem in one direction, two and a half weeks in the other. Dekker seems ultimately to be protecting "Dejection" from Wordsworth by minimizing the formative role of Wordsworth's Ode of 1802 in the genesis of Coleridge's poem. He counts but two "distinct echoes" of the Ode in the Verse Letter—the most conservative estimate on record—and he adds that "these lines bear all the marks of impromptu writing" (49). Like the other bad stuff in the poem, Beaumont and Fletcher did it, or caused it.

One can understand Dekker's territorial fervor. Great poem that it is, "Dejection" has had the misfortune to live in the shadow of Wordsworth's Ode. By the time Coleridge's poem received its first published praise (and from a relative), Wordsworth's Ode was arguably the most important cultural document of its age.[3] Dekker wants us to know that "Dejection" was *Coleridge's* poem, and that far from beginning in an occasionally mawkish and often rambling response to a work of the friend to whom he was so strongly devoted, it was a poem that Coleridge had, in one way or another, been writing all his life. And further, that it was a poem that English poetry had been trying to bring forth for half a century.

I sympathize with Dekker's motives as strongly as I disagree with his interpretation of the available evidence on the Verse Letter. "Dejection" is undoubtedly Coleridge's poem, and Dekker's citations from the poet's earlier letters and notebooks show decisively that Coleridge, fascinated by the eighteenth century's obsession with the plight of genius, had been playing upon and around the Verse Letter's topics and even phrasings for many years. It is eerie to watch the way in which Coleridge's playful poses become realities. Not only had he been shaping this poem all his life, it had been shaping him. But—at least until further evidence arises which might confirm the earlier existence of the poem—Coleridge did not begin writing what became "Dejection" as a poem until he had heard or read, or both, Wordsworth's fragmentary Ode of 1802. Wordsworth's Ode triggered Coleridge's Verse Letter by giving him something concrete to respond to, to set and measure himself against, and, in a deeply reflexive fashion, to complete. Dekker suggests that we not take the Verse Letter "too seriously as an aesthetic object which surely it was never meant to be" (51). The physical manuscript from which he is working, described so vividly by Fruman, argues against such a view. The manuscript is prepared with meticulous care; its very heading, "A Letter to ————," suggests not the salutation of a piece of correspondence but the title of a work of literature in a traditional form, the verse epistle.

The following pages depart considerably from the emphases of the preceding chapter on Wordsworth's Ode. The things least in doubt about Coleridge's poem are its sources, although some fresh formal analogies will be suggested. Coleridge's anxieties, as overdetermined in the Verse Letter as Wordsworth's are obscure in the Ode, have been traced to various roots in his relationship with Sara Hutchinson, in his psychosexual development, in his philosophy of nature, in his spiritual experience, in his ideas on love, and in his extensive readings in the literature of sensibility.[4] This chapter concentrates instead on the Verse Letter as a draft toward a poem, and more specifically as a kind of poem which exists in creative tension with the work which is its obvious and overwhelming source, Wordsworth's Ode of 1802. Such a way of reading the Verse Letter is hardly new. It was sketched out by Thomas McFarland in a masterful study which has been the most influential single piece of scholarship dealing broadly with the relationship between the two poets as poets.[5] McFarland is persuasive on the "principle of polar opposition" which enriched the collaboration of the two friends while it prohibited their "blending . . . into one literary entity" (276).

As an indication of the way in which Wordsworth's and Coleridge's collaboration worked, McFarland calls special attention to a famous passage from the *Biographia Literaria*. Coleridge says of their work on *Lyrical Ballads*:

> it was agreed, that my endeavours should be directed to persons and characters supernatural, or at least romantic; yet so as to transfer from our inward nature a human interest and a semblance of truth sufficient to procure for these shadows of imagination that willing suspension of disbelief for the moment, which constitutes poetic faith. Mr. Wordsworth, on the other hand, was to propose to himself as his object, to give the charm of novelty to things of every day, and to excite a feeling analogous to the supernatural, by awakening the mind's attention from the lethargy of custom, and directing it to the loveliness and the wonders of the world before us. (*BL* 2:6–7)

If Coleridge is spinning a nostalgic fiction in this passage, it is probably somewhere in the general direction of truth. However the collaboration was planned, this must have been something like the way it worked out. Coleridge could almost be describing directly the relationship between his own narrative masterpiece, *The Rime of the Ancient Mariner*, and Wordsworth's *Peter Bell*, which was begun about the same time but not completed to Wordsworth's satisfaction for any of the issuings of *Lyrical Ballads*.[6] The example is germane, because the Verse Letter gestures in one line toward both poems. Looking at "Yon crescent Moon, as fix'd as if it grew / In it's own

cloudless, starless Lake of Blue" (39–40), Coleridge is reminded of
"A Boat becalm'd! dear William's Sky Canoe" (41). The first half of
the line recalls the dreadful calm in which Coleridge's mariner is
held, while the second loses these nightmarish associations in memories of Wordsworth's wayward but playful craft in the Prologue to
Peter Bell.[7] Reflexive currents flowed both ways in the relationship.
Peter Bell discovered its countertext in Coleridge's *Rime*, while Wordsworth's Ode served the same function for Coleridge's Verse Letter.

The following discussion, borrowing upon one of Harold Bloom's
concepts, views Coleridge's Verse Letter as an antithetical completion
of Wordsworth's Ode of 1802. It approaches the limits of the shaky
fiction which ultimately underpins intertextual analysis of all kinds,
the myth of perfect complementarity. A study that is serious about
the ways in which poems impinge on one another has little choice
but to assume potential meaningfulness in the differences as well as
similarities between companion poems. The one area of comparison
which will not concern me, ideational differences in the poems, has
generated the bulk of existing commentary on the works. It seems
inappropriate to compare the ideas of the two poems, because Wordsworth's fragmentary Ode of 1802 had no ideas. The completed work
grows a goodly number of them in 1804, and my penultimate chapter pursues them at length. At this stage of his poem's development,
though, Coleridge is not responding to ideational content: he is responding to poetic form, to images, to latent but powerful emotional
currents in Wordsworth's work, and to his own formulations of
Wordsworth the poet and Coleridge the poet. He is not engaging in
a conceptual struggle with this particular text. Indeed, it may be the
Ode's freedom from conceptualization that leaves Coleridge free to
pursue his own conjectures. When Wordsworth moves toward conceptualization of the fragment in 1804, he will do so in the face of
repeated philosophical readings of his work which have already been
performed by Coleridge.

In Chapter Two I remarked that it was odd that Wordsworth
should have begun an ode at all, and Magnuson has pointed out that
it is equally rare to find a fixed idea of genre in advance of Wordsworth's compositional activity.[8] It was Coleridge who was the odist.
Much of his early fame (or notoriety) as an active political poet had

been based on "Ode to the Departing Year" (1796) and "France: an Ode" (1798), declamatory works in the highest and most public English Pindaric tradition. In beginning an ode of the higher sort, whatever its subject, Wordsworth was trespassing into his friend's poetic territory. What are we to make, then, of Coleridge's responding with a verse epistle? Among expressive forms, the ode and the epistle stand near opposite ends of any traditional scale of poetic elevation. Higher odes are public in outlook, wrapped in the trappings of prophetic intent, and are normally addressed to a god and only overheard by any human audience. Verse epistles are inherently private, circumstantial, and colloquial. As Horace has shown, a versatile poet can work in both forms; but as posterity's response to his works has also shown, he may not seem to work in them equally happily. *Letter to the Pisones* must have left a dozen contented readers for every one of the *Carmen Saeculare*. Both are about serious business, but in very different ways.

Two possible explanations for Coleridge's generic swerve present themselves. Coleridge may be abasing himself in Wordsworth's presence, resigning to his friend the arena of higher utterance. Such an explanation is consonant with much of the emotional matter of the Verse Letter, and yet Coleridge's poem, while beginning colloquially, does rise to pitches of utterance commensurate with anything in Wordsworth's Ode of 1802. It uses as well, as Dekker has pointed out, a stanzaic pattern that would be completely at home in an English irregular Pindaric ode (48). It seems equally likely that Coleridge selected the form of the epistle as a way of commenting indirectly on the inappropriateness of the matter of Wordsworth's fragment to its chosen form. Wordsworth's poem maintains its power and elevation through its generality. Without specifying the cause of its discontents, it conveys intensity of feeling by adopting imagery and expressions derived ultimately from the conventions of erotic pastoral. Coleridge chooses a form which is solidly within the traditions of erotic literature. When we look for counterparts to his Verse Letter in English and classical poetry, we will not find them in the line of the "ethic epistle," which Jay Arnold Levine has traced from Horace through Pope's *Epistles to Several Persons*.[9] Instead, Coleridge intersects an epistolary form which traditionally has been given over to the exploration of the psychology of suffering, the erotic verse epistle, which is rooted in Ovid's *Heroides*, is codified for the eighteenth century by Pope's "Eloisa to Abelard," and may lie behind much of the epistolary prose fiction of sensibility, in which, as Dekker has demonstrated, Coleridge was deeply immersed.

A progress of rhymes, perhaps coincidental, is suggestive. Pleading for a letter from Abelard, Pope's Eloisa cries, "Then share thy pain, allow that sad relief; / Ah more than share it! give me all thy grief." [10] Wordsworth writes: "To me alone there came a thought of grief / A timely utterance gave that thought relief" (22–23). Coleridge tells Sara of

> A Grief without a pang, void, dark, & drear,
> A stifling, drowsy, unimpassion'd Grief
> That finds no natural Outlet, no Relief
> In word, or sigh, or tear.
>
> (17–20)

Coleridge's qualifications of his personal grief—"without a pang, void, dark, & drear, / A stifling, drowsy, unimpassion'd Grief"— seem designed to remove erotic implications from his feelings, or more properly his lack of feelings. He is akin not to Pope's Eloisa, who has burned and yearned rather too pointedly for many readers, but to her description of Abelard:

> For thee the fates, severely kind, ordain
> A cool suspense from pleasure and from pain;
> Thy life a long, dead calm of fix'd repose;
> No pulse that riots, and no blood that glows.
>
> (249–52)

Coleridge seems to interpret Wordsworth's "timely utterance" as an expression of grief by the poet himself, and an expression within established conventions of erotic longing—"word, or sigh, or tear"— all of which Eloisa supplies in abundance. By setting the relief of vocal utterance or even wordless expression of sorrow in apposition with "natural Outlet," which must itself be read in apposition with Wordsworth's "timely utterance," Coleridge is subtly eroticizing the sense of satisfaction available to Wordsworth but denied himself. Coleridge frames his emotional situation by means of a reflexive commentary on his construction of Wordsworth's, which reads through his friend's text to the conventions which underpin it.

Much of the tension between Wordsworth's Ode and Coleridge's Verse Letter is generic in origin. As Paul Fry has intriguingly described the desires of the higher ode, it is a form which insists on presence. It yearns to confront its deity directly, without mediation, and Fry appropriately calls its aesthetic mode presentational rather than representational. With aspirations so unbounded, the ode is often doomed to failure, and in English verse its theme may become its own inability to achieve or sustain presence.[11] Something of this sort happens in stanzas III and IV of Wordsworth's Ode. The poet is not so much describing a landscape as calling forth a season. A May setting, for example, is created for this poem written in late March. For reasons not fully clear in the text of 1802, the presence of May cannot be maintained, and Wordsworth's last lines question and lament the failure of, among other things, his created season. In direct contrast, the erotic verse epistle is grounded in absence. Separated by an unbridgeable distance which is a measure of physical, emotional, and spiritual alienation, its writer yearns for a presence which is always known to be impossible. Eloisa may call for Abelard, but he will not and cannot come to her. They are separated by distance, by convent walls, by the fact of his emasculation, and by the laws of man and God. By responding to Wordsworth's Ode with a variant of the erotic verse epistle, Coleridge accentuates both the hopefulness of his friend's situation and the desperate hopelessness of his own. Coleridge simply does not read or respond to the last seven lines of Wordsworth's fragment, which tell of the "tree of many one," the "single field," and the "pansy," all of which bespeak the loss of the "visionary gleam." Indeed, the last seven lines of the Ode of 1802 may not have been written in March, but may be the "little" more which Dorothy records having been added to the poem on 17 June (*DWJ* 137). Such a conjecture is not necessary for my point, however, because the Wordsworth whom Coleridge creates in his Verse Letter *is* a poet capable of achieving presence in all aspects of his life, while the Coleridge he creates is condemned to absence.

The sexual roles implied by the two forms also deserve comment. The higher ode has been in Coleridge's practice a strenuous and manly form. (One can hardly avoid a term the poet used so widely.) In "Ode to the Departing Year" and "France: An Ode" he girds his loins and addresses the nation as a wholly masculine prophet. Self-doubt may have existed in his past responses to the events of which he speaks, but not in the present of his utterance.[12] The erotic verse epistle, on the other hand, is established by Ovid as a feminine form. Twenty-one letters constitute the canon of the *Heroides*, all but three of which are written through the personae of women. The three exceptions, epistles from Paris to Helen, Leander to Hero, and Acontius to Cydippe, serve as occasions for responses by the heroines addressed, who are given the final words in the exchanges. Adaptations of the form in England in the sixteenth and seventeenth centuries were more even-handed, especially in the most famous work in the tradition, Michael Drayton's *Englands Historicall Epistles* (1597–99), which presented twenty-four letters arranged in pairs. Whatever claims may be made for the psychological penetration of Drayton's verse letters, though, it is reasonably clear that he is finally more interested in history than in passion, and we find in his work nothing even approaching the sensual intensity of *Heroides* 15 (Sappho to Phaon).

When Pope takes up the matter of Eloisa and Abelard from John Hughes's French adaptation of the Latin letters (1713), he condenses the exchange of correspondence into a single verse epistle, written by Eloisa in the late stages of her despair.[13] He is doing little more than acknowledging the dominant tendency of the form since its inception. The Horatian "ethic epistle" is a masculine form, while the Ovidian erotic epistle is feminine. The proclivity of the male writer to masquerade as a woman in order to explore passion which borders on or crosses over into madness is fascinating, and clearly deserving of a broader cultural critique than is offered in these pages.

In his complaints—a form at least distantly related to the erotic verse epistle—Wordsworth can be observed using female impersonation to such ends three times in the *Lyrical Ballads* of 1798: "The Female Vagrant," "The Mad Mother," and "The Complaint of a forsaken Indian Woman." Aside from Coleridge's very slight "The Complaint of Ninathome," written in 1793 and published in 1796, there are no examples of his presenting an entire poem through the persona of a woman. Some of the discomfort critics have confessed about Coleridge's Verse Letter can be attributed to the effect of encountering a feminine genre written in a masculine voice, and a voice which has, at best, extreme doubts about its own sexual identity. The major topics of Coleridge's poem—alienation from the beloved and the loss of song—are the stuff of Ovid's *Heroides* 15, written by Sappho as she recalls the history of her thwarted love for Phaon and anticipates her suicide.

In contiguous notebook entries of December 1801, Coleridge proposed for himself either one or two closely related projects:

To write a *series* of Love Poems—truly Sapphic, save that they shall have a large Interfusion of moral Sentiment & calm Imagery on Love in all the moods of the mind—Philosophic, fantastic, in moods of high enthusiasm, of simple Feeling, of mysticism, of Religion—/comprize in it all the practice, & all the philosophy of Love—

A lively picture of a man, disappointed in marriage, & endeavoring to make himself a virtuous & tender & brotherly friendship with an amiable Woman—the obstacles—the jealousies—the impossibility of it.—Best advice that he should as much as possible withdraw himself from the pursuits of morals &c—& devote himself to the abstract sciences—(*CNB* 1:1064–65)

The relevance of these entries to Coleridge's "Dejection" has never been in doubt.[14] What is puzzling is what Coleridge meant by "truly Sapphic." In a notebook entry from the German winter of 1798–99 he speaks with some security of Sappho's metrical practices, but makes no references to her as a love poet (*CNB* 1:373). Reading Sappho's fragments is itself an experience vaguely comparable to reading Coleridge's notebooks, as words and lines suggesting one of the moods of love are juxtaposed against diametrically opposed emotions. For some notion of what the idea of Sappho meant within poetic tradition, we might turn to "Longinus," in his comments upon a fragment he preserved, now known as fragment 31:

> Do you not admire the way in which she brings everything to-gether—mind and body, hearing and tongue, eyes and skin? She seems to have lost them all, and to be looking for them as though they were external to her. She is cold and hot, mad and sane, frightened, and near death, all by turns. The result is that we see in her not a single emotion, but a complex of emotions. Lovers experience all this; Sappho's excellence, as I have said, lies in her adoption and combination of the most striking details.[15]

The poetry of Sappho was read and understood as a poetry of moods and volatile changes, and the intimate voice of her monodies has frequently been contrasted to the public voice of Pindar's choric works. Sappho's addressees seem more often single and personal than corporate, and the erotic verse epistle would not be the worst analogue for attempting to recover the lost forms of her work. Indeed, Ovid's *Heroides* 15 became quasi-canonical as a result of its being one of the major sources of lore about the obscure poetess.[16] When, in a notebook entry of September 1803, Coleridge compares a "High Bridge" of the Scottish mountains to "Sappho's Leap," he intersects not the Sapphic canon but the myth of her suicide perpetuated by Ovid. And Coleridge was certainly reading the *Heroides* shortly after he wrote the Verse Letter: in a letter to William Sotheby of 26 August 1802, the first letter to Sotheby following the one of 19 July in which he included altered stanzas from the Verse Letter (described as having been addressed to Wordsworth), Coleridge quotes two lines from *Heroides* 12 (Medea to Jason), in outlining an idea for a tragedy on the subject of Medea (*STCL* 2:813–19, 855–59).

My interest is not so much in Coleridge's sources as in what his chosen form allows him to do in the face of Wordsworth's fragmentary Ode. Chapter Two considered at length the Ode's lack of a concrete physical setting, a space for its meditations more secure than the idyllic landscape called forth in stanzas III–IV. As a part of their attempt to bridge a void between writer and reader, verse epistles pay particular attention to the environmental circumstances of their composition. After his colloquial and seemingly random reference to the "grand old Ballad of Sir Patrick Spence" (2), Coleridge attempts to describe for Sara the specific setting in which he is writing:

> This Night, so tranquil now, will not go hence
> Unrous'd by winds, that ply a busier trade
> Than that, which moulds yon clouds in lazy flakes,
> Or the dull sobbing Draft, that drones & rakes
> Upon the Strings of this Eolian Lute,
>   Which better far were mute.
> For lo! the New Moon, winter-bright!
> And overspread with phantom Light,
> (With swimming phantom Light o'erspread
> But rimm'd & circled with a silver Thread)
> I see the Old Moon in her Lap, foretelling
> The coming-on of Rain & squally Blast—
>
>   (3–14)

Coupled with his dating of the poem in its title ("April 4, 1802"), Coleridge's opening lines establish his work as the product of a time and place. While Wordsworth's despair at the beginning of the Ode was unfocused and free-floating, Coleridge's emotions, although not created by their setting, interact throughout with the environment in which he is writing of them. The poet's heart, mind, and eye are in process, and subtle rhetorical gestures provide his verse with a sense of spontaneity. The amplifying parenthetical expressions throughout the poem ("With swimming phantom Light o'erspread / But rimm'd & circled with a silver Thread") give the sense of a mind that is recording its first impression, but then circling back to give a clearer sense of what it is perceiving. Such touches may, as Dekker suggests, be well lost when the poem is transformed into an ode, but within the form of the verse letter they add measurably to its effects.[17]

Coleridge could have had another motivation for beginning his poem with detailed natural description. His work is as competitive as it is complementary. His opening description as well as his observation of the skies in the second verse paragraph recall his seemingly effortless evocations of scene and mood in such poems as "This Lime-tree Bower my Prison" (1797) and "Frost at Midnight" (1798), which achieve delicate scenic effects as far beyond the reach of Wordsworth as, say, Wordsworth's passage from the *Prelude* on crossing the Alps is beyond the reach of Coleridge. It is sad that Coleridge consistently undervalued his gift in comparison to his friend's, but the countless notebook passages in which he works painstakingly to develop his observational abilities demonstrate that he did take it seriously. The following passage, then, might profitably be read against Wordsworth's catalogue of earthly light in stanza II of the Ode:

> All this long Eve, so balmy & serene,
> Have I been gazing on the western Sky
> And it's peculiar tint of Yellow Green—
> And still I gaze—& with how blank an eye!
> And those thin Clouds above, in flakes & bars
> That give away their Motion to the Stars;
> Those Stars, that glide behind them, or between
> Now sparkling, now bedimm'd, but always seen;
> Yon crescent Moon, as fix'd as if it grew
> In it's own cloudless, starless Lake of Blue—
> A Boat becalm'd! dear William's Sky Canoe!
> —I see them all, so excellently fair!
> I see, not feel, how beautiful they are.
>
> (31–43)

A countertext for Coleridge's passage may be found in four lines from Wordsworth's Ode:

> The Moon doth with delight
> Look round her when the heavens are bare
>   Waters on a starry night
> Are beautiful and fair
>
> (12–15)

Coleridge's scene is both "fair" and "beautiful" (42–43), and it is much more fully observed. He has reflected the basic elements of Wordsworth's lines, the solitary moon and star-filled heavens, and with his reference to the "Lake of Blue" and "dear William's Sky Canoe" (40–41), he has gestured as well toward Wordsworth's image of reflected light. Other intertextual resonances are also remarkable. The description of the "thin clouds" giving "away their Motion to the Stars" (35–36) points toward one of Wordsworth's most impressive early poems, "A Night-Piece" (January 1798), and by invoking *Peter Bell,* Coleridge also calls forth memories of his own "A Soliloquy of the full Moon, She being in a Mad Passion" (1800–1801), the first work by Coleridge entered in "Sara Hutchinson's Poets" (DC MS. 41), and one of the most exuberant of those works George Whalley has identified as Asra Poems.[18] In "A Soliloquy" the moon rants at having been transformed into a "little Canoe" (32) by Wordsworth, the "Rogue" (26) who is "The head of the Gang" (27) of "muttering / Spluttering / Ventriloquogusty / Poets" (10–13). Coupled with his allusion to his own "Rime," the pattern of references ties together the time both of Coleridge's greatest productivity in his relationship with Wordsworth and of the early, and apparently happiest, days of his love for Sara Hutchinson.

Coleridge's scene is doubly beautiful, then, both in itself and in the memories of happier times which his description recalls. He creates this sense of the beauty of external things, of course, only to deny his own responsiveness to them: "I see, not feel, how beautiful they are" (43). For the Coleridge of the Verse Letter it is immaterial that the Wordsworth of the Ode is presenting feelings of chronic and acute depression; the important thing is that Wordsworth is *feeling*. Throughout Coleridge's second verse paragraph the emphasis is on lack of emotion, on a void at what should be the heart of his emotional life. His "Grief" of lines 17–20 is so heavily qualified as to empty it of all possible qualities of feeling. His mood is "heartless" (23). The throstle "That pipes within the Larch-tree, not unseen" (25), which should with "all the tender Sounds & gentle Sights / Of this sweet Primrose-month" (28–29) woo him "to mild Delights" (27)—implicitly to erotic sensation—woos in vain (29).[19] Coleridge's pains are not within the breast, as they are in conventional erotic literature; they are more like a "smoth'ring Weight" (46) *upon* the breast, which cannot be removed by the beauty of things external to the self:

> It were a vain Endeavour,
>   Tho' I should gaze for ever
> On that Green Light, which lingers in the West!
> I may not hope from outward Forms to win
> The Passion & the Life, whose Fountains are within!
> These lifeless Shapes, around, below, Above,
>   O what can they impart?
>
> (47–53)

As much as anything in Wordsworth's Ode of 1802, these lines from Coleridge's poem direct Wordsworth's ultimate completion of his fragment in 1804. Stanzas V–XI of the Ode will become to a striking degree a meditation on a setting sun, from which image something is *won*: "Another race hath been, and other palms are w[on?]" (193). Wordsworth's adoption of Coleridge's image is particularly striking because, for all the natural phenomena catalogued in the Ode of 1802, there had been no sunset.

Coleridge's depiction of the last vestiges of sunset brings him back to thoughts of Sara. Even the thought that she may be viewing the same sight as he, "Sweet Thought it is—yet feebly stirs my Heart!" (57). By simple verbal association, reminiscent of his practices in the conversation poems, the word *feebly* moves him to recreate an equivalent time within the history of his own feelings to Wordsworth's time of the visionary gleam. He recalls the time "In my first Dawn of Youth that Fancy stole / With many secret Yearnings on my Soul" (60–61). For the unspecified time of glory suggested by Wordsworth, Coleridge substitutes the period of the beginnings of romantic feeling. In keeping with the peculiarly anerotic biases of this erotic verse letter, this was a time of purity as well as intensity of feeling. While he has been but "feebly" stirred by imagining Sara gazing at the skies, there was a time when he could not imagine a

> Man so stripp'd of good affections
> As not to love to see a Maiden's quiet eyes

Uprais'd, and linking on sweet Dreams by dim Connections
To Moon, or Evening Star, or glorious western Skies.

(68–71)

When he was a schoolboy this "Thought," as he calls it, "became a kind of Vision to me!" (72–73). Coleridge converts Wordsworth's time of the celestial light into the time when he was possessed by a visionary idea of romantic love. Once that vision has been recollected, he can re-enact partially Wordsworth's recovery from his thought of grief: "I spake with rash Despair, / And ere I was aware, / The weight was somewhat lifted from my Breast" (77–79). Imagining Sara's present situation more vividly, whether in "the weather-fended Wood" (80) or sitting "Upon the sod-built Seat of Camomile" (86), he becomes able to feel—"I feel my spirit mov'd" (92)—and can experience the relief of articulation: "And I, dear Sara—*I am blessing thee!*" (98).

Coleridge shapes his poem from a double rhetorical perspective that is characteristic of the literary verse epistle. On the one hand, the Verse Letter at least pretends to be a piece of personal correspondence. It is addressed to a single individual, written from a specific location, at a particular time, and prompted by a singular occasion. The occasion of Coleridge's Verse Letter is not finally made clear until lines 111–29, when we find that he is writing in response to a letter of Sara's reporting that she is ill, apparently as a consequence of a "complaining Scroll" he himself had sent to her. On the other hand, the literary verse epistle has a public audience beyond its addressee. Coleridge's reading the verses to Wordsworth and Dorothy on 21 April, his referring to them as having been addressed to Thomas Poole in a letter of 7 May (*STCL* 2:801), his sending large sections of the poem's less intimate stanzas to Sotheby on 19 July, with a statement that it had been written to Wordsworth (*STCL* 2:814–819), his including two passages in a letter to Southey on 29 July (*STCL* 2:831–32), and his providing for Thomas Wedgwood on 20 October the passage dealing with his abstruse researches, which he had omitted from the version of "Dejection" published in the Morning Post (*STCL* 2:875), all suggest the larger audience envisioned for the Verse Letter. The poem is simultaneously written

to Sara and *for* Coleridge's more or less immediate circle of friends.
With so many quotations from the poem in the extant correspondence of mid-1802, one wonders how many letters containing segments of it have not survived.

A full reading of the problems of multiple audience implicit in
the Verse Letter, coupled with a full study of the poem's intertextual
resonances, might end up demonstrating conclusively only that art
is indeed long and life short. The remainder of this chapter addresses
first those formal and topical components of Coleridge's Verse Letter
which seem to be generically determined, and then those which are
most fruitfully explained in terms of the poem's intertextual mission,
which is largely to differentiate the poetic impulses, strategies, and
practices of Coleridge from those of Wordsworth.

This discussion of the generic qualities of the Verse Letter is
framed against the practices of the form as they are represented in
Ovid's *Heroides* 15 (Sappho to Phaon), a work already mentioned.
Although to some extent this procedure is arbitrary, the poet who
was reworking a poem of Wordsworth's for the *Morning Post* in late
1800, and signing it Alcaeus in response to Mrs. Mary "Perdita"
Robinson's Sappho, had more than a passing interest in Sapphic
lore.[20] The presiding topic of Ovid's poem is the disastrous effect of
the loss of Phaon on Sappho's life and art.[21] She burns like fields
driven by the east winds (9–10), but her craft is not impelled by the
winds of inspiration (71–72), because poetry must be the work of a
mind free of cares (14). The wind is the presiding image of Ovid's
poem as it is of Coleridge's. Sappho worries that the winds which
carry her words of complaint away from Phaon, so that her prayers
accomplish nothing, are the same betraying winds which will not fill
the sails which could carry Phaon back to her (207–14). Sappho's
leap into the Leucadian wave, which the poem foreshadows, is implicitly her way of giving herself over to the winds, either to become
free from her consuming passions or to be killed. Her love for Phaon
is presented as one of a series of emotional upheavals that has alien-
ated the poetess from her art. The early death of her father, the
enmity of her brother, and the weariness brought about by caring for
her daughter have also been contributing factors (59–70).
Sappho's emotional misfortunes have left her stripped of all which

might have the power to engage her heart. She no longer delights in the embraces of the Lesbian daughters whom she has loved before (15–20). She alternates between praises of the beauty of Phaon and depreciation of her own charms (21–40), which have decayed drastically since her lover's desertion, as she takes no care in personal adornment (71–96). Ovid has Sappho move from emotion to emotion with volatile rapidity. A lyrical recollection of her lovemaking with Phaon (45–50) will lead abruptly to jealousy of the Sicilian maidens now imagined as enjoying his love (51–56). She dreams voluptuously of her lover (123–34), and when hated daylight comes, she roams the woods seeking out the spots which recall their passion. Her desire has carried her to the point where she is beyond pride: she pleads that Phaon return not to love her, but simply to let himself be loved (93–96).

Even the barest summary of the major topics of Ovid's poem shows its relevance to Coleridge's Verse Letter. Before recovering the feeling that leads to his initial prayer and blessing for Sara (97–98), Coleridge imaginatively revisits her favored haunts (80–91). After his blessing, he recalls a moment laden with erotic memories, but eroticism of the purified kind which the poem insists upon throughout:

> It was as calm as this, that happy night
> When Mary, thou, & I together were,
> The low decaying Fire our only Light,
> And listen'd to the Stillness of the Air!
> O that affectionate & blameless Maid,
> Dear Mary! on her Lap my head she lay'd—
>   Her Hand was on my Brow,
>   Even as my own is now;
> And on my Cheek I felt thy eye-lash play.
> Such Joy I had, that I may truly say,
> My Spirit was awe-stricken with the Excess
> And trance-like Depth of it's brief Happiness.
>   (99–110)

This, the first appearance of the crucial word *Joy* in the Verse Letter, embeds it in questions of interpersonal relationships. The happy

memory is no sooner evoked, though, than Coleridge castigates himself for not having let it prevent him from sending the letter which
has led to Sara's present illness and misery.

After several lines of self-recriminations, Coleridge rouses himself
to an act of heroic renunciation, a recurrent moment in Ovid's *Heroides*, pledging to be happy in the happiness of the Wordsworth circle
in his friend's impending marriage to Mary. He promises only moments of infrequent regrets, "Dreaming of all your Loves & Quietness" (143), while he in isolation wears "away / In no inglorious Toils
the manly Day" (139–40). He will absent himself from their felicity,
for fear that seeing their joy might tempt him to repine, and even to
blight their spirits:

> While *ye* are *well* & *happy*, twould but wrong you
> If I should fondly yearn to be among you—
> Wherefore, O wherefore! should I wish to be
> A wither'd branch upon a blossoming Tree?
>   (165–68)

As Coleridge pits Grasmere's imagined lot against his own—"It is,
& will remain, Indifference or Strife" (164)—it becomes apparent
that his promises of contentment are primarily an inversion of a common topic of the erotic verse epistle—the topic of jealousy. Grasmere
has become Sicily to Keswick's Lesbia.

Coleridge's renunciation is short-lived. After imagining the Wordsworth circle in perfect health and happiness, he imagines Sara lying
ill in the future, and vows to fly to her side to comfort her and
attempt to bring her health. He is roused from his morbid imaginings—"The dark distressful Dream" (185)—by the sound of the
wind, which leads him into musings about poetry which are more
properly a part of the Wordsworthian direction of the poem. Another
prayer for Sara then leads him to comparisons between her situation
and his own, in which he lapses into the well-known analysis of his
own marriage:

> my coarse domestic life has known
> No Habits of heart-nursing Sympathy,

> No Griefs, but such as dull and deaden me,
> No Hopes of it's own Vintage, None, O! none—
> (258–61)

Like Sappho's daughter, Coleridge's children become, in these circumstances, a burden and a curse:

> Those little Angel Children (woe is me!)
> There have been hours, when feeling how they bind
> And pluck out the wing-feathers of my Mind,
> Turning my Error to Necessity,
> I have half-wish'd, they never had been born!
> (277–81)

After Coleridge's furthest descent into exploring his personal misery, he once again rouses himself to a discussion of the sources and consequences of Joy, addressed to Sara but directed at Wordsworth. He ends with a final prayer that she "may'st . . . ever, evermore rejoice!" (339). In the context established by the genre of the poem, Coleridge's final prayer and blessing are not easily read as evidence of his recovery from his emotional crisis. Too many waxings have been followed by too many wanings for the reader to see in the poem's conclusion much more than a temporary termination. The erotic verse epistle, in any event, is predominantly a work of the tragic or pathetic mode, and often Ovid will ironically pose the hopefulness of a heroine's conclusion against the reader's knowledge of what is to follow in the myth.[22] For Coleridge in the Verse Letter, a wish of happiness for Sara has too frequently been an act of renunciation of his own hopes for the reader to see the conclusion as much more than a final heroic gesture. More importantly, love letters do not and cannot resolve their dilemmas. The problem of absence inherent in the very circumstances of their composition cannot be resolved through their completion. Spirits may be lifted and psychological intimacy temporarily re-established, but at the end the unbridgeable gulf between the writer and his beloved remains as it was at the beginning.

If Coleridge's using the form of the erotic verse epistle does not quite enable him to accomplish the goals mentioned for the series of love poems in his notebook entry—to trace "Love in all the moods of the mind"—it has allowed him to depict with some credibility an astonishing range of emotions, including "a large Interfusion of moral Sentiment & calm Imagery" as well as emotions stemming from moods more characteristically Sapphic. The form justifies the fits and turns of his psychological responses, and the work does manage to impersonate an extempore performance, as any love letter should, however much it may have been revised. Its self-referentiality, including its notation of time passing in line 216 ("Tis Midnight! and small Thoughts have I of sleep"), is characteristic of the verse epistle, and handled by Coleridge with unusual subtlety. At least he spares us the tear stains on the page provided by Ovid's Sappho (97–98) and Pope's Eloisa (13–16).

It would be an understatement to say that the erotic verse epistle has not enjoyed a good critical press. Ovidians hold the *Heroides* in some disdain, Popians tiptoe nervously around "Eloisa to Abelard," and Coleridgeans seem generally relieved that the writer decided to turn the Verse Letter into an ode. Some may wish he had burned it. The infrequent analyses of these works consequently have a tendency to turn into polemical defenses.[23] My discussion of its generic properties has not claimed transcendent greatness for Coleridge's poem. I maintain only that it is what it is, and that it manages to be so in an interesting manner, especially when its formal strategies are read against those of both its tradition and of Wordsworth's Ode.

Now for those parts of Coleridge's poem which suggest that it is also more than it is: if much of the Verse Letter is in keeping with its genre, much is also in excess of any need to fulfill its form. A Wordsworth may have been necessary to give the erotic verse epistle its edge of jealousy and sexual envy, however muted, but the presence of this Wordsworth is out of all proportion to his role as a girl of Sicily, who will become upon marrying her sister the intimate of Coleridge's beloved object as well. The remainder of this chapter explores the poem's interactions with its secondary audience, which may be loosely described as Wordsworth and more specifically as the Wordsworth who emerges from Coleridge's reading of the Ode of 1802. While this Wordsworth is related to the one who is the center of the circle to contain Sara—"one happy Home, / One House, the dear abiding Home of All" (134–35)—he is also Wordsworth the Poet, with whom Coleridge engages in dialogue on rather more equal terms. This matter is concentrated into four continuous passages from the last half of the Verse Letter, all of which frame the differences between the two poets as Coleridge saw them, some of which are marked by direct allusions to Wordsworth's Ode, and all of which survive, to a greater or lesser extent, in the received text of "Dejection."

After Coleridge has so vividly imagined Sara lying ill in her bed and himself unable to come to her aid, a reverie which he labels "The dark distressful Dream" (185), he turns his attention from his somber introspections once more to his surroundings. It is clear at this point in the poem that he can be roused and moved, at least by retrospection and sympathetic imagination, but his response to the external world is still in doubt. In stanzas III and IV of the Ode, Wordsworth has been able to feel with the season, at least temporarily, and even when his mood of sympathetic delight fades, strong feeling remains, however negative. Coleridge's turn from his self-absorption to the external scene, then, obliquely parallels the turn which Wordsworth makes at the beginning of his third stanza:

> I turn from it, & listen to the Wind
> Which long has rav'd unnoticed! What a Scream
> Of agony by Torture lengthen'd out
> That Lute sent forth!
>
> (186–89)

The relationship between the passage describing the poet's responses to the sounds of the wind on the eolian lute (184–215) and the rest of the poem is obscure. There is no way of determining whether we are to see the reawakened harp as equivalent to the poetic spirit of the writer, who is now being roused and driven like it by external forces, or whether the harp is set in ironic contrast to his spirit, which cannot be moved even by forces capable of wringing from an inanimate object a simulacrum of song.

Dekker has mounted an impressive argument for taking with great seriousness the revised version of this passage in the received text of

"Dejection," showing that Coleridge's concern is not so much the fairly recent novelty of the wind harp as the ancient tradition of the winds of inspiration, a tradition which does not necessarily suggest that the poet is wholly passive and played upon (Dekker 101–41). Perhaps. However, the sequence of poetic moods suggested by the wind's activity argues against any reading of the passage as evidencing more than a fleeting recovery of imaginative powers. The lute's "Scream / Of agony" (187–88) which first catches the poet's attention is a reflection of the state of his spirit during the "dark distressful Dream" (185). The wind first suggests a setting for that scream, a setting which reflects both Coleridge's and Wordsworth's youthful preoccupations with the scenic paraphernalia of gothic horror: [24]

> Jagg'd Rock, or mountain Pond, or blasted Tree,
> Or Pine-grove, whither Woodman never clomb,
> Or lonely House, long held the Witches' Home,
> Methinks were fitter Instruments for Thee,
> Mad Lutanist!
>
> (190–94)

At the season of the beginnings of rebirth, the wind is making "Devil's Yule, with worse than wintry Song / The Blossoms, Buds, and timorous Leaves among" (196–97). When Coleridge attempts to hear within this Gothic setting the stories told by the wind, addressed as a perfect tragic actor and mighty (if frenzied) poet, he is able to make out two.

The first is a tale of war: "Tis of the Rushing of an Host in Rout—/ And many Groans from men with smarting Wounds—/ At once they groan with smart, and shudder with the Cold!" (201–203). Within these lines we may hear faint echoes of one of Coleridge's most cherished projects. On 20 October 1802, in a letter which included lines taken from the Verse Letter, he was to tell Thomas Wedgwood: "I have since my twentieth year meditated an heroic poem on the Siege of Jerusalem by Titus—this is the Pride, & the Stronghold of my hope. But I never think of it except in my best moods" (*STCL* 2:877). If the passage from the Verse Letter proceeds from one of the poet's best moods, which seems unlikely, that mood is certainly fleeting. The wind drops immediately, bringing a "Trance of deepest Silence" (204), which is followed by "other Sounds, and all less deep, less loud" (207). If the first tale had been Coleridge's, the second is clearly his friend's:

> A Tale of less Affright,
> And temper'd with Delight,
> As William's Self had made the tender Lay—
>   Tis of a little Child
>   Upon a heathy Wild,
> Not far from home—but it has lost it's way—
> And now moans low in utter grief & fear—
> And now screams loud, & hopes to make it's Mother hear!
>   (208–15)

What has happened in the passage seems clear enough. Coleridge has been roused by the wind and the harp to envision an appropriate setting for their sounds, a setting which comes out garden-variety Gothic. As he is moved to imagine a story appropriate to this setting, he first reaches for the heroic strain, evoking the pet topic before which every other subject for a modern epic would pale, or so he believed. His subject can be sustained only momentarily, and with a shift in the wind, his clashing armies are both overthrown by a Wordsworthian child. The echo of "Lucy Gray" reveals the Coleridge of epic desires overcome by Wordsworth the modest balladeer, and by the end of the stanza, the moans and screams have become not so much the wind's and the harp's, or even the lost child's, but the poet's. Wordsworth would seem once more to have descended upon Coleridge, as he had written to William Godwin a year earlier, and "by shewing to him what true Poetry was . . . made him to know, that he himself was no Poet" (*STCL* 2:714).

Support for such a construction comes a few lines further along in the Verse Letter. After a prayer that Sara may not suffer from his sleeplessness, Coleridge asks that she write to inform him of her health and cheerful spirits. His need for "good Tidings" (225) leads to a comparison of his past and present emotional states which rings

heavily of Wordsworth's Ode. "For, oh! beloved Friend!" he tells
Sara,

> I am not the buoyant Thing, I was of yore—
> When, like an own Child, I to *Joy* belong'd;
> For others mourning oft, myself oft sorely wrong'd,
> Yet bearing all things then, as if I nothing bore!
>
> (227–30)

Although Coleridge is borrowing Wordsworth's vague temporal designation, "of yore," he seems to have in mind a time of adult experience in which he belonged *like* a child to Joy, and had an emotional
resilience which he now lacks. The lines provide an odd measure of
Joy—the ability to bear wrongs and mourn for others—which gives
a strong sense of the lesser expectations of the poet of the Verse Letter. We are a far distance from Wordsworth's desire to behold once
more a world "Apparel'd in celestial light."

Coleridge will pick up his friend's garment metaphor in lines
which follow directly, working them into an increasingly nightmarish pattern of spiritual bondage:

> Yes, dearest Sara! Yes!
> There *was* a time when tho' my path was rough,
> The Joy within me dallied with [?Di]stress;
> And all Misfortunes were but as the Stuff
> Whence Fancy made me Dreams of Happiness:
> For Hope grew round me, like the climbing Vine,
> And Leaves & Fruitage, not my own, seem'd mine!
> But now ill Tidings bow me down to earth—
> Nor care I that they rob me of my Mirth—
> But oh! each Visitation
> Suspends what Nature gave me at my Birth,
> My shaping Spirit of Imagination!
>
> (231–42)

Coleridge has no golden age to offer in place of Wordsworth's time of
the celestial light. He remembers instead a time of hardships made
bearable by the presence of Joy. He had already differentiated the

course of his life from Wordsworth's in his recollections of his vision of ideal romance: he had felt that Joy while "cloister'd in a city School" (63), looking through a "barr'd window" (65), at a sky which was all he "knew of Beautiful" (64). His Joy could dally once with distress, using it as the raw material for building dreams of future bliss. One must wonder here at the precise nature of Coleridge's response to the loss Wordsworth chronicles in the first four stanzas of the Ode, remembering that Coleridge probably heard at the same time "To a Cuckoo," in which Wordsworth had played with nostalgic depression only to claim in the end that he could have it all, that loss was not loss but gain.

When Coleridge had prostrated himself before Wordsworth in his letter to Godwin of 25 March 1801, it was on the basis of three of Wordsworth's poems—"The Brothers," "Ruth," and "Michael"—which manage to salvage joy from the otherwise pathetic wreckage of human lives (*STCL* 2:714). Coleridge may well have seen the first stanzas of the Ode as a continuation of a typically Wordsworthian procedure of intensifying despair in order to claim a higher and more improbable happiness. Something is surely necessary to explain the contradictions in Coleridge's analysis here: his own Joy is internal, while Hope is outside him, growing parasitically like "the climbing Vine, / And Leaves & Fruitage, not my own, seem'd mine!" (236–37). One way of explaining the contradiction is to see the leaves and fruitage of Hope as Wordsworth's, the products of his tragic and pathetic modes, which had led Coleridge in his Joy to feeling that he was a participant in the same sort of process.[25] Without Joy, the ill tidings—which can range from reports of Sara's illness to Wordsworth's most recent dalliances with distress—are parasitic growths which pull Coleridge "down to earth" (238). Coleridge is of course echoing Wordsworth's "The Thorn":

> Up from the earth these mosses creep,
> And this poor thorn they clasp it round
> So close, you'd say that they were bent
> With plain and manifest intent,
> To drag it to the ground.
>
> (*LB* 70; 16–20)

Instead of leading Coleridge to creative imitations, as they once did, afflictions or reports of afflictions now suspend his "shaping Spirit of Imagination" (242). Coleridge may be doing something more than asking for newsy, cheerful letters: he may be implicitly naming the sources of much of Wordsworth's strength as oppressive to him.

Several lines further on, Coleridge explains why his response to sorrow is to "complain" rather than "mourn" (254–55): his

> coarse domestic Life has known
> No habits of heart-nursing Sympathy,
> No Griefs, but such as dull and deaden me,
> No Hopes of it's own Vintage, None, O! none—
> Whence when I mourn'd for you my Heart might Borrow
> Fair forms & living Motions for it's Sorrow.
>   (258–63)

Here we are almost back to the principles Wordsworth had sketched out in his narrative of Drummond in *The Pedlar*: "Unoccupied by sorrow of its own / His heart lay open" and "He could afford to suffer / With those whom he saw suffer" (*RC&P* 361). Coleridge may in some way have identified Drummond with Wordsworth and used the pedlar as a way of distinguishing between the poetic responses of the two friends to suffering. One mourns, which is a fitting act of a higher ode; the other complains, as he does in the Verse Letter. Mourning is an act of responsive, creative joy, while complaining is essentially unpoetic and uncreative, as well as joyless. Denied mourning, Coleridge's recourse against complaining has become a habit of abstraction:

> For not to think of what I needs must feel,
> But to be still & patient all I can;
> And haply by abstruse Research to steal
> From my own Nature all the Natural Man—
> This was my sole Resource, my wisest plan!
> And that, which suits a part, infects the whole,
> And now is almost grown the Temper of my Soul.
>   (264–70)

The impact of Coleridge's analysis of his situation, and implicitly of the differences between his character and Wordsworth's, appears to have haunted Wordsworth.

Barron Field recalls a conversation with Wordsworth, which probably took place no earlier than 1827, in which the poet spoke at length of the effects of Coleridge's unhappiness on his poetry:

> It was poor dear Coleridge's constant infelicity that prevented him from being the poet that Nature had given him the power to be. He had always too much personal and domestic discontent to paint the sorrows of mankind. He could not "afford to suffer / With those whom he saw suffer." I gave him the subject of his Three Graves; but he made it too shocking and painful, and not sufficiently sweetened by any healing views.[26]

Wordsworth was to tell Justice Coleridge in 1836 that "Latterly he thought . . . [Coleridge] had so much acquired the habit of analysing his feelings, and making them matter for a theory or argument, that he had rather dimmed his delight in the beauties of nature and injured his poetical powers."[27] We have no way of knowing how often or how early Wordsworth and Coleridge had discussed the relationships between happiness and poetry or analytical thought and poetry. Certainly the principle of pleasure is a dominant topic in Wordsworth's discussion of the character of the poet added to the preface to *Lyrical Ballads* early in 1802 (*Prose* 1:137–43). It is Coleridge, though, who first frames even semi-publicly those distinctions between himself and his friend through which Wordsworth would come to understand both their characters.

The final movement of the Verse Letter contains Coleridge's most extended commentary on Wordsworth's Ode. Leaving the subject of his mixed emotions about his children, he turns to his larger environment:

> These Mountains too, these Vales, these Woods, these Lakes,
> Scenes full of Beauty & of Loftiness
> Where all my Life I fondly hop'd to live—
> I were sunk low indeed, did they *no* solace give;

> But oft I seem to feel, & evermore I fear,
>   They are not to me now the Things, which once they were.
>
>   (289–294)

Like Wordsworth at the beginning of the Ode, Coleridge is questioning his response to the surroundings that are supposed to sustain
him. Self-evidently, they are specifically Wordsworthian surroundings. Unlike the Wordsworth of the Ode, he has come to understand
why they have lost their wonted power. He speaks to Wordsworth
through Sara, who has by this time become only a fictive convenience
of the poem:

> O Sara! we receive but what we give,
> And in *our* Life alone does Nature live.
> Our's is her Wedding Garment, our's her Shroud—
> And would we aught behold of higher Worth
> Than that inanimate cold World allow'd
> To the poor loveless ever-anxious Crowd,
> Ah! from the Soul itself must issue forth
> A Light, a Glory, and a luminous Cloud
>   Enveloping the Earth!
>
>   (295–303)

Coleridge works intricate variations upon Wordsworth's opening
stanza. The garment metaphor—"Apparel'd in celestial light"—is
first refigured literally. The inner quality of our lives determines
whether the nature we perceive wears festal adornments or the weeds
of death. These possible garments are then transformed into a kind
of light which emanates from the soul and clothes creation. Wordsworth's celestial light is shown to come from within the self alone.
In speaking of the "Light" and "Glory" Coleridge echoes the Ode;
his embellishment, the "luminous Cloud," will, in conjunction with
the image of the setting sun discussed previously, provide Wordsworth with the basic imagistic materials needed to complete his
poem. The sunrise which symbolizes our birth will become the setting of our life's star in another existence. We come to earth not

utterly naked but "trailing clouds of glory." Wordsworth's first four stanzas included no setting sun, and they were also cloudless.

Coleridge is not content just to locate the source of the vanished light within the self. He goes on to make the light into the voice of poetry itself:

> And from the Soul itself must there be sen[t?]
> A sweet & potent Voice, of it's own Birth,
> Of all sweet Sounds the Life & Element.
> O pure of Heart! thou need'st not ask of me
>   What this strong music in the Soul may be,
> What, & wherein it doth exist,
> This Light, this Glory, this fair luminous Mist,
> This beautiful & beauty-making Power!
>
> (304–311)

Coleridge's conflations are dazzling. The innocent pronoun *it* of line 309 collapses the light projected by the soul into the music which it also originates, making the two indistinguishable, and the conjoint light and sound then stand in apposition to the "beautiful & beauty-making Power," which must be the shaping spirit of the imagination. Throughout the remainder of his work on the Ode, Wordsworth will resist Coleridge's conflations. The Ode of 1802 was about neither the death of song nor the decline of the imagination. And the poem will never take up these topics, however often commentators assume that it does. Wordsworth will use a major part of Coleridge's completion of his fragment, but he will resist this expansionary movement.

Coleridge finally gathers together all the elements he has identified—the music, the voice, the light, the cloud, the glory, the beautiful and beauty-making power—and attributes them to a single cause:

> *Joy*, innocent Sara! Joy, that ne'er was given
> Save to the Pure, & in their purest Hour,
> *Joy*, Sara! is the Spirit & the Power,

> That wedding Nature to us gives in Dower
>   A new Earth & new Heaven
> Undreamt of by the Sensual & the Proud!
> Joy is that strong Voice, Joy that luminous Cloud—
>   We, we ourselves rejoice!
> And thence flows all that charms or ear or sight,
> All melodies the Echoes of that Voice,
> All Colors a Suffusion of that Light.
>
>   (312–22)

Coleridge has effectively reduced both life and art to a single principle. His recourse to the metaphor of marriage—Joy is the dower
given by our marrying nature to ourselves—puts him outside his
crucial monism, away from "all that charms or ear or sight" (320).
Wordsworth's sense of the reciprocity of mind and nature in "Tintern
Abbey"—of all the mighty world / Of eye and ear, both what they
half-create, / And what perceive" (*LB* 116; 106–08)—had been
questioned by his Ode. Coleridge has forced the questioning further,
and asserts that all must be created *before* it can be perceived. The
Wordsworth created within Coleridge's poem possesses the requisite
joy for perception and creation, as does the entire Grasmere circle.
The Coleridge it has created does not.

If Coleridge's emblematic use of the sacrament of marriage has in
some ways authorized his description of his personal union earlier in
the poem—providing for his complaints a larger context—it also
could point back toward one of Wordsworth's most significant uses
of the metaphor. My previous chapter on the Ode omitted reference
to Wordsworth's possible work on *Home at Grasmere* in the spring of
1802. In the absence of any documentary evidence, dating the early
stages of composition on what was to remain the only substantially
completed part of *The Recluse* proper is at best a fragile enterprise.
However, Mark L. Reed is willing to hypothesize that the best-
known portion of this work—the lines which which become the Prospectus to *The Excursion*—was completed before Coleridge's Verse
Letter.[28] He sees in Coleridge's use of the marriage metaphor a response to Wordsworth's ringing prophetic challenge to the subject
matter of the traditional (read Miltonic) epic:

> Paradise and groves
> Elysian, fortunate islands, fields like those of old
> In the deep ocean—wherefore should they be
> A History, or but a dream when minds
> Once wedded to this outward frame of things
> In love, find these the growth of common day?
> (*HG* 102; 996-1001)

Reed even suspects a reciprocal influence from Coleridge's Verse Letter—that Wordsworth's later elaboration of the metaphor ("spousal verse" [1003]; "this great consummation" [1004]), can be attributed to Coleridge's use of it in his poem.

The possibility that Coleridge's response to the Ode was partially conditioned by his recollections of portions of *Home at Grasmere*, and especially the possibility that he might have heard lines from the Prospectus section of that poem at the same time that he first heard the fragmentary Ode, helps to explain the strong, self-confident, joyous Wordsworth he has created in his Verse Letter. In the light of *Home at Grasmere*, the Wordsworth of the Ode would have seemed a temporary aberration, one who may for a moment have lost contact with the sources of his strength, but whose security and joy would inevitably lead to his recuperation. Consequently, Coleridge's primary reflexive strategy at the end of the Verse Letter is to pit this strong Wordsworth against the Coleridge it has created in such woeful detail, a Coleridge who is Alone at Keswick.

It is difficult to keep an understanding of the Verse Letter from becoming colored by knowledge of Coleridge's later revisions. Coleridge's letter to Sotheby of 19 July 1802, which claims that the poem was originally addressed to Wordsworth, elides most of the matter which would qualify the original poem as an erotic verse epistle. Sara is gone, as are the passages of quasi-erotic nostalgia, muted sexual jealousy, and complaints about his marriage. The substitution of Wordsworth for Sara in the final passages of the poem, which I have just been discussing, seems only a modest reassignment to their proper addressee, because they were directed at his friend all along. The Wordsworth always implicit in the Verse Letter becomes explicit in the lines sent to Sotheby:

Calm stedfast Spirit, guided from above,
O Wordsworth friend of my devoutest choice,
Great Son of Genius! full of Light & Love!
    Thus, thus dost thou rejoice.
To Thee do all things live from pole to pole,
Their Life the Eddying of thy living Soul!
Brother & Friend of my devoutest Choice,
Thus may'st thou ever, ever more rejoice!
                                        (*STCL* 2:817–18)

Coleridge's refocusing of his poem can be partially attributed to Wordsworth's responses to the Verse Letter in "The Leech-Gatherer" and "Resolution and Independence."

The problem with progressive analyses of the genesis of "Dejection: An Ode," such as that of Stephen F. Fogle, is that they turn the history of the poem into a matter of refinement.[29] We seem to see unwieldy matter attaining form before our eyes, as the poet discovers what part of his earlier work is truly germane to his aesthetic purpose. Processes of reading and writing are not that simple. Within its dialogical context Coleridge's Verse Letter has more to say to Wordsworth's Ode than any subsequent use of its material will ever have. The way in which Coleridge's implicit genre, the erotic verse epistle, brings to the surface the latent eroticism of Wordsworth's Ode is extremely important. Nor is Coleridge's response to Wordsworth's poem singular. In his lecture on *Romeo and Juliet*, William Hazlitt set Shakespeare's blunt acknowledgment of the passions against what he considered Wordsworth's spurious spiritualizing of childhood at the expense of passionate adolescence.[30] When Shelley responded to the completed Ode in "Alastor," he performed a similar transformation. William Keach has discussed brilliantly the point at which the crisis of Shelley's poem intersects Wordsworth's: "The narrator recounts the wandering poet's self-projective erotic dream, in which a veiled maiden whose 'voice was like the voice of his own soul' . . . appeared to speak and sing to him, and to fold him in her arms just as both dream and dreamer dissolved into vacancy. Upon waking the protagonist found that his 'vacant brain' . . . now perceived a 'vacant' world instead of the rich 'natural bower' in which he had fallen asleep."[31] As Keach points out, the language of the narrator's questions about this experience echoes the questions at the end of Wordsworth's fourth stanza:

> Whither have fled
> The hues of heaven that canopied his bower
> Of yesternight? the sounds that soothed his sleep,
> The joy, the exultation!
>
> (196–200)

Keach goes on: "Wordsworth's 'visionary gleam' is elaborated eroti- cally into the 'Alastor' protagonist's 'vision' of a maiden with 'glow- ing limbs' . . . and 'beamy bending eyes' . . . ; Wordsworth's 'dream' becomes in Shelley 'a dream of hopes that never yet / Had flushed his cheek' " (Keach 40). Coleridge and Shelley have identified the same underlying motivation for Wordsworth's vague but power- ful nostalgic yearnings, have displaced his golden time into the age of the beginnings of adolescent sexuality, and have given startlingly similar depictions of that time's visionary content, however strongly they may disagree on the value of the vision. The dream of perfect erotic love dulls the taste of Shelley's protagonist for the things of this world and ends up destroying him. But then, however treasured, the dream doesn't appear to have done much for Coleridge's happiness either.

Coleridge's Verse Letter is a rich and fascinating work, both on its own terms and as an antithetical completion of Wordsworth's Ode. Its historical importance can hardly be overestimated. When Words- worth responds to it with "The Leech-Gatherer," his major concerns will not be the passages Coleridge rewrites for Sotheby and uses as the basis for the received text of "Dejection" but those suppressed passages of erotic complaint. When Wordsworth risks once more the figures and topics of erotic pastoral, he will do so with a firmer sense of their hidden and treacherous powers. The verses which Coleridge sent to Sotheby, "improved" as they might seem, could not have called forth "The Leech-Gatherer" and "Resolution and Indepen- dence." The Verse Letter did.

4

Wordsworth's "The Leech-Gatherer"

There was a roaring in the wind all night
The rain came heavily and fell in floods
But now the sun is rising calm and bright
The Birds are singing in the distant woods
Over his own sweet voice the stock-dove broods   [5]
The Jay makes answer as the magpie chatters
And all the air is fill'd with pleasant noise of waters

All things that love the sun are out of doors
The sky rejoices in the morning's birth
The grass is bright with rain drops: on the moor   [10]
The Hare is running races in her mirth
And with her feet she from the plashy earth
Raises a mist which glittering in the sun
Runs with her all the way wherever she doth run.

I was a Traveller upon the moor   [15]
I saw the hare that rac'd about with joy
I heard the woods and distant waters roar
Or heard them not, as happy as a Boy
The pleasant season did my heart employ

My old remembrances went from me wholly [20]
And all the ways of men so vain & melancholy

But as it sometimes chanceth from the might
Of joy in minds that can no farther go
As high as we have mounted in delight
In our dejection do we sink as low [25]
To me that morning did it happen so
And fears and fancies thick upon me came
Dim sadness & blind thoughts I knew not nor could name.

I heard the sky lark singing in the sky
And I bethought me of the playful hare [30]
Even such a happy child of earth am I
Even as these happy creatures do I fare
Far from the world I live & from all care
But there may come another day to me
Solitude pain of heart distress & poverty. [35]

My whole life I have liv'd in pleasant thought
As if life's business were a summer mood:
Who will not wade to seek a bridge or boat
How can he ever hope to cross the flood?
How can he e'er expect that others should [40]
Build for him, sow for him, and at his call
Love him who for himself will take no heed at all?

I thought of Chatterton the marvellous Boy
The sleepless soul who perished in his pride
Of Him who walked in glory & in joy [45]
Behind his Plough upon the mountain's side
By our own spirits are we deified
We Poets in our youth begin in gladness
But thereof comes in the end despondcey and madness.

Now whether it was by peculiar grace [50]
A leading from above, a something given

Yet it befel that in that lonely place
When up & down my fancy thus was driven
And I with these untoward thoughts had striven
I to the borders of a Pond did come   [55]
By which an Old man was, far from all house or home

He seem'd like one who little saw or heard
For chimney-nook, or bed, or coffin meet
A stick was in his hand wherewith he stirr'd
The waters of the pond beneath his feet   [60]
Him
But
How [came he here, thought I or what can he be doing?]

He [?c]
Prov   [65]
But
Comi[ng together as in their pilgrimage;]
As i[f some dire constraint of pain, or rage]
Of [sickness felt by him in times long past,]
Wh[?i]   [70]

He [wore a Cloak the same as women wear]
As [one whose blood did needful comfort lack;]
His [face look'd pale as if it had grown fair,]
An[d furthermore he had upon his back]
Be[neath his Cloak a round & bulky Pack]   [75]
A [load of wool or raiment as might seem]
Bu[t on his shoulders lay as if it clave to him.]

The
B
U[pon the muddy water which he conn'd]   [80]
A[s if he had been reading in a book

Lines 61–112: A leaf is torn from Dove Cottage MS. 41. Lines supplied in
brackets are conjectured by Curtis, *WET*.

[And now such freedom as I could I took]
[And, drawing to his side, to him did say,]
"[This morning gives us promise of a glorious day."]

[?A] [gentle answer did the Old Man make]   [85]
[?I][n courteous speech which forth he slowly drew;]
[?A][nd him with further words I thus bespake,]
"[What kind of work is that which you pursue?]
[This is a lonely place for one like you."]
[He answer'd me with pleasure & surprize,]   [90]
[And there was while he spake a fire about his eyes.]

[His words came feebly from a feeble] chest
[Yet each in solemn order follow'd each]
[With something of a pompous utterance drest,]
[Choice word & measur'd phrase, beyond the reach]   [95]
[Of ordinary men, a stately speech,]
[Such as grave livers do in Scotland use,]
[Religious Men, who give to God & Man their] dues.

. . . .

I yet can gain my bread tho' in times gone   [125]
I twenty could have found where now I can find one

Feeble I am in health these hills to climb
Yet I procure a Living of my own
This is my summer work in winter time
I go with godly Books from Town to Town   [130]
Now I am seeking Leeches up & down
From house to house I go from Barn to Barn
All over Cartmell Fells & up to Blellan Tarn

Lines 99–124. Almost four full stanzas are lost because of the sheet torn from the manuscript. Line endings readable from the stubs are "last" (105), "home" (106), and "'d" (112). Because they correlate with no line endings in extant versions, they give no clue to the content of the stanzas.

With this the Old Man other matter blended
Which he deliver'd with demeanor kind   [135]
Yet stately in the main & when he ended
I could have laugh'd myself to scorn to find
In that decrepit man so firm a mind
God said I be my help & stay secure
I'll think of the Leech-gatherer on the lonely Moor.   [140]

THE HISTORY of Wordsworth's and Dorothy's direct responses to Coleridge's Verse Letter can be quickly told. Dorothy reports that "On Tuesday [April] 20th when we were sitting after Tea Coleridge came to the door. I startled Wm with my voice. C. came up palish but I afterwards found he looked well. William was not well and I was in low spirits" (*DWJ* 113). Coleridge's notebooks record in a dated entry one detail from his visit: "Tuesday Evening, 1/2 after 7 / Cut out my name & Dorothy's over the S.H. at Sara's Rock" (*CNB* 1 : 1163). No one's spirits would improve the following day:

> William and I sauntered a little in the garden. Coleridge came to us and repeated the verses he wrote to Sara. I was affected with them and was on the whole, not being well, in miserable spirits. The sunshine—the green fields and the fair sky made me sadder; even the little happy sporting lambs seemed but sorrowful to me. The pile wort spread out on the grass a thousand shining stars. The primroses were there and the remains of a few Daffodils. The well which we cleaned out last night is still but a little muddy pond, though full of water. I went to bed after dinner, could not sleep, went to bed again. Read Ferguson's life and a poem or two—fell asleep for 5 minutes and awoke better. We got tea. Sate comfortably in the Evening. I went to bed early. (*DWJ* 113–14)

Heath has pointed to the astonishing "number of connections that can be drawn between Dorothy's brief account of her response to Coleridge's poem and William's own poems of the same period" (Heath 107). She is reacting to Coleridge's evening letter in the midst of the springtime brightness of the idealized landscape of the Ode, and even her reading of the life of Robert Fergusson has significance, because, as Heath notes, Fergusson could easily have been added to the more familiar pair of doomed poets—Chatterton and Burns—who will become crucial figures in "The Leech-Gatherer."

Dorothy's account may be most fascinating, though, because it is the only one we have. Coleridge's visit lasted until 25 April (*CMY* 164), and there is a lacuna of over a month in the extant Wordsworth correspondence. The next letter preserved by either brother or sister is Wordsworth's highly formal response to John Wilson of 7 June (*EY* 352–58), and the next to an intimate is a joint letter to Sara Hutchinson of 14 June (*EY* 361–68), which refers to a number of letters, now lost, sent in the previous weeks. In all of their surviving papers neither Wordsworth nor Dorothy ever breaks silence about Coleridge's Verse Letter or any of its subsequent mutations. Heath speculates that "Coleridge's propensity for uninhibited self-interest and uncritical self-expression must often have been an embarrassment to the Wordsworth household. Whatever terms they chose for expressing the conduct of their own lives, they must have thought that a position like that which Coleridge takes, language such as he uses, in the verse letter to Sara was not appropriate to poetry or useful in the decorous conduct of everyday life" (Heath 108). In the light of Dorothy's recorded response to Coleridge's poem, their ominous silence confirms Heath's judgment of the poem's impact.

An established critical and biographical tradition connects Wordsworth's two major poems of the following months, "The Leech-Gatherer' and "Resolution and Independence," with Coleridge's Verse Letter.[1] As a responsive reading of an earlier poem, though, "The Leech-Gatherer" is vastly different from Coleridge's Verse Letter. If the letters, journals, and manuscripts of this period had entirely vanished, we could still conclude that Wordsworth's completed Ode and Coleridge's "Dejection" were interlocking poems, because their formal and verbal correspondences are too striking to be coincidental. We might have argued about which poem anticipated and influenced which, as commentators did before the chronology was straightened out, but we would know that they belonged together in some way. Even the meager documentary evidence with which we are blessed may have blinded us to the strangeness of "The Leech-Gatherer" as an "answer" to Coleridge's poem. Wordsworth avoids any reflections of the poetic texture of Coleridge's work, and he avoids more than a limited, and highly revisionary, contact with the topics of his own Ode, which had generated Coleridge's poem. What he does with the materials of the Ode can be attributed to the ways in which Coleridge had appropriated them.

Those searching for undesignated odes in the Wordsworth canon, for example, have never seized upon "The Leech-Gatherer" or "Resolution and Independence" as examples. Both of the poems employ a fixed stanzaic form, a variant of rhyme royal with which Wordsworth had been working in his translations of Chaucer and Clanvowe, and a form which, as both poets had demonstrated, is easily adaptable to narrative, descriptive, or reflective ends. Wordsworth varies the classic stanza by closing on an alexandrine, a touch he could be adopting from the Spenserian stanza or could have learned, in this particular manifestation, from the works of Milton or Chatterton.[2] The concluding alexandrine enhances stanzaic closure, lending to both poems a sense of ordered, incremental progression. Stanzas are not enjambed, either syntactically or conceptually. Indeed, it is the lack of conceptual enjambment that will allow so much of "The Leech-Gatherer" to remain intact when Wordsworth drastically changes the poem into "Resolution and Independence."

The larger form of the earlier poem is a familiar Wordsworthian hybrid. To the extent that the work is dominated by the voice of the poet's persona, it is surely a lyric poem, but to the extent that its procedures are those of serial narrative, with a beginning, middle, and end, moved along by external as well as psychological events, it is not easily assimilable to the developmental strategies of the Ode, or of "Tintern Abbey," or of Coleridge's conversation poems, to say nothing of the fits and starts, progressions and regressions of the Verse Letter. In its fixed stanzaic form and steady linear progress, the earlier version of the poem in particular seems to be an implicit commentary on the dangers of undisciplined utterance uncovered by both the Ode and the Verse Letter. If "The Leech-Gatherer" evidences a retreat from psychologically treacherous generic territory, it is a retreat to familiar ground. To some extent it blends the emphases of two poems from the 1798 *Lyrical Ballads*, both concerned with encounters with old men: "Simon Lee" and "The Last of the Flock." Like the former, it features detailed description of and reflections upon the figure of the anecdote; like the latter, it presents the figure's story in his own words. More than either of these earlier poems, though, it depends heavily upon the predispositions which the poetic persona brings with him to the encounter with the aged figure. For a vastly foreshortened version of "The Leech-Gatherer" we must turn, as Stephen Parrish has pointed out, to a slightly earlier poem of 1802, "The Sailor's Mother," which Wordsworth completed on 11–12 March.[3]

"The Sailor's Mother" can serve as a formal gloss for "The Leech-Gatherer" because it contains virtually every distinctive strategic feature, however greatly reproportioned and repositioned, of the later and larger poem. It begins, for example, in strict circumstantiality:

> The day was cold and rain and wet;
> A foggy day in winter time,
> —A Woman in the road I met
> Not old, but something past her prime.[4]

The "Leech-Gatherer" begins with an extended description of the environment and climate of the day of the encounter with the old man, coupled with meditations on the state of the poet's spirits and hopes and fears about his future, before moving to an equally blunt account of his chance meeting: "I to the borders of a Pond did come / By which an Old man was, far from all house or home" (55–56). In each case the visual impact of the figure moves the poet to a preliminary assessment of the person. To the woman he responds:

> —Majestic seem'd she as a mountain storm;
> A Roman Matron's gait—like feature & like form

> The ancient spirit is not dead;
> Old times thought I, are breathing there;

Proud was I that my country bred
Such strength, a dignity so fair,
—She begg'd an alms, like one of low estate;
I look'd at her again, nor did my pride abate.

(5–12)

If it is apparent that the poet's response has come both from the visual image of the woman and from his predispositions toward such a figure, it is even clearer that his initial depiction of the leech-gatherer has been colored by his gloomy musings. What we have of the opening description labels the man's appearance as that of "one who little saw or heard / For chimney-nook, or bed, or coffin meet" (57–58), and apparently follows the later text in attributing his bent figure, with head and feet "Comi[ng together in their pilgrimage]" (67), to "[some dire constraint of pain, or rage] / Of [sickness felt by him in times long past]" (68–69). In "The Sailor's Mother" the poet refers to his initial impression of the woman as a consequence of his "lofty thoughts" (13), from which he awakens and begins to speak with her. We might say that the opening depiction of the leech-gatherer has been produced by the poet's morbid thoughts, from which he also must awaken in order to speak with the old man.

"The Sailor's Mother" ultimately finds the woman's voice surer and more revealing than the poet's eye and imagination. The story which she tells, about the singing bird which belonged to her dead son and which she is carrying back from Hull to Mary-port ("A weary way" [29]), makes the earlier poetical description of her, puffed as it is with historical and patriotic associations, seem woefully inadequate either to the reality of her situation or to her emotional strength:

"The Bird and cage they both were his,
"'Twas my Son's Bird;—and neat and trim
"He kept it—many voyages
"This singing-bird hath gone with him;
"And I, God help me! for my little wit
"Trail't with me, Sir! he took so much delight in it!"

(31–36)

The tale told by the leech-gatherer, largely lost because of the page ripped out of DC MS. 41, apparently served a similar function. The poet's eye has misread the situation of the old man, whose extended account of himself and his life, which probably ran five stanzas originally, leaves the poet stunned at the inadequacy of his own first impressions: "I could have laugh'd myself to scorn to find / In that decrepit man so firm a mind" (137–38). If the obvious topic of "The Leech-Gatherer" is despondency corrected, its formal procedures suggest that it shares with "The Sailor's Mother" a larger and more aesthetically pointed topic—superficiality transcended.

The similarities between "The Sailor's Mother" and "The Leech-Gatherer" are important because the earlier poem was to become an object of contention between Wordsworth and Coleridge. In the *Biographia Literaria* Coleridge cited it as "the only fair instance that I have been able to discover in all Mr. Wordsworth's writings, of an *actual* adoption, or true imitation, of the *real* and *very* language of *low and rustic life*, freed from provincialisms" (*BL* 2:71). Coleridge's reservations about the poem concern its dynamics: he wonders whether the concluding stanza of the poem is not an "abrupt downfall" from the second stanza, because of the tonal shift from the poet's eloquent musings to the woman's colloquial account (*BL* 2:71). Coleridge suggests a destructive tension between the two voices of the poem. In its latter half he feels a "sense of oddity and strangeness . . . here in finding *rhymes at all* in sentences so exclusively colloquial" (*BL* 2:70).[5] Coleridge had arrived at Dove Cottage for a three-day visit on 19 March, a week after Wordsworth's completion of "The Sailor's Mother" (*CMY* 154). If he at that time expressed reservations about the poem (none are recorded), Wordsworth's use of it as a model for his response to the Verse Letter takes on added meaning. Every stricture which applies to "The Sailor's Mother" could apply doubly to "The Leech-Gatherer." Indeed, Coleridge was later to point to "Resolution and Independence," even though it is shorn of the colloquial speech of the old man, as an example of Wordsworth's defect of inconstancy of style (*BL* 2:125). In all likelihood Coleridge did voice reservations about "The Sailor's Mother" on his visit to Grasmere. His basic taste in things Wordsworthian changed less over the years than the growing theoretical framework he used to buttress his views. If my surmise is correct, Wordsworth's elaboration of this poetic model in "The Leech-Gatherer" is intentional and directly related to his response to the Verse Letter.

The Verse Letter had placed the burden of all perception and creation within the self. We see by our own lights, we hear our own music. In "The Sailor's Mother" as well as "The Leech-Gatherer" Wordsworth seems inclined to grant Coleridge half his argument. Vision can be tyrannical, and we often do see what we are disposed to see. But the voice of another figure is a thing external to the self. All sounds do not proceed from the soul, and there are other harmonies, other accents, if we have ears to hear them. A crucial passage from the preface to *Lyrical Ballads* of 1802 makes the point eloquently. Here Wordsworth discusses the limitations of the poet's powers of sympathetic imagination, his ability to call up within himself passions akin to those produced by real events:

> But whatever portion of this faculty we may suppose even the greatest Poet to possess, there cannot be a doubt that the language which it will suggest to him, must, in liveliness and truth, fall far short of that which is uttered by men in real life, under the actual pressure of those passions, certain shadows of which the Poet thus produces, or feels to be produced, in himself.
>
> However exalted a notion we would wish to cherish of the character of a Poet, it is obvious, that while he describes and imitates passions, his situation is altogether slavish and mechanical, compared with the freedom and power of real and substantial action and suffering. (*Prose* 1 : 138)

For Wordsworth at this time, a sympathetic recognition of the authority of human voices outside the self appears to be the surest defense against poeticizing solipsism. "The Sailor's Mother" and its more ambitious derivative, "The Leech-Gatherer," could have been written to illustrate this important addition to the preface. For Wordsworth to respond to Coleridge's invitation to solipsism with a form which depends upon the power and authority of an external voice, then, is appropriate. If Wordsworth was aware of Coleridge's misgivings about the form, the response is even more fitting.

The following pages trace in some detail the extent to which the concerns of "The Leech-Gatherer" parallel and deviate from those of both the Verse Letter and the Ode. First, though, it will be useful to gain some perspective on what the Ode had meant to Wordsworth from the time of its first composition, and to suggest the extent to which Coleridge's Verse Letter had altered that meaning. Four of Wordsworth's poems can be firmly dated as having been composed between 27 March and 21 April 1802: "Among All Lovely Things My Love Had Been" (12 April), "Written While Resting on the Bridge Near the Foot of Brother's Water" (16 April), "The Redbreast Chasing the Butterfly" (18 April), and "To a Butterfly" ("I've watch'd you now a full half hour," completed 20 April).[6] While none of the poems could be classified as major works, they show no signs that Wordsworth is in the midst of any crisis of poetic productivity. Nor do they deal with any diminution of the poet's responses to natural objects. If they invoke no celestial light, neither do they lament losses or absences. Heath has called "Among All Lovely Things" an oblique love poem to Dorothy, and pointed out that it was written only a few hours after Wordsworth "had left Mary, as he was return-ing from an apparently urgent visit occasioned by William and Do-rothy's conclusion a few weeks earlier that the wedding would take place after William and Dorothy went to France to see Annette and Caroline" (Heath 113). He takes Wordsworth's giving it to Dorothy as "a kind of reassurance" to his sister and her "sending it immedi-ately to Mary something less than generous-spirited." Heath is prob-ably right, although at the same time he has noted little outside the normal dialectic of lovers and bothers, sisters and fiancées. From the vantage point of the Ode, though, the poem shows a perfectly shared response to a thing of natural beauty—"O joy it was for her, and joy for me" (20)—and the glowworm's having survived the anxious day-light hours in which the poet "hop'd with fear" (17) that his gift would still be there and alive for his Emma to see, shows that all treasured lights have not failed in the spring of 1802.

"Written . . . Near . . . Brother's Water" is even less problemati-cal in its treatment of natural beauty. In this short piece, which gives the illusion of an extempore performance, the poet accedes wholly to the sights and sound of the season:

> The cock is crowing,
> The stream is flowing,
> The small birds twitter,
> The Lake doth glitter,
> The green field sleeps in the sun.
>
> (1–5)

Wordsworth is content to register the details around him, the horse plowing, the cattle grazing, the snow retreating in the spring warmth, the plowboy whooping, the blue sky, and the departed rain. Again, there is no indication that the spirits of the poet are not in total accord with the joy of the mountains which surround him. Nor does "The Redbreast Chasing the Butterfly" lend itself to a dark reading of the poet's spirits. Wordsworth expresses mock surprise at this rather benign spectacle of nature red in tooth and claw, exhorting the bird in the name of all man's fond regards for him to cease pursuing "A beautiful creature that is gentle by nature" (29). The poem's desire for natural concord is of course exaggerated, but surely the exaggeration is a product of the observing poet's sense of harmony and well-being, which he would spread to all creation. If the plea to the robin—"O pious Bird whom man loves best / Love him, or leave him alone" (41–42)—overlooks basic facts about the relations of birds and insects, it does so from a feeling of human delight in the season so extreme as to desire a temporary moratorium in the habits of its creatures. In the second poem on the butterfly ("I've watch'd you now a full half hour"), finished the day before Coleridge's reading of the Verse Letter, Wordsworth takes up the preceding month's concerns with relationships between childhood and adulthood. Having watched the butterfly at rest in his orchard, the poet invites it to use the plot as a sanctuary "whenever you are weary":

> Come often to us, fear no wrong
> Sit near us on the bough
> We'll talk of sunshine and of song
> And summer days when we were young
> Sweet childish days that were as long
> As twenty days are now.
>
> (14–19)

Differences between past and present are remarked, but not as a cause for regrets. If the butterfly does not bring back the golden time entirely, it is at least a stimulus to pleasantly nostalgic conversation about the days of childhood.

Writing the first four stanzas of the Ode did not change Wordsworth's life. He felt no compulsion to linger on its ground, searching for the vanished gleam. Wordsworth's immediate movement from the Ode to unproblematical expressions of joy in nature reinforces my suspicion that the poem had begun as a rather conventional literary experiment. There is just no evidence that Wordsworth was haunted by its topics. His first poem in a somber mood comes the day after Coleridge's reading of his verses to Sara, and it is composed in a free stanzaic form reminiscent of the first two stanzas of the Ode. The first part of the poem ("These chairs they have no words to utter") portrays a moment of housebound solitude, with the poet "Happy and alone," in which he dismisses anxieties akin to those expressed by his friend:

> Oh! who would be afraid of life?
> The passion the sorrow and the strife
> When he may lie
> Shelter'd so easily
> May lie in peace on his bed
> Happy as those who are dead.
> (*WET* 176; 7–12)

The second part, designated "*Half an hour afterwards*," recants any desires to die: "The things which I see / Are welcome to me / Welcome every one" (13–15), and finds in life itself "A deep delicious peace" (25) with "Sweetness & Breath with the quiet of death" (29). Wordsworth never published the poem, which is found, with so many of the poems of spring 1802, in DC MS. 41. Although the poem reveals a darker side to the poet's experience of the period, that side—with its misanthropic desire for a solitude approaching the state of death—surfaces during Coleridge's visit. Wordsworth's lines are occasional musings, stimulated by Coleridge's visit, and largely unrelated to the poet's productions of these particular months.[7] As

poem follows poem in the days leading up to "The Leech-Gatherer"—
"The Tinker" (27—29 April), "Foresight" (28 April), and the two
poems on the lesser celandine (30 April-1 May)—it becomes more
and more difficult to make a case for the centrality of the Ode to
Wordsworth's poetic experience at this time. Coleridge's response to
the poem seems more important than Wordsworth's work itself, and
the Verse Letter will define the issues Wordsworth treats in "The
Leech-Gatherer" and "Resolution and Independence."

The dialogue of "The Leech-Gatherer" with the Verse Letter begins immediately in its stringently delineated setting and occasion:

> There was a roaring in the wind all night
> The rain came heavily and fell in floods
> But now the sun is rising calm and bright.
>
> (1—3)

Although Wordsworth does not supply a date for his fictive experience, the reader can suggest one without being overly ingenious. It
seems to be 5 April 1802, the morning after the storm of the Verse
Letter. Coleridge had responded to Wordsworth's morning poem
with a night piece, and Wordsworth is here continuing the cyclical
dialogue. By stressing the renewed joy which followed the breaking
of the storm,

> All things that love the sun are out of doors
> The sky rejoices in the morning's birth
> The grass is bright with rain drops: on the moor
> The Hare is running races in her mirth,
>
> (8—11)

Wordsworth is able to associate the gloom of the Verse Letter with
the darkness and storm of its fictive setting. Of course there are night
thoughts, but they are followed by those of the morning. Indeed,
throughout the poem Wordsworth will concentrate on a symptomatology of acute and circumstantial depression, evading almost wholly
the feelings of chronic loss which underpin parts of both his Ode and
the Verse Letter.

Wordsworth's statements to Miss Fenwick about the emotional state depicted at the beginning of the poem are intriguing: "I was in the state of feeling described in the beginning of the poem, while crossing Barton Fell from Mr. Clarkson's, at the foot of Ullswater, towards Askam. The image of the hare I then observed on the ridge of the Fell" (*PW* 2:510). Heath has determined that the most likely time for Wordsworth to have been making the journey in question was "the day William left Middleham to see Mary—April 7th, his thirty-second birthday. . . . Wordsworth, . . . going to meet the woman he had promised to marry, about to cross through or near the estate of Lord Lonsdale, the man who had been responsible for his own financial distress, might well have thought of the anxious prospects facing a poet" (Heath 123). Indeed he might—even the happiest of men is entitled to a case of premarital jitters. However, the crucial point of Wordsworth's experience, found in this poem which he did not begin for almost a month, is that the significance of it did not become clear to him until after he had heard Coleridge's Verse Letter.

Heath describes "The Leech-Gatherer" as a spring elegy, a designation with which I have no quarrel, and gives a brief history of the convention as Wordsworth would have encountered it in works by Michael Bruce, James Graeme, John Langhorne, John Scott, and Robert Fergusson. He discusses as well the relevance of Wordsworth's translation of "The Cuckoo and the Nightingale," in which the poet had been working with a forerunner of this late eighteenth century convention (Heath 123–27). The burden of such poems is that everything in nature is blooming and bursting with happiness except the speaker of the poem, who, as Heath notes, is usually a rejected lover. As I remarked in my reading of stanzas III and IV of Wordsworth's Ode, it is the presence of this conventional figuration which enables such erotic readings of the poem's motivations as Coleridge, Hazlitt, Shelley, Jeffrey Robinson, and I have supplied. Wordsworth's strategies in "The Leech-Gatherer" attempt to preclude such readings, and only the most persistent biographical critic will be able to insist on them.

While Wordsworth is tracing the fluctuations of his spirits on the morning in question, his work is thoroughly in keeping with the conventions Heath has described:

> The pleasant season did my heart employ
> My old remembrances went from me wholly
> And all the ways of men so vain & melancholy
> But as it sometimes chanceth from the might
> Of joy in minds that can no farther go
> As high as we have mounted in delight
> In our dejection do we sink as low
> To me that morning did it happen so
> And fears and fancies thick upon me came
> Dim sadness & blind thoughts I knew not nor could name.
>
> (19–28)

We are waiting only for the unspecified source of uneasiness, so much like that which remained unspecified in the Ode, to reveal itself in fears of the loss of some Daphne or Belinda. The pattern traced here has marked similarities to the one which lies behind "Strange fits of passion I have know": "fond and wayward thoughts . . . slide / Into a Lover's head," after which he cries, "O mercy! . . . / If Lucy should be dead" (*LB*; 25–28).

But in "The Leech-Gatherer" the sadness and thoughts are almost immediately named, and in such a way as to jerk the poem from its moorings in erotic convention:

> I heard the sky lark singing in the sky
> And I bethought me of the playful hare
> Even such a happy child of earth am I
> Even as these happy creatures do I fare
> Far from the world I live & from all care
> But there may come another day to me
> Solitude pain of heart distress & poverty.
>
> My whole life I have liv'd in pleasant thought
> As if life's business were a summer mood:
> Who will not wade to seek a bridge or boat
> How can he ever hope to cross the flood?
> How can he e'er expect that others should

> Build for him, sow for him, and at his call
> Love him who for himself will take no heed at all?
> (29–42)

These lines place the poet's anxieties far outside the boundaries of conventional erotic longing. If he is concerned about solitude and pain of heart, as well as others' love for him, his misgivings stem from a position which makes him at once carefree and dependent. Distress and poverty threaten to wait upon the child of nature who will not build and sow for himself. While the poem has followed much of the symptomatology of acute depression found in both the Ode and the Verse Letter—feelings of joy which descend suddenly into dejection—it has ascribed them to causes which neither poem had even entertained. The speaker has been too much a child of the season, acting as if "life's business were a summer mood" and unwilling or unable to take the common steps which would help to assure his own survival. The Ode had nothing to do with any crisis of the will; the Verse Letter had presented itself as a crisis of the heart, which Wordsworth seems here to be revising into a crisis of the will.

In an important recent article, Samuel E. Schulman has drawn attention to the way in which "self-descriptive passages of the first half of . . . ["The Leech-Gatherer"] derive from [James] Thomson's Spenserian moralizing in *The Castle of Indolence*."[8] Thomson anticipates Wordsworth in describing sudden irrational descents from delight to despair:

> But not even Pleasure to Excess is good,
> What most elates then sinks the Soul as low;
> When Spring-Tide Joy pours in with copious Flood,
> The higher still th' exulting Billows flow,
> The farther back back again they flagging go,
> And leave us grovelling on the dreary Shore.
> (1.62)

In addition, Schulman points out that both Thomson and Wordsworth echo the Sermon on the Mount in describing the life of the carefree, "liv'd in pleasant thought":

> Behold the merry Minstrels of the Morn,
> The swarming Songsters of the careless Grove,
> . . . .
> They neither plough, nor sow; ne, fir for Flail,
> E'er to the Barn the nodding Sheaves they drove;
> Yet theirs each Harvest dances in the Gale,
> Whatever crowns the Hill, or smiles along the Vale.
>
> (1.10)

The probability of a direct influence of Thomson's poem on "The Leech-Gatherer" is enhanced by Wordsworth's having begun on 9 May, two days after he completed the poem on the old man, "Stanzas Written in My Pocket-copy of Thomson's 'Castle of Indolence,' " a work which playfully mocks the volatility of poets' spirits through quaintly exaggerated sketches of himself and his Coleridge.

It is left for Wordsworth's next stanza in "The Leech-Gatherer" to establish that the poem is about the joys and miseries of poets, taken as a class:

> I thought of Chatterton the marvellous Boy
> The sleepless soul who perished in his pride
> Of Him who walked in glory & in joy
> Behind his Plough upon the mountain's side
> By our own spirits are we defied
> We Poets in our youth begin in gladness
> But thereof comes in the end despondcey and madness.
>
> (43–49)

These lines perform complicated tasks within the poem. To begin with, they establish the mode of the reflections which have preceded them, assuring us that we are indeed dealing with a lament of sensibility about the decline and decay of genius. They also take up the concluding sections of Coleridge's Verse Letter: "By our own spirits are we deified" is a succinct and fairly adequate gloss of Coleridge's insistence on joy as the ultimate source of all that is worthwhile in life; and Wordsworth's lines entertain, at least for the moment, the logical consequence of the position which Coleridge has taken in his poem, as the inevitable fall from the gladness of youth can lead only to despondency and madness. In responding to Coleridge's poem, Wordsworth appears to have read through both its specific complaints and particular occasion to the literary convention in which he perceives it to exist, and to the psychological convention—no less dangerous for its conventionality—which it implies. Such lines from the Verse Letter as the following, which are particularly relevant to "The Leech-Gatherer," can be picked almost at random from the poetry of sensibility: "The transientness is Poison in the Wine, / Eats out the pith of Joy, makes all Joy hollow, / All Pleasure a dim Dream of Pain to follow!" (160–62). Wordsworth explores the conventions which lie behind Coleridge's complaint by displacing his problems into and mediating them through the figures of two forerunners, Chatterton and Burns, one of whom was a hero of the cult of sensibility, the other of whom was perhaps the most accomplished poet to devote himself to its conventions.

As Dekker has shown, Chatterton is far easier to identify with Coleridge than with Wordsworth himself.[9] In his "Monody on the Death of Chatterton" (1893) Coleridge had traced in the young suicide currents of "the silent agony of Woe" (*CPW* 1:68; 14) akin to those which surface in his letter to Sara. In the Verse Letter, of course, Coleridge appears to have forgotten his closing prayer that he may resemble Chatterton in all except his fate: "But ah! when rage the Waves of Woe, / Grant me with firmer breast t'oppose their hate, / And soar above the storms with upright eye elate!" (88–90). The grounds of Wordsworth's association of Coleridge with Burns are more obscure, but within the poem the association is more profound.

Both Wordsworth and Coleridge had, after all, long outlived their Chattertonian possibilities. If their candles had not burned to the socket, they had surely lasted the night. In an odd way Chatterton's fate is a dream of sensibility—to cease upon the midnight with no pain—while Burns's is its grim reality. Like Burns, Coleridge had long ago entered the world of adult responsibilities. With his wife, children, and many close friends, he was not alone in a garret, as he very well knew. With Dekker, I would locate Wordsworth's linkage of Coleridge and Burns in the poet's first reading of James Currie's life of Burns (1800), an event to which Wordsworth refers in his open letter about the poet in 1816: "I well remember the acute sorrow

with which, by my own fire-side, I first perused Dr. Currie's Narrative, and some of the letters, particularly of those composed in the
latter part of the poet's life" (*Prose* 3 : 1 1 8). The date of Wordsworth's
first reading of Currie is untraceable; but, given the work's notoriety,
his abiding interest in its subject, and his friend's early knowledge of
it, it seems unlikely that Wordsworth's access would have been long
delayed. Coleridge was in Liverpool when it came out, met Currie
several times, and pronounced his work "a masterly specimen of
philosophical Biography" (*STCL* 1 : 607). Charles Lamb, one of
Burns's most enthusiastic advocates, was less impressed, describing
it as "very confusedly and badly written, and interspersed with dull
pathological and *medical* discussions." [10]

It is just those pathological and medical discussions which Wordsworth would have read with startled recognition as well as sorrow.
Currie attributes Burns's failings as well as his virtues to the "extraordinary sensibility of his mind," adding that the "fatal defect in his
character lay in the comparative weakness of his volition, that superior faculty of the mind, which governing the conduct according to
the dictates of the understanding, alone entitles it to be denominated
rational." [11] Such a formulation of the problem (though perhaps
without such a smug judgment) could come from Coleridge's analysis
of the character of Hamlet, or from anybody's biography of Coleridge. According to Currie, Burns lacked the sort of regular habits
of life, including a settled vocation, which could have helped him to
counterbalance the excesses of his sensibility. Currie's analysis of the
effects of alcohol on the man of sensibility is worth quoting at length:

In proportion to its stimulating influence on the system (on which
the pleasurable sensations depend), is the debility that ensues; a
debility that destroys digestion, and terminates in habitual fever,
dropsy, jaundice, paralysis, or insanity. As the strength of the body
decays, the volition fails; in proportion as the sensations are
soothed and gratified, the sensibility increases; and morbid sensibility is the parent of indolence, because, while it impairs the
regulating power of the mind, it exaggerates all the obstacles to
exertion. Activity, perseverance, and self-command, become more
and more difficult, and the great purposes of utility, patriotism, or

of honourable ambition, which had occupied the imagination, die away in fruitless resolutions, or in feeble efforts. (1:245–46)

Ominously, Currie had begun his discussion of the effects of liquor on the will, of which this is the conclusion, with a digressive footnote comparing the effects of alcohol and opium (1:242–43). While Currie declines "to apply these observations to the subject of our memoirs" (1:246), Wordsworth could not have failed to apply them to Coleridge as well as Burns. When he heard or read Coleridge's Verse Letter chronicling his emotional and spiritual misfortunes, he must have been led inevitably to think of Burns.

Wordsworth's early and continuing admiration of the poetry of Burns is as readily demonstrable, as well known, and as little regarded as any fact of his poetic life.[12] Our problems in associating the two writers arise from their glaring superficial differences, which were remarked as early as William Hazlitt's *Lectures on the English Poets*. In the midst of his spiteful commentary on Wordsworth's apologetic pamphlet of 1816, *A Letter to a Friend of Robert Burns*, Hazlitt remarks that "It is hardly reasonable to look for a hearty or genuine defence of Burns from the pen of Mr. Wordsworth; for there is no link of sympathy between them. Nothing can be more different or hostile than the spirit of their poetry. Mr. Wordsworth's poetry is the poetry of mere sentiment and pensive contemplation: Burns's is a very highly sublimated essence of animal existence."[13] Hazlitt's Burns is the Burns of our common experience: he singles out poems like "The Twa Dogs," "Halloween," "To a Haggis," "Scotch Drink," and—supremely—"Tam O'Shanter" for his warmest praise. He has as little tolerance as the modern reader, though, for the Burns of "English serious odes and moral stanzas," who loomed surprisingly large in the Kilmarnock edition of 1786, to which the young Wordsworth responded so immediately and enthusiastically.

Extremes of melancholy are fully as pronounced in the Kilmarnock poems as flights of high animal spirits. In "Despondency, an Ode," which Wordsworth described to Coleridge in 1799 as a poem he could "never read without the deepest agitation" (*EY* 256), Burns envies the lot of the hermit, to whom "By unfrequented stream, / The *ways of men* are distant brought, / A faint-collected dream."[14]

The poem ends with despair over "The fears all, the tears all, / Of dim declining *Age!*" (159). The flower turned down by the plow in "To a Mountain-Daisy" prefigures the fall of the poet himself:

> Such is the fate of simple Bard,
> On Life's rough ocean luckless starr'd!
> Unskilful he to note the card
>   Of *prudent Lore*,
> Till billows rage, and gales blow hard,
>   And whelm him o'er!
>
> (172)

Dekker notes the habits of thought and feeling which link such passages to the opening stanzas of "The Leech-Gatherer" (66–75). I would add that Burns's own emphases in his lines are practically a guide to the topics of Wordsworth's poem.

With his phrase "We poets" (48), Wordsworth has identified his vocational class as that most prone to suffer from volatile fluctuations of emotion, and as the class which is as a consequence doomed to the fates of Chatterton and Burns. A moment's thought will enable us to see how unusual such a class identification is in Wordsworth. The burden of his 1802 additions to the preface to *Lyrical Ballads*, after all, was to narrow the distance between poets and the rest of mankind. In this recent theoretical elaboration, poets did not constitute an elect, but rather represented the inherent powers of all men. In the poetry of Burns, though, we find poets commonly treated as a class distinct from the rest of society. Such poems as the "Epistle to Davie, a Brother Poet," "On a Scotch Bard Gone to the West Indies," "Epistle to J. L*****k, an Old Scotch Bard," and "To W. S*****n, Orchiltree," all celebrate the fraternal order of bardies in which Burns places himself. The composite poet created by the Kilmarnock volume might best be described as a patient, as a completely feeling soul. He is a pure but fragile sensibility existing precariously at the mercy of fate, of finance, and of his own fierce passions. "A Prayer, in the Prospect of Death" is marked by special pleading:

> Thou know'st that Thou hast formed me,
>   With Passions wild and strong;

And list'ning to their witching voice
Has often led me wrong.

(169)

Even the confessional lines of "A Bard's Epitaph" minimize the role of the will in a poet's life: "thoughtless follies laid him low, / And stain'd his name" (235). In such formulations the active force always seems to lie outside the self. Error becomes the fault of the creator, who made passions too strong to be controlled. Follies are somehow external forces which destroy the self and damage its reputation.

The poem by Burns which is closest to Wordsworth's depiction of the poet's dilemma in "The Leech-Gatherer" is "The Vision," in which Burns appears to confront directly and triumphantly that improvidence, so oddly compounded of selflessness and self-indulgence, which is assumed throughout the volume to be peculiar to poets. The work describes the poet's return from a cold autumn's day of work in the fields to an evening of pensive reflection by the fireside:

All in this mottie, misty clime,
I backward mus'd on wasted time,
How I had spent my *youthfu' prime*,
    An' done nae-thing,
But stringing blethers up in rhyme
    For fools to sing.

Had I to guid advice by harket,
I might, by this, hae led a market,
Or strutted in a Bank and clarket
    My *Cash-Account*;
While here, half-mad, half-fed, half-sarket,
    Is a' th' amount.

(88–89)

When Wordsworth changes "The Leech-Gatherer" into "Resolution and Independence," this remarkable poem will serve as his formal model. For now, I will only point out that the apparent incompatibility between poetry and self-interest with which it deals is the ultimate source of the anxieties presented in "The Leech-Gatherer."

One more extract from the writings of Burns demonstrates his identification of poetry as a joy which leads to misery, and especially his association of the miserable joys of poetry and of sexuality. This is from a letter reprinted by Currie, "To Miss C****," dated August 1793:

> The fates and characters of the rhyming tribe often employ my thoughts when I am disposed to be melancholy. There is not, among all the martyrologies that ever were penned, so rueful a narrative as the lives of the poets.—In the comparative view of wretches, the criterion is not what they are doomed to suffer, but how they are formed to bear. Take a being of our kind, give him a stronger imagination and a more delicate sensibility, which between them will ever engender a more ungovernable set of passions than are the usual lot of man; implant in him an irresistible impulse to some idle vagary, such as, arranging wild flowers in fantastical nosegays, tracing the grasshopper to his haunt by his chirping song, watching the frisks of the little minnows in the sunny pool, or hunting after the intrigues of butterflies—in short, send him adrift after some pursuit which shall eternally mislead him from the paths of lucre, and yet curse him with a keener relish than any man living for the pleasures that lucre can purchase; lastly, fill up the measure of his woes by bestowing on him a spurning sense of his own dignity, and you have created a wight nearly as miserable as a poet. To you, Madam, I need not recount the fairy pleasures the muse bestows to counterbalance this catalogue of evils. Bewitching poetry is like bewitching women; she has in all ages been accused of misleading mankind from the counsels of wisdom and the paths of prudence, involving them in difficulties, baiting them with poverty, branding them with infamy, and plunging them in the whirling vortex of ruin; yet, where is the man but must own that all our happiness on earth is not worthy the name—that even the holy hermit's solitary prospect of paradisaical bliss is but the glitter of a northern sun, rising over a frozen region, compared with the many pleasures, the nameless raptures that we owe to the lovely Queen of the heart of Man! (2:422–23)

Of course Burns is being arch and courtly in this letter. But, as Currie had pointed out in his biography, it was the pursuit of just such a philosophy which had helped to lead to his early death. And however different their moods, the same tensions animate this letter and Coleridge's Verse Letter. Joy is the principle of the poet's life, and the sensibility which gives him a finer relish of life's pleasures makes him more susceptible to its pains. In the absence of joy, his life would have no pleasures, and the poet would be ground under by his despondency. The "Queen of the heart" with whom Burns concludes is simultaneously muse and mistress, as Sara could be to Coleridge, did not other circumstances of his life fate him to enjoy neither. Wordsworth has framed his response to Coleridge's Verse Letter through a topical dialectic taken largely from the canon of Burns.

The answer which "The Leech-Gatherer" offers to its Burnsian impasse reflects simultaneously the concerns of Coleridge's Verse Letter, concerns of the earlier Wordsworth canon, and the writings of Burns himself. The poet's somber musings on despondency and madness are interrupted by his coming unexpectedly upon an alien figure:

> Now whether it was by peculiar grace
> A leading from above, a something given
> Yet it befel that in that lonely place
> When up & down my fancy thus was driven
> And I with these untoward thoughts had striven
> I to the borders of a Pond did come
> By which an Old man was, far from all house or home
>
> (50–56)

Wordsworth's insistence upon the exteriority of both the event and the figure is a response to the extreme interiority of Coleridge's Verse Letter. Important things can happen outside the self, even when it is engaged in the most despairing and self-absorbed reflections. Without claiming that the encounter is transcendental in nature, Wordsworth signals its adventitiousness by a heightened rhetoric which places the event at a remove from the self akin to the difference between the transcendent and the quotidian. He suggests that the appearance of the figure may have been the result of "peculiar grace / A leading from above," or, at any event, "a something given" (50–51). We do not, as Coleridge claims in the Verse Letter, "receive but what we give" (296).[15] Wordsworth's rhetoric in this passage has been taken to suggest that he is moving from a faith in the natural order of things to a more orthodox reliance on providence.[16] Although such a reading is surely allowable, it sorts oddly with the facts of the leech-gatherer's situation and story, which emphasize above anything else his existence as part of common suffering humanity. Wordsworth is strongly juxtaposing the world of internal meditation, in which the fancy is driven up and down, against the world of external happenings, which can offer correctives to self-pity. He will make his theoretical intentions clear in his letter to Sara Hutchinson of 14 June: "I describe myself as having been exalted to the highest pitch of delight by the joyousness and beauty of Nature and then as depressed, even in the midst of those beautiful objects, to the lowest dejection and despair. A young Poet in the midst of the happiness of Nature is described as overwhelmed by the thoughts of the miserable reverses which have befallen the happiest of all men, viz Poets—I think of this till I am so deeply impressed by it, that I consider the manner in which I was rescued from my dejection and despair *almost* an interposition of Providence" (*EY* 366, emphasis added).

Wordsworth wants the reader first to suspect something supernatural, but then to be surprised by the commonplaceness of both the figure and event: "A person reading this Poem with feelings like mine will have been awed and controuled, expecting almost something spiritual or supernatural—What is brought forward? 'A lonely place, a Pond' 'by which an old man *was*, far from all house or home'—not stood, not sat, but '*was*'—the figure presented in the most naked simplicity possible. This feeling of spirituality or supernaturalness is again referred to as being strong in my mind in this passage—'*How came he here* thought I or what can he be doing?'" (*EY* 366). Both figure and event are thoroughly natural. Why should there not be an old man by a pond on a moor, as well as a poet? The sense of supernatural surprise is a result of the poet's strongly introspective mood, which leaves him shocked to find anything at all existing outside the self.

For a detailed description of the leech-gatherer and his story, we must turn to Dorothy's journal of 3 October 1800, which records their meeting with such a man, and which Wordsworth certainly used, probably quite literally, when composing the passages which are wholly or partially destroyed in DC MS 41. I give the entire passage:

When Wm and I returned from accompanying Jones we met an old man almost double, he had on a coat thrown over his shoulders above his waistcoat and coat. Under this he carried a bundle and had an apron on and a night cap. His face was interesting. He had dark eyes and a long nose. John who afterwards met him at Wythburn took him for a Jew. He was of Scotch parents but had been born in the army. He had had a wife 'and a good woman and it pleased God to bless us with ten children.' All these were dead but one of whom he had not heard for many years, a sailor. His trade was to gather leeches, but now leeches are scarce and he had not strength for it. He lived by begging and was making his way to Carlisle where he should buy a few godly books to sell. He said leeches were very scarce partly owing to this dry season, but many years they have been scarce—he supposed it owing to their being much sought after, that they did not breed fast, and were of slow growth. Leeches were formerly 2/6 [per] 100; they are now 30/. He had been hurt in driving a cart, his leg broke his body driven over his skull fractured. He felt no pain till he recovered from his first insensibility. It was then late in the evening, when the light was just going away. (*DWJ* 42)

Conjectural readings based on the stubs of Sara's notebook suggest how closely Wordsworth has followed Dorothy's account. He has apparently described the old man's bent stature, his cloak, and the bundle which he bears beneath it. After the poet has drawn near to him and engaged him in conversation, the old man's speech reflects the Scottish heritage Dorothy had remarked:

> [His words came feebly from a feeble] chest
> [Yet each in solemn order follow'd each]
> [With something of a pompous utterance drest,]
> [Choice word & measur'd phrase, beyond the reach]
> [Of ordinary men, a stately speech,]
> [Such as grave livers do in Scotland use,]
> [Religious Men, who give to God & Men their] dues.
>
> (92–98)

Dorothy had not, of course, commented on any peculiarities of the old man's speech. Wordsworth appears to be drawing upon a recurrent contrast in the Burns canon, where the "grave livers" of Scotland are frequently depicted, but only to be set as figures of sport against the poet and his cronies, who are themselves lighthearted souls of fellowship, imprudence, and good cheer. In his age, decrepitude, pomposity, and religiosity, Wordsworth's leech-gatherer is a figure whom Burns had alternately feared, scorned, and ignored.

Indeed, a possible formal model for both "The Leech-Gatherer" and Wordsworth's earlier encounter poems may be found in another of the Kilmarnock poems, "Man Was Made to Mourn; a Dirge." This lament on mutability presents an encounter between the poet and an old man:

> One ev'ning, as I wand'red forth,
>   Along the banks of AIRE,
> I spy'd a man, whose aged step
>   Seem'd weary, worn with care;
> His face was furrow'd o'er with years,
>   And hoary was his hair.
>
>   (160)

After this opening stanza the poem consists solely of the monologue of the old man, a narrative procedure Wordsworth was to follow in "The Last of the Flock" and "The Mad Mother" in the 1798 *Lyrical Ballads*. The "story" told by the aged figure Burns encounters is not terribly complex, and a single stanza will serve to give a sense of its tone and substance.

> O man! while in thy early years
>   How prodigal of time!
> Misspending all thy precious hours,
>   Thy glorious youthful prime!
> Alternate follies take the sway;
>   Licentious Passions burn;
> Which tenfold force give Nature's law,
>   That Man was made to mourn.
>
>   (162)

As recompense for Nature's law of universal decline and decay, the old man can offer only "Death! the poor man's dearest friend, / The kindest and the best" (164).

In "The Leech-Gatherer" Wordsworth has presented a Burnsian dilemma about the relationship of poetic joy and misery, and has addressed the problem through depicting an encounter with a Burnsian figure in a Burnsian situation. What we can piece together of the old man's tale, though, has no parallel in the canon of Burns. Wordsworth clearly wanted this story to be the center of the poem. His response to the faint praise of Sara and Mary tells us as much as we can know of what it contained:

> . . . this I can *confidently* affirm, that, although I believe God has given me a strong imagination, I cannot conceive a figure more impressive than that of an old Man like this, the survivor of a Wife and ten children, travelling alone among the mountains and all lonely places, carrying with him his own fortitude, and the necessities which an unjust state of society has entailed upon him. You say and Mary (that is you can say no more than that) the Poem is *very well* after the introduction of the old man; this is not true, if it is not more than very well it is very bad, there is no intermediate state. You speak of his speech as tedious; everything is tedious when one does not read with the feelings of the Author—"*The Thorn*" is tedious to hundreds; and so is the *Idiot Boy* to hundreds. It is in the character of the old man to tell his story in a manner which an *impatient* reader must necessarily feel as tedious. But Good God! Such a figure, in such a place, a pious self-respecting, miserably infirm . . . Old Man telling such a tale!
>
> My dear Sara, . . . it is of the utmost importance that you should have had pleasure from contemplating the fortitude, independence, persevering spirit, and the general moral dignity of this old man's character. (*EY* 366–67)

In the midst of bullying his reluctant readers, Wordsworth tells us what the leech-gatherer's tale generally was. It was a story of pain and loss, from his own mouth, at least largely akin to that preserved in Dorothy's notebook. But it is one of those tales of sorrow that is not pain to hear of, for the glory that redounds therefrom to human kind. The old man has suffered and been diminished—Wordsworth especially concentrates on his domestic losses, as he has survived a wife and ten children (one more than in Dorothy's record of the actual meeting). He is alone, and he must support himself in the face of the

burdens placed on him by "an unjust state of society." The sole surviving passage of his account of himself suggests his attitude toward
his hardships:

> I yet can gain my bread tho' in times gone
> I twenty could have found where now I can find one
>
> Feeble I am in health these hills to climb
> Yet I procure a Living of my own
> This is my summer work in winter time
> I go with godly Books from Town to Town
> Now I am seeking Leeches up & down
> From house to house I go from Barn to Barn
> All over Cartmell Fells & up to Blellan Tarn
>
> (127–33)

While the leech-gatherer acknowledges the difficulty of his life, he is
less concerned with his hardships than with his success in overcoming
them. The old man seems immune to self-pity, and any reflections
on the injustices of society surely belong to the observing poet rather
than the speaker. The poem works from an ironic disjunction between the pathetic matter of the story and "the fortitude, independence, persevering spirit, and general moral dignity" of the voice in
which it is told. This man was not made to mourn.

The contrast could hardly be clearer between the poet's early fearful musings about his own destiny and the old man's acceptance of a
lot as bad as any the poet might have envisioned. The poet's ultimate
response is not tears for the old man's life but laughter at his own
self-centered anxieties:

> I could have laugh'd myself to scorn to find
> In that decrepit man so firm a mind
> God said I be my help & stay secure
> I'll think of the Leech-gatherer on the lonely Moor.
>
> (137–40)

Without a text for the bulk of the tale, we can relate it only in a
general way to Coleridge's Verse Letter. It seems likely, though, that
Wordsworth was responding in it primarily to Coleridge's chronicle

of his domestic discontents, that "house-hold Life" of "Indifference or Strife" (163–64). Where Coleridge laments "those habitual ills / That wear out Life, when two unequal Minds / Meet in one House, & two discordant Wills" (243–45), Wordsworth presents a figure who has lost his wife and has no home. Where Coleridge's "little Angel Children (woe is me!)" (277) may "bind / And pluck out the Wing-feathers of my Mind" (278–79), the leech-gatherer has lost ten children to death. He has no occasion to half-wish "they never had been born" (281).

"The Leech-Gatherer" suggests that the anxieties of the poet before his encounter with the old man can be attributed to his having been thinking about himself as something apart from the common run of mankind, as a creature of a different emotional constitution. Wordsworth is reading Coleridge's Verse Letter as a lament of sensibility like those of Burns, all of which are predicated on the assumption that poets are something different, finer, more fragile, less suited to bear the burdens of common life. Its offered cure is that Coleridge remove himself from the company of poets and reintroduce himself to the company of men. The poetic necessity of such a movement is evident throughout Wordsworth's 1802 additions of the preface to *Lyrical Ballads.*

Wordsworth has used as the basis of his poem an experience in which Coleridge did not participate; however, the poem seems designed to stimulate recollections of another poem commemorating an event in which Coleridge did take part, the fourth of the "Poems on the Naming of Places" in the second volume of *Lyrical Ballads* (1800), "A narrow girdle of rough stones and crags." [17] On a calm September morning, Wordsworth and his "two beloved Friends" (*LB* 223; 66), Dorothy and Coleridge, go for a stroll along the eastern shore of Grasmere. The language of the first part of the poem reinforces the sense of leisure in their walk, as they saunter, play with their time, observe in "vacant mood" (16) odd bits of vegetation on the lake, trifle, and pause. They hear all the while "the busy mirth / Of Reapers, Men and Women, Boys and Girls" (42–43). Suddenly they come upon another man by the shore:

> Through a thin veil of glittering haze, we saw
> Before us on a point of jutting land

> The tall and upright figure of a Man
> Attir'd in peasant's garb, who stood alone
> Angling beside the margin of the lake.
>
>   (48−52)

As they walk toward him, they self-righteously proclaim him

> An idle man, who could thus lose a day
> Of the mid harvest, when the labourer's hire
> Is ample, and some little might be stor'd
> Wherewith to chear him in the winter time.
>
>   (57−60)

When they finally reach the lone fisherman, they discover him to be "a man worn down / By sickness, gaunt and lean, with sunken cheeks / And wasted limbs" (64−66), who is clearly "Too weak to labour in the harvest field" (69). Instead, he is "using his best skill to gain / A pittance from the dead unfeeling lake / That knew not of his wants" (70−72). Because of this experience, the three friends jointly have named the place where the man was standing "POINT RASH-JUDGMENT" (86). The mechanisms of the poem are those of "The Leech-Gatherer": presuppositions about life, developed in the midst of an immersion in seasonal happiness, are corrected by an actual encounter with an alien figure. As Parrish has pointed out, both poems also look backward to other similar and powerful Words-worthian encounters, such as those of the various figures who meet "The Old Cumberland Beggar" and the poet's meeting with the discharged soldier, recorded in the early drafts of what would become Book IV of *The Prelude*.[18]

My discussion of "The Leech-Gatherer" began by remarking that it is a strange reading of and response to Coleridge's Verse Letter. It is time to classify its reflexive strategies more fully. "The Leech-Gatherer" is absolutely silent on Coleridge's erotic discontents, and it also wholly ignores the artistic problem which Coleridge has enunciated briefly but powerfully, the loss of his shaping spirit of imagination. It treats despairing thoughts about the future as the idle work of a fancy which has insufficient sympathy with problems met and overcome by ordinary mortals in the course of common life. It treats

poetic despair—whether Chatterton's, Burns's, Coleridge's, or Wordsworth's own—as wholly acute anxiety, denying it the dignity of the
sense of chronic and permanent loss which echoes throughout both
the Verse Letter and Wordsworth's own Ode. "The Leech-Gatherer"
is a stern reply to Coleridge's Verse Letter, but it operates parodically
and reductively. The parody is not mean-spirited by any means, and
certainly is is well-intentioned. In itself, "The Leech-Gatherer" is
a solid Wordsworthian poem in an established mode; but when set
as it was written against the Verse Letter, it seems to verge upon
travesty. It accentuates and parodically subverts the intense self-
centeredness and self-consciousness of the poet of sensibility in a way
that strips him of any real powers. If Burns and Chatterton were
destroyed by the problems which afflict the narrator of "The Leech-
Gatherer" (or rather, which he inflicts upon himself), they must have
been fragile indeed. Both predecessors, and Coleridge by extension,
are trivialized.

Despite the vehemence of Wordsworth's defence of "The Leech-
Gatherer" to Sara Hutchinson, he was not long happy with the
poem. In a little over a month he would begin the revisions which
convert the poem into a work close to the one we know as "Resolution and Independence." Many commentators have seen Wordsworth's
continued work on the poem as an accession to Sara's criticism. That
is to say, they envision Wordsworth reacting to his own poem as a
poetic unit, deciding that, yes, it is too much to expect a reader to
sit still through the old man's speech, and so forth, and determining
how best to say what he had had in mind. Part of the problem with
such a view is that "The Leech-Gatherer" and "Resolution and Independence," while sharing half their stanzas, don't say the same
things. Another problem is that this view makes of "The Leech-
Gatherer" something akin to an exercise to be corrected. It is not. It
is a strong and moving poem which, so far as we can judge without
the central part of the old man's dialogue, could easily stand beside
other works in Wordsworth's dramatic mode, such as "The Thorn,"
"The Mad Mother," and "The Sailor's Mother." This is good company. The following chapter will argue that Wordsworth was not just
attempting to make "The Leech-Gatherer" a better poem, but was
specifically addressing its weaknesses in terms of the dialogue set in
motion by the Ode and the Verse Letter.

Wordsworth's "Resolution and Independence"

There was a roaring in the wind all night;
The rain came heavily, & fell in floods;
But now the sun is rising calm and bright,
The birds are singing in the distant woods;
Over his own sweet voice the stock dove broods,   [5]
The jay makes answer as the magpie chatters;
And all the air is fill'd with pleasant noise of waters.

All things that love the sun are out of doors;
The sky rejoices in the morning's birth,
The grass is bright with rain-drops, on the moors   [10]
The hare is running races in her mirth,
And with her feet she from the plashy earth
Raises a mist, which, glittering in the sun,
Runs with her all the way wherever she doth run.

I was a Traveller then upon the Moor,   [15]
I saw the hare that rac'd about with joy,
I heard the woods and distant waters roar,
Or heard them not, as happy as a Boy;
The pleasant season did my heart employ,

My old remembrances went from me wholly,　　　　　　　　[20]
And all the ways of men so vain and melancholy.

But, as it sometimes chanceth from the might
Of joy in minds that can no farther go,
As high as we have mounted in delight
In our dejection do we sink as low　　　　　　　　　　　[25]
To me that morning did it happen so;
And fears and fancies thick upon me came,
Dim sadness & blind thoughts I knew not, nor could name

I heard the sky-lark singing in the sky,
And I bethought me of the playful hare;　　　　　　　　[30]
Even such a happy Child of earth am I,
Even as these happy creatures do I fare;
Far from the world I walk & from all care
But there may come another day to me;
Solitude, pain of heart, distress and poverty.　　　　　　[35]

My whole life I have liv'd in pleasant thought
As if life's business were a summer mood,
And they who liv'd in genial faith found nought
That grew more willingly than genial good
But how can he expect that others should　　　　　　　[40]
Build for him, sow for him, and at his call
Love him who for himself will take no heed at all.

I thought of Chatterton, the marvellous Boy,
The sleepless soul who perish'd in his pride;
Of him who walk'd in glory and in joy　　　　　　　　[45]
Behind his plough upon the mountain side;
By our own spirits are we deified:
We Poets in our youth begin in gladness;
But thereof comes in the end despondency & madness.

Now whether it was by peculiar grace,　　　　　　　　[50]
A leading from above, a something given,

Yet it befel that in that lonely place,
When up and down my fancy thus was driven,
And I with these untoward thoughts had striven,
I spied a Man before me unawares;   [55]
The oldest Man he seem'd that ever wore grey hairs.

My course I stopp'd as soon as I espied
The Old Man in that naked wilderness;
Close by a Pond upon the hither side
He stood alone: a minute's space, I guess,   [60]
I watch'd him, he continuing motionless.
To the Pool's further margin then I drew,
He all the while before me being full in view.

As a huge stone is sometimes seen to lie
Couch'd on the bald top of an eminence,   [65]
Wonder to all that do the same espy,
By what means it could thither come & whence;
So that it seems a thing endued with sense,
Like a Sea-beast crawl'd forth, which on a shelf
Of rock or sand reposeth, there to sun itself.   [70]

Such seem'd this Man, not all alive nor dead,
Nor all asleep; in his extreme old age
His body was bent double, feet and head
Coming together in their pilgrimage,
As if some dire constraint of pain, or rage   [75]
Of sickness felt by him in times long past
A more than human weight upon his age had cast.

Himself he propp'd, both body, limbs and face
Upon a long grey staff of shaven wood;
And still as I drew near with gentle pace   [80]
Beside the little Pond or moorish flood
Motionless as a cloud the Old Man stood,
That heareth not the loud winds when they call,
And moveth altogether if it moves at all.

He wore a Cloak the same as women wear   [85]
As one whose blood did needful comfort lack;
His face look'd pale as if it had grown fair,
And furthermore he had upon his back
Beneath his Cloak a round & bulky Pack,
A load of wool or raiment as might seem   [90]
That on his shoulders lay as if it clave to him.

At length, himself unsettling, he the Pond
Stirr'd with his staff, & fixedly did look
Upon the muddy water which he conn'd
As if he had been reading in a book;   [95]
And now such freedom as I could I took
And, drawing to his side, to him did say,
"This morning gives us promise of a glorious day."

A gentle answer did the Old man make
In courteous speech which forth he slowly drew;   [100]
And him with further words I thus bespake,
"What kind of work is that which you pursue?
"This is a lonesome place for one like you."
He answer'd me with pleasure & surprize,
And there was while he spake a fire about his eyes.   [105]

His words came feebly from a feeble chest,
Yet each [i]n solemn order follow'd each
With something of a pompous utterance dress'd
Choice word & measur'd phrase, beyond the reach
Of ordinary men, a stately speech   [110]
Such as grave livers do in Scotland use,
Religious Men who give to God & Man their dues.

He told me that he to the Pond had come
To gather Leeches, being old and poor,
That 'twas his calling, better far than some,   [115]
Though he had many hardships to endure:
From Pond to Pond he roam'd from Moor to Moor,

Housing with God's good help by choice or chance,
And in this way he gain'd an honest maintenance.

The Old Man still stood talking by my side, [120]
But soon his voice to me was like a stream
Scarce heard, nor word from word could I divide,
And the whole body of the Man did seem
Like one [w]hom I had met with in a dream;
Or like a Man from some far region sent [125]
To give me human strength, & strong admonishment.

My former thoughts return'd, the fear that kills,
The hope that is unwilling to be fed,
Cold, pain, and labour, & all fleshly ills,
And mighty Poets in their misery dead; [130]
And now, not knowing what the Old Man had said,
My question eagerly did I renew,
"How is it that you live? & what is it you do?"

He with a smile did then his words repeat
And said, that wheresoe'er they might be spied [135]
He gather'd Leeches, stirring at his feet
The waters of the Ponds where they abide,
Once he could meet with them on every side;
But fewer they became from day to day,
And so his means of life before him died away. [140]

While he was talking thus the lonely place,
The Old Man's shape & speech all troubl'd me;
In my mind's eye I seem'd to see him pace
About the weary Moors continually,
Wandering about alone and silently. [145]
While I these thoughts within myself pursu'd,
He, having made a pause, the same discourse renew'd.

And now with this he other matter blended
Which he deliver'd with demeanor kind,

Yet stately in the main; & when he ended   [150]
I could have laugh'd myself to scorn to find
In that decrepit Man so firm a mind;
"God," said I, "be my help & stay secure!
"I'll think of the Leech-gatherer on the lonely Moor

OR FIVE WEEKS after its completion on 7 May 1802, "The Leech-Gatherer" evidently sat unaltered. Indeed, as Curtis points out (*WET* 100), Wordsworth's response to Sara Hutchinson's objections to the poem, contained in his letter of 14 June, suggests that the poem is very nearly unalterable. Some of Wordsworth's letter was cited in the preceding chapter, as a means of reconstructing the import of the mutilated text of "The Leech-Gatherer." Wordsworth's moral satisfaction with his work surely passes the boundary into smugness:

> My dear Sara, it is not a matter of indifference whether you are pleased with this figure and his employment; it may be comparatively so, whether you are pleased or not with *this Poem*; but it is of the utmost importance that you should have had pleasure from contemplating the fortitude, independence, persevering spirit, and the general moral dignity of this old man's character. Your feelings upon the Mother, and the Boys with the Butterfly, were not indifferent: it was an affair of whole continents of moral sympathy. I will talk more with you on this when we meet—at present, farewell and Heaven for ever bless you! (*EY* 366–67)

Even after making allowances for the defensiveness created by Wordsworth's readily bruised feelings, one finds in this letter little to suggest that the poem is about to change materially. The old man and his story are fixed: it is Sara who will have to change, for the good of her soul, to fit the poem.

It comes as a surprise, then, to find Dorothy recording in her journal that on 2 July she had "transcribed the alterations in the

Leech gatherer" (*DWJ* 144). Her phrasing suggests that her brother's work may already have been in progress for some days, perhaps beginning as early as 26–28 June, a period for which a page has been torn from her journal. Subsequent entries record Wordsworth's having "finished the Leech gatherer" on 4 July and Dorothy's having copied the poem "for Coleridge and for us" the following day (145).

Scholars have long assumed that the state which "The Leech-Gatherer" reached on 5 July is essentially that found in the earliest extant manuscript of the revised poem, which Coleridge sent to Sir George and Lady Beaumont on 13 August 1803 (Pierpont Morgan MS. MA 1581). Certainly a fresh copy of the poem was sent to the Beaumonts, because Coleridge records Dorothy's having worked on it the day before (*STCL* 2:965). Since Dorothy made the transcription at Keswick, though, she was probably working from the copy which she had made for Coleridge the summer before. The relationship of Dorothy's 1803 text to Wordsworth's 1802 revisions is complicated by an unpublished letter from Beaumont to Coleridge, which is undated but which clearly acknowledges receipt of both the revised "Leech-Gatherer" and several stanzas of "Dejection," which he had not seen previously. Beaumont writes: "I delight in the lines on dejection, were I to tell you what they make me feel it would seem like fulsome flattery." After inserting the wish that Coleridge "will recover the remainder" of the poem, Beaumont adds, "I more and more admire the beginning of the Leech gatherer & I think the latter part greatly improved" (Pierpont Morgan MS. MA 1857, #6). One line may be missing from the page of the letter, and whatever else Beaumont may have had to say about Wordsworth's poem is lost. The question of what version of the poem Beaumont had previously seen is tantalizing. Coleridge's first mention of their acquaintance at Keswick comes in a letter to Wordsworth of 23 July 1803 (a scant three weeks before Dorothy's copy of the revised poem), in which he told his friend that "Sir G. & Lady B . . . are half-mad to see you" (*STCL* 2:957). In the excitement of meeting the Beaumonts and actively and successfully promoting their interest in and patronage of Wordsworth, Coleridge must have shown or given them copies of the unpublished work which he had at hand, including his copy of the unrevised version of "The Leech-Gatherer." There is no evidence that

Wordsworth worked further on the poem between July 1802 and the date when Dorothy transcribed it in 1803.

Building upon important analyses of the two poems by Helen Darbishire, A. W. Thomson, and William Heath, among others, Curtis has sketched out clearly the tendency of Wordsworth's revisions which turned "The Leech-Gatherer" into Resolution and Independence."[1] Curtis argues that Wordsworth's revisions resulted in a poem in a different genre entirely, transmuting what had been "ballad-like" in its origins to something ultimately "fable-like" in its effects by replacing "the language of men" represented in the old man's original speech with "the language of vision" found in the heavily figurative additions which Wordsworth made to the poem (*WET* 111). My discussion differs from Curtis's in its greater detail, in its greater emphasis on intertextual motivations for Wordsworth's revisions, and its different understanding of the function of the figurative passages Wordsworth added.

Wordsworth seems to have decided—and critics since Beaumont have agreed with his judgment—that little needed to be changed in his initial presentation of the speaker's dilemma in the poem. In "Resolution and Independence" the initial depiction of the scene and the speaker's meditations which arise from it remain substantially unchanged. The change in the weather first generates the lifting of the poet's spirits, which then change as abruptly and arbitrarily as the weather: "And fears and fancies thick upon me came, / Dim sadness & blind thoughts I knew not, nor could name" (27–28). The speaker still compares himself to the happy creatures of earth, threatened by impending catastrophes which may assail him at some time in the future.

Wordsworth's first substantial change in the poem suggests the extent to which "Resolution and Independence" will more fully engage the concerns of Coleridge's Verse Letter. After questioning his life "liv'd in pleasant thought / As if life's business were a summer mood" (35–36), the speaker of "The Leech-Gatherer" urged himself to activity: "Who will not wade to seek a bridge or boat / How can he ever hope to cross the flood?" (37–38). "Resolution and Independence" suspends its exhortation briefly, describing more fully the expectations of those who live in the mood of summer: "And they who liv'd in genial faith found nought / That grew more willingly than genial good" (38–39). Wordsworth echoes the "genial spirits" which have failed in Coleridge's Verse Letter, assuming in his lines at least a portion of the wordplay which had underlain Coleridge's phrase. Genial faith and genial good largely carry their meaning in a kind of amiability, until their relations to poetic genius are set in motion by the references to Chatterton and Burns, which follow closely (43–46). Even this very early textual revision suggests that "Resolution and Independence" is taking rather more seriously Coleridge's topic of the failed imagination. Certainly, the new lines ease the way into the matter of the poetic forerunners, which had intruded abruptly in the earlier version.

Wordsworth's second major revision is in his initial presentation of the leech-gatherer himself. In both versions the appearance of the old man is suspended until the end of the eighth stanza. The first five lines heralding the old man's coming remain unchanged. The stanza still begins with its speculations about "peculiar grace, / A leading from above, a something given" (50–51), and recapitulates the turmoil of the speaker's feelings on this particular morning. "The Leech-Gatherer" continues: "I to the borders of a Pond did come / By which an Old man was, far from all house or home" (55–56). In his letter to Sara Hutchinson of 14 June, Wordsworth had insisted on the importance of the verb of being in the clause which begins the second line: "What is brought forward? 'A lonely place, a Pond' 'by which an old man *was*, far from all house or home'—the figure presented in the most naked simplicity possible" (*EY* 366). The lines which replace this couplet in "Resolution and Independence" reverse entirely the earlier emphasis: "I spied a Man before me unawares; / The oldest Man he seem'd that ever wore grey hairs" (55–56). While the earlier formulation had centered on the old man's being, the revision shifts its attention to the speaker's perception. What the man is in himself is now subordinated to what he appears to be to the observer who spies him.

"The Leech-Gatherer" moved directly to a description of the old man's appearance and actions, mediated of course by the speaker's perceptions, but still concentrating on the figure itself—his age and apparent decrepitude, his stirring the waters of the pond, the sense projected of past pain or sickness, his clothing, and his pack. Four stanzas of alternate description and reflection upon what was being observed brought us at last to the speaker's first remarks to the man. The final two of these stanzas survive only in bits in "Resolution and Independence," where Wordsworth creates in their place four new stanzas, among the most justly celebrated in the poem, which belong almost solely to the observer himself rather than the object of his attention.

The first of these stanzas fixes attention on the speaker's responses and actions:

> My course I stopp'd as soon as I espied
> The Old Man in that naked wilderness;
> Close by a Pond upon the hither side
> He stood alone: a minute's space, I guess,
> I watch'd him, he continuing motionless.
> To the Pool's further margin then I drew,
> He all the while before me being full in view.
>
> (57–63)

The observer's interventions are inescapable in the passage: "I stopp'd . . . I espied . . . I guess . . . I watch'd . . . I drew . . . before me." The reader's attention is shifted from the "naked simplicity" of the figure to watching a mind, itself anything but nakedly simple, ponder and approach such a figure. With all the advantages of hindsight, we can feel the appropriateness of the change. The movement from the speaker's self-absorption to a regard for something external to the self had come easily in the earlier text, perhaps too quickly for it to be given full credence. The encounter with the man is retarded in the revised text, suspended so that we can see first what a mind such as the speaker's will make of such a figure in such unusual circumstances.

What it makes is brilliant but humanly inadequate poetry. The observing poet attempts to assess the importance of the unexpected figure through a complex and shifting heroic simile, which ironically does more to dissolve than to fix the identity of the man himself:

> As a huge stone is sometimes seen to lie
> Couch'd on the bald top of an eminence,

Wonder to all that do the same espy,
By what means it could thither come & whence;
So that it seems a thing endued with sense,
Like a Sea-beast crawl'd forth, which on a shelf
Of rock or sand reposeth, there to sun itself.

Such seem'd this Man, not all alive nor dead,
Nor all asleep; in his extreme old age
His body was bent double, feet and head
Coming together in their pilgrimage,
As if some dire constraint of pain, or rage
Of sickness felt by him in times long past
A more than human weight upon his age had cast.

(64–77)

Wordsworth's well-known analysis of this passage in the preface to the edition of 1815 deserves both repetition and elaboration: "The stone is endowed with something of the power of life to approximate it to the sea-beast; and the sea-beast stripped of some of its vital qualities to assimilate it to the stone; which intermediate image is thus treated for the purpose of bringing the original image, that of the stone, to a nearer resemblance to the figure and condition of the aged Man; who is divested of so much of the indications of life and motion as to bring him to the point where the two objects unite and coalesce in just comparison" (*Prose* 3 : 33). Wordsworth is speaking here, of course, of "the conferring, the abstracting, and the modifying powers of the Imagination" (*Prose* 3 : 33). He describes its activity as an attempt to capture how the old man "seem'd," how he had seemed to a particular speaker on a particular day, when he had been entertaining certain thoughts about the nature and course of human life. That is, the tenor itself—an aged man "not all alive nor dead, / Nor all asleep"—is an invention of the poet's, authorized only by his perception, as of course are the speculations that the man's condition is the product of "some dire constraint of pain, or rage / Of sickness felt by him in times long past." The vehicle created to communicate the nature of the tenor, an image mediate between the sea-beast and stone, itself affects the tenor, as the old man "is divested of so much of the indications of life and motion as to bring him to the point where the two objects unite and coalesce in just comparison." Just, one may well ask, but to what? Not to the man, who is being transformed through a comparison which initially set out to illuminate him. The only firm answer can be that the comparison is just to the poet's sense of things on this morning, with the provision that the figure simultaneously reveals and shapes his perceptions.[2]

The persistent passive voice of Wordsworth's commentary, in which the stone "is endowed," the sea-beast "stripped," and the man "divested," effectively cloaks the subject of the passage, which is not external reality at all, but the activity of the poet's mind. Where "The Leech-Gatherer" had figured the fate of poets in terms of their passion and passivity, which make them vulnerable to the vagaries of fate, it had left them devoid of power, even of the power of language. "Resolution and Independence" redresses this balance. Coming as it does after the narrator's earlier fears of the inevitability of decline and decay, this passage demonstrates the way in which the poetic imagination can put such materials to use. It provides a powerful visual and visionary confirmation of the speaker's previous surmises about the devolutionary course of human existence, as the figure places the old man at a juncture between mineral and animal existence. The figure, which is compelling in a way that the earlier vacillations had not been, affirms the power and integrity, if not the truth and accuracy, of the darker musings of Burns, Coleridge, and other kindred poets of sensibility.

The passage is interesting in another way, which has gone unremarked. It is a rare example in Wordsworth of an imaginative figure which has not grown from a perception. Nothing remotely like it occurs in Dorothy's journals, in "A narrow girdle of rough stones and crags," or in "The Leech-Gatherer." The figure is a new creation, something highly uncharacteristic of Wordsworth's revisionary activity. The textual growth of *The Prelude* suggests that the visionary elements of his work appear early, while the poem grows around them. That "Resolution and Independence" reverses this pattern, adding newly composed visionary passages, reinforces the possibility that it was revised with an eye on one or more external formal models. At the very least it is fair to say that Wordsworth discusses the stanzas so brilliantly in the preface of 1815 because they do precisely what he meant them to.

The most interesting recent commentaries on this figurative passage stress the traditional qualities of Wordsworth's poetic activity. Theresa M. Kelley holds that Wordsworth is drawing, in characteristically romantic fashion, upon the classical figure of Proteus:

> Because he is *like* a stone, the old man of Wordsworth's poem recalls the god's transformations into a stone. Both are old and reside, or seem to reside, in the sea or on its edge. Both are therefore "amphibious," at least momentarily, since they exist on the border between opposing environments or states of existence. As Proteus takes up successive animate and inanimate forms for his life, so does the leech-gatherer acquire similitudes to animate and inanimate forms. But the resemblance which secures the leech-gatherer as a figure for the Romantic Proteus is the one implied by the speaker's similes. Like the god's transformations, they construct an identity which is meticulously unfixed and fixed along a continuum of proximate similes.[3]

Kelley feels that the consoling power of the figure lies directly in the poet's capacity to invent it, the only consolation "which a poet who fears the possible loss of imagination wants" (644). The problem with Kelley's reading is that the poet (or at least the poem) has not for a moment feared the loss of imagination—the loss of happiness, companionship, health, and financial security, to be sure, but not imagination. Indeed, it might be argued that the poet's anxiety is itself an imaginative construction, which has identified present joy with the joy of poets generally and projected from that identification pain and sorrow which will necessarily follow. The Protean qualities of the invented figure recapitulate in a more powerful fashion the lack of a continuous character implied in the passionate volatility of the poet-speaker himself. For Wordsworth, the activity of the imagination has no necessary truth value.[4]

Kelley's essay refers to Spenser on numerous occasions, but not in dealing specifically with "Resolution and Independence." Certainly, when we speak of metamorphic figuration, Spenser is the English poet whose example comes to mind. Samuel E. Schulman has found in Wordsworth's epic simile an allusion to Spenser's animate "Rocke of vile Reproch, encountered by Guyon and the Palmer on their voy-

age to Acrasia's bower. . . . Like Wordsworth's bald-topped eminence, it is encrusted with living or once-living things:

> that perilous Rocke,
>   Threatning it selfe on them to ruinate,
>   On whose sharp clifts the ribs of vessels broke,
>   And shiuered ships, which had been wrecked late,
>   Yet stuck, with carkasses exanimate
>   Of such, as hauing all their substance spent
>   In wanton ioyes, and lustes intemperate,
>   Did afterwards make shipwracke violent,
> Both of their life, and fame for euer fowly blent."[5]

As Schulman goes on to say, the rock is glossed in the episode (*Faerie
Queene* 2.12) as an emblem of luxury and waste, products of misspent
lives, and it is consequently apt for "Wordsworth's poem about
spendthrift young poets" (42).

Whether Wordsworth's allusion is direct and intentional remains
questionable, but Schulman's juxtaposition of Wordsworth's and Spenser's passages does help to clarify some elements of the former. Like
Spenser's, Wordsworth's figure is a trope of dread, which furnishes a
nightmarish consummation of his earlier fears about the course of
human life. But Wordsworth's poem is not a call for moral rearma-
ment, not a plea that young poets mend their ways and balance their
checkbooks before it is too late. It is precisely the poet's *fears*, of
which this figure is so compelling a product, which are to be laughed
to scorn. Schulman's reading, like Kelley's, presumes that a necessary
moral force must reside in a figure which Wordsworth has discussed
as a product of the imagination. Their problem, like that of many
other readers, comes from attempts to center the poem on this figurative passage. They consequently ignore the rhetorical development
of the poem, which shows the way in which even this compelling
specter is revised and transcended.[6]

Wordsworth's Spenserianism in "Resolution and Independence"
works somewhat differently than Schulman suggests. Wordsworth
turns to Spenser not so much for the substance of his magnificent figure as for gestures which are found in his diction and in his management of the extended simile. In "The Faerie Queene" one elaborated

figure becomes virtually a signature. It is a simile inverted so that
the vehicle, introduced by "as" at the beginning of a stanza, precedes
the tenor. The vehicle is given a narrative development which often
runs a full stanza. In such cases the tenor is suspended until the
beginning of a new stanza, introduced by a relational "so." A single
example will show Spenser's characteristic use of the figure:

> As a tall ship tossed in troublous seas,
>> Whom the raging windes, threatning to make the pray
>> Of the rough rockes, doe diuersly disease,
>> Meets two contrary billowes by the way,
>> That her on either side do sore assay,
>> And boast to swallow her in greedy graue;
>> She, scorning both their spights, does make wide way,
>> And with her brest breaking the fomy wave,
> Does ride on both their backs, and faire her self doth save;
>
> So boldly he him beares, and rusheth forth
>> Betweene them both, by conduct of his blade.
>
>   (2.2.24–25)

Such a passage, in this case descriptive of Sir Guyon's becoming em-
broiled in a fight between Sir Huddibras and Sansloy, which he was
only trying to stop, has interesting effects. It simultaneously heightens the effect of the action and suspends it. The figure retards the
narrative proper by framing it in a more global context, increasing
narrative suspense while it adds another form of suspense as well, as
the reader wonders how the poet will ever manage to bring the discordant vehicle into conjunction with the surrounding context of the
poem.

Wordsworth manages his figure in "Resolution and Independence"
to similar ends. The halting of the narrative echoes the narrator's own
halted, watchful state. The elaborated figure heightens on the one
hand the importance of the old man, postulating a significance which
can be communicated only through tortuous indirection; on the other
hand, the figure turns the old man into a creation of the poet himself,
or at least refuses to let him be seen except as he appears to the poet's
consciousness. Language loses its transparency in an extended simile

of this sort, as the strenuous attempt to convey the importance and meaning of the old man ends up calling attention primarily to the actions of the poet's mind. The romantic poets learned many things from Spenser, but self-effacement was not among them.

The only Spenser evoked in "The Leech-Gatherer" had been the Spenser of the eighteenth century. There Wordsworth's diction had shown signs of neo-Spenserian mannerisms, and certainly his presentation of the plight of the helpless poet had been reminiscent of the Thomsonian lassitude parodied so lovingly in "Stanzas Written in My Pocket-Copy of Thomson's 'Castle of Indolence.'" What "Resolution and Independence" adds to the sensibilitarian doctrine and archaic mannerism of the earlier poem is true Spenserian energy. This poet is a poet not by his ineptitude in the world of affairs, although that remains, but by the considerable imaginative power he manifests in the heroic simile I have been discussing. That power increases rather than decreases his vulnerability. His enhanced imagination gives him the ability to translate his anxieties about the future into his frightening representation of the old man he has encountered. More than coincidentally, the created figure of the old man plays a role in "Resolution and Independence" analogous to that played by Coleridge's projection in the Verse Letter of his beloved Sara, lying deathly ill and himself unable to come to her aid. "Resolution and Independence" offers a critique of the Verse Letter which attributes the poet's problems not to the *death* of the shaping spirit of imagination but to an *excess* of it.

To this point in the revised poem, we can remark the following tendencies in Wordsworth's alterations: the old man has become a far more dominant figure, as his otherworldly potential has been enhanced by the elaborate Spenserian simile through which he is seen. At the same time, the role of the poet has been enlarged, as the old man is no longer securely grounded in the realm of being ("an Old man was"), but is part of a world of shifting appearances ("Such seem'd this Man"). On the whole, the situation of the despondent poet is greatly intensified in the revised work. The poet is more vulnerable because more imaginatively powerful, and his imagination makes of the ominous figure with which it is confronted a more threatening prophecy of the course of human life. To the degree to which "Resolution and Independence" is rehearsing and recasting the concerns of the Verse Letter, it is granting them far greater seriousness. Where "The Leech-Gatherer" had evaded the question of imaginative power and its loss, concentrating instead on spoofing the Verse Letter's emphasis on poetic improvidence, "Resolution and Independence" confronts the issue of imaginative power directly, standing it on its head. For Coleridge the decay of the imagination had been presented as one of a series of catastrophes; for Wordsworth the strength of the imagination has the capacity to beget visions of catastrophe, to create a vision of the future so forbidding as to destroy the present.

The rhetorical burden of the poem after the majestic Spenserian simile is to demonstrate the inadequacy of that figure, to show that it has come from the state of the poet's mind rather than the state of things. The process begins immediately, as the poet draws nearer to the old man:

> Himself he propp'd, both body, limbs and face
> Upon a long grey staff of shaven wood;
> And still as I drew near with gentle pace
> Beside the little Pond or moorish flood
> Motionless as a cloud the Old Man stood,
> That heareth not the loud winds when they call,
> And moveth altogether if it moves at all.
>
> (78–84)

The passage corrects those which have gone before in a number of significant ways. Even the reflexive construction which begins the stanza ("Himself he propp'd") belies the absolute passivity attributed to him by the simile. The huge stone might "lie," and the sea-beast crawl and repose, but the old man "stood." True he is "motionless," but the new comparison to a cloud makes his lack of movement contingent rather than absolute.

Revision of the poet's first impressions is intensified in the next two stanzas. Immediately after the conclusion of the stone-sea-beast-old man figure, the narrator had remarked upon the man's stature, interpreting it as a product of pain and sickness: "His body was bent double, feet and head / Coming together in their pilgrimage" (73–74). Now, as he approaches the man more closely, he notes that he has

> upon his back
> Beneath his Cloak a round & bulky Pack,
> A load of wool or raiment as might seem
> That on his shoulders lay as if it clave to him.
> (88–91)

Much of the ominously symbolic doubleness of the figure, so crucial to understanding him as a sign for last things, is quietly explained away. He bears not a "more than human weight" (77) but a "round & bulky Pack." His posture is further explained in his subsequent activities:

> he the Pond
> Stirr'd with his staff, & fixedly did look
> Upon the muddy water which he conn'd
> As if he had been reading in a book.
> (92–95)

The combined descriptions of the old man's garb and behavior, seen upon closer view, severely undermine the conjectures about the figure embedded in the marvelous figure through which he is first apprehended. The visionary sense must yield before plain visual sense.

These descriptions of the old man apparently existed almost intact in "The Leech-Gatherer." In that poem, though, there had been no strong imaginative apprehension of the old man to give them rhetorical point. Set against the despondent poet's vision of last things in "Resolution and Independence," both the descriptive elements and the old man's ensuing speech gain added force. As all scholars who have compared the two texts have noted, Wordsworth chooses to compress the old man's monologue, which had taken up five stanzas of the earlier poem. The framing passage remains intact, in which the oddly elevated nature of the old man's utterance is stipulated—"Choice word & measur'd phrase, beyond the reach / Of ordinary men, a stately speech" (109–10)—but Wordsworth avoids direct quotation entirely, perhaps in deference to the response of Sara Hutchinson, who had found the speech tedious, but more probably to avoid the disjunction between matter and manner evident even in the remaining scrap of original dialogue. Lines from "The Leech-Gatherer" like "From house to house I go from Barn to Barn / All over Cartmell Fells & up to Blellan Tarn" (132–33) are difficult to reconcile with earlier descriptions of the manner of the man's speech.

Wordsworth also buries utterly the litany of personal tragedies and hardships which must have formed the bulk of the man's speech, as it did in Dorothy's journal entry. The narrator's summary is of the direct answer to his initial question, "What kind of work is that which you pursue?" (102):

> He told me that he to the Pond had come
> To gather Leeches, being old and poor,
> That 'twas his calling, better far than some,
> Though he had many hardships to endure:
> From Pond to Pond he roam'd from Moor to Moor,
> Housing with God's good help by choice or chance,
> And in this way he gain'd an honest maintenance.
>
> (113–19)

Wordsworth's suppression of the domestic traumas of the old man's life makes his reported speech a far less direct commentary on the domestic discontents chronicled in Coleridge's Verse Letter. Indeed, as I have suggested earlier, the old man of "Resolution and Independence" is not proposed as a moral example in the way he had been in the earlier poem. The revised poem is less about dealing with hardships and discontents than about dealing with fear. If that fear is itself a potential by-product of the imaginative life, endemic to the very essence of being a poet, the moral example of the man on the street (or the man on the moor) loses its relevance. When "Resolution and Independence" proposes a model for the Coleridge of the Verse Letter, it is not the leech-gatherer himself but the narrator of the poem.

The extent to which external reality, that "something given" by the old man's voice, has lost its compelling authority in the revised poem is suggested by the narrator's reverie during the speech:

> The Old Man still stood talking by my side,
> But soon his voice to me was like a stream
> Scarce heard, nor word from word could I divide,
> And the whole body of the Man did seem
> Like one [w]hom I had met with in a dream;
> Or like a Man from some far region sent
> To give me human strength, & strong admonishment.
>
> My former thoughts return'd, the fear that kills,
> The hope that is unwilling to be fed,
> Cold, pain, and labour, & all fleshly ills,
> And mighty Poets in their misery dead;
> And now, not knowing what the Old Man had said,
> My question eagerly did I renew,
> "How is it that you live? & what is it you do?"
>
> (120–33)

In *The Prelude* Wordsworth will speak of "spots of time" which "re-tain / A Renovating virtue" (1805, 11.257–59). These passages, he will say, are found primarily

> Among those passages of life in which
> We have had deepest feeling that the mind
> Is lord and master, and that outward sense
> Is but the obedient servant of her will.
>
> (1805, 11.269–72)

In the two stanzas above, added to "Resolution and Independence," Wordsworth has created a spot of time which may serve to underline a truth of *The Prelude* which is seldom acknowledged: although the mind may be lord and master, it is not necessarily right. External sense pales before the imagination of the poet, which makes a talkative old man first into a dreamlike figure and then into a more than natural visitant, sent specifically to provide spiritual guidance.

Perhaps because the poet's mind has too readily dissolved reality, this act of the imagination leads to a recurrence of his earlier imaginative fears. Every act of the imagination does not bring salvation, particularly if it prematurely obliterates or absurdly elevates the reality which has set it into motion. Only when the narrator asks the

man again to tell his story, and when he attends to it, is he able to
create a symbolic projection which is both adequate to the old man's
situation and an answer to his own fears:

> While he was talking thus the lonely place,
> The Old Man's shape & speech all troubl'd me;
> In my mind's eye I seem'd to see him pace
> About the weary Moors continually,
> Wandering about alone and silently.
> While I these thoughts within myself pursu'd,
> He, having made a pause, the same discourse renew'd.
>
> And now with this he other matter blended
> Which he deliver'd with demeanor kind,
> Yet stately in the main; & when he ended
> I could have laugh'd myself to scorn to find
> In that decrepit Man so firm a mind;
> "God," said I, "be my help & stay secure!
> "I'll think of the Leech-gatherer on the lonely Moor
>
> (141–54)

The concluding passage insists on the simultaneity of inner and outer
perspectives, the balanced authority of internal musings and external
sense. In so doing, of course, it sets into ironic perspective the beginning of the poem, in which inner terrors had been allowed to
obliterate the joys of a beautiful spring morning.

Curtis distinguishes the narrator's final imaginative conception of
the leech-gatherer from those which have preceded it, noting that we
are left "not with a simile, or even a double simile, but with a frankly
mythical vision." He observes that the old man "shares with Tantalus
and Sisyphus, with the Wandering Jew and the old man of Chaucer's
'Pardoner's Tale,' [the] quality of purposive but ceaseless activity. . . .
Thus fabled by the imagination, 'the mind's eye,' Wordsworth's old
man is lifted out of the immediate circumstances as he was in the
previous stanza, but now retains his own shape, becomes his own
metaphor" (*WET* 110). Finally, the leech-gatherer has done nothing
except talk; it is the mind of the poet, working with and from what
he has said, which has made him move and live an heroic existence,

just as that mind had before incapacitated him to a subhuman level. In "The Leech-Gatherer" it was external reality alone which rescued the poet from imaginative fears; in the revised poem imagination—working with fidelity to external reality, which includes the old man's account of his everyday, ordinary heroism—can cure its own diseases.

If not more faithful than "The Leech-Gatherer" to the concerns of Coleridge's Verse Letter, "Resolution and Independence" is at least more willing to grant seriousness to the crises of a poet's life. The counsel of the earlier work was very nearly that the poet must become less of a poet, or at least dwell less on himself as a poet and more as a man in general. Its bipartite structure had offered the outlook embodied in the old man's speech as an adequate solution to imaginative fears. It was able to do this only by minimizing those fears, removing from them all real or potential external causation and turning them into stock responses of the literature of sensibility. When "Resolution and Independence" grants its poet-figure genuine imaginative power, through the elaborate Spenserian simile which ends the first movement of the poem, the leveling urge of the earlier poem becomes inadequate. It may be possible to correct daydreams with good sense, but good sense will not, as Anthony E. M. Conran argues in an otherwise excellent study of the poem, chase nightmares.[7] In responding to Coleridge's Verse Letter in his revised poem, Wordsworth more nearly echoes its own movements, shifting back and forth between outer and inner realities, between the external world and what the mind makes of it. Its argument seems to be that the mind which is capable of creating figures of disaster is capable going beyond them as well. Coleridge needs not just to lift himself from his morbid broodings to the external world (the "storm without"), but to imagine more fully and more deeply, creating figures which will sustain rather than incapacitate him.

Because "Resolution and Independence" is the first poem in the sequence I have been tracing to reach anything like its first public form, and because the overall thrust of my study has been to pursue all the poems' entanglements in convention and tradition, some remarks on just what form it finds would be appropriate. Nor would these remarks be out of keeping with traditions of commentary upon it. No other major lyric of Wordsworth's has generated such ranging speculation on sources and analogues which help to clarify its grounds of being. We are variously led to view the poem through the conventions of the dream vision, running from Chaucer through Spenser, Milton, and Chatterton;[8] to understand its strategies in terms of the spring elegies of such writers as Bruce, Graeme, John Scott, and Fergusson;[9] to note its affinities with the traditions of radical protestant spiritual autobiography;[10] or, staying within the canon of Wordsworth, to see it as a mutated form of earlier lyrical ballads.[11] In contrast to such studies, even the most sophisticated formal commentaries on "Tintern Abbey" and the Ode have done little more than explain the poems' internal explanations. Certainly, and rightly or wrongly, it has seldom been suggested that the obstacles these works present to our understanding are essentially generic. Critical consideration of "Resolution and Independence" seems convinced of the rugged splendors of the visible edifice but unsure of its foundations.

The prevalent methodological concern of studies of the poem has coexisted uneasily with the assertion of Coleridge, which has been echoed and underscored by most recent critics, that "this fine poem is *especially* characteristic of the author" (*BL* 2 : 126). If this were so, descriptions of its formal characteristics would hardly be so indirect. If we strip away everything about the poem that is peculiarly Wordsworthian, and view it purely as a map of an emotional experience, its singularity emerges clearly. Its passional range is "from the might / Of joy in minds that can no farther go" (22–23) to

> the fear that kills
> The hope that is unwilling to be fed,
> Cold, pain, and labour, & all fleshly ills,
> And mighty Poets in their misery dead.
> (127–30)

Such an emotional spectrum has no close parallel in Wordsworth's other "confessional" lyrics. Further, the peaks and depths of this poem are confined within an unusually compressed time span, a morning's walk on the moors. The Wordsworth who was "not used to make / A present joy the matter of my song" (1805 *Prelude* 1.55–56) was equally unaccustomed to tracing seismographically the momentary fluctuations of the mind and spirit. "Resolution and Independence" consequently lacks the stability which other lyrics gain by Wordsworth's characteristic mediative devices, through which a potential emotional crisis may be lightened by greatly expanding its temporal dimensions ("To the Cuckoo") or by translating it into the terms of some more or less formal epistemological system ("Tintern Abbey"). The emotional fluidity of "Resolution and Independence" places it closer to "The Eolian Harp," or "Ode to a Nightingale," or "Stanzas, Written in Dejection, Near Naples," than to "Tintern Abbey." When recent criticism has marked the unusual features of the poem, it has often suggested that they are, in effect, more Wordsworthian than the poet's normal practices. Again, such thinking would seem to have the sanction of Coleridge. "Resolution and Independence," the feeling goes, gives us Wordsworth au naturel, or at least with his mediations down. Consequently, the anxieties it lays bare can help us to see past the skillful rhetorical conciliations of "Tintern Abbey" and the completed Ode to the unresolved dilemmas that fester beneath their surfaces.

My discussion throughout this chapter suggests reasons why "Resolution and Independence" is an especially treacherous choice as a characteristically Wordsworthian poem. To begin with, it is generated in the course of an intertextual dialogue, each step of which has expanded enormously the problems of ascribing an expression to any originating motive, certainly to personal psychological motives. The dilemma of the poet expressed in the first seven stanzas of both "Resolution and Independence" and "The Leech-Gatherer" is written in response immediately to Coleridge's Verse Letter and indirectly to the mode which Wordsworth himself was exploring in his fragmentary Ode. Coleridge's poem forced Wordsworth to examine this mode critically. If those opening stanzas of the Ode could bring about Coleridge's devastating complaints, they possessed a power which the poet himself might never have guessed. With "The Leech-Gatherer" Wordsworth begins distancing himself from the mode, parodically heightening and exaggerating its depiction of the despondent poet by intersecting more directly the conventions of the poetry of sensibility in which both he and Coleridge were steeped. Certainly the archaisms of the poem had no other function than to signal conventionality of sentiment, as Wordsworth could have very well made do without such locutions as "doth" and "chanceth." In short, "The Leech-Gatherer" began with revisionary motives, calling into question a school of poetic feeling and expression beyond which both Wordsworth and Coleridge felt they had gone. "Resolution and Independence" is at a further remove in the dialogue, a revision of a revision. It is simultaneously a critique of "The Leech-Gatherer" and a reconsideration of the Verse Letter and the Ode. We should not be at all surprised that it is more literary than the poem which it succeeds, supplementing the corrective of "reality" supplied by the old man's artless narrative with a series of strong but no less conventional imaginative interventions on the part of the poet-narrator.

I will take the search for a generic base for "Resolution and Independence" a step further than it has gone to now, offering a poem from the age of sensibility as at least a working model for what Wordsworth has done. The work, mentioned in passing in my discussion of "The Leech-Gatherer," is "The Vision" by Robert Burns, which is cited by Wordsworth more frequently than any other of his works and certainly plays a stronger role in Wordsworth's later poetry about his predecessor than any other poem in the Burns canon. The terms of the poets' dilemmas in "The Vision" and "Resolution and Independence" are nearly identical. In both works the life of a poet seems threatened by the very things which make him a poet. Burns has returned from a cold day's labor in the fields to reflect by the fireside on the way he has spent his life, "stringing blethers up in rhyme / For fools to sing." [12] That course of life is contrasted to the life of the provident, who take their part in the world of markets, banks, and cash-accounts. The poet, on the other hand, is left "half-mad, half-fed, half-sarket." He swears in his despair to "be *rhyme-proof* / Till my last breath" (89). Like Burns, Wordsworth contrasts the fate of the happy child of earth to those who attend more fully to life's business and whom he, consequently, must expect to care for him.

At the moment of greatest despair in "The Vision," the poet's repudiation of his calling, the work abruptly changes direction, and Burns triumphs over the threatening consequences of that improvidence which throughout the Kilmarnock poems is presumed to be peculiar to poets. The snap of the latchstring announces the entrance of "A tight, outlandish *Hizzie*, braw, / Come full in sight" (89), wearing a wreath of holly which betokens her mission:

> I took her for some SCOTTISH MUSE,
>   By that same token;
> And come to stop those reckless vows,
>   Would soon been broken.
>
>   (90)

Her address to the poet, occupying almost half the work, reassures him that he has followed the proper path. She is but one of "many a light, aerial band" (92), who oversee the soldiers, patriots, and poets of Scotland. Coila, as she is called, has watched over Burns's poetic career from the moment of his birth:

> 'I mark'd thy embryo-tuneful flame,
>   'Thy natal Hour.
>
> 'With future hope I oft would gaze,
> 'Fond on thy little, early ways,
> 'Thy rudely-caroll'd chiming phrase,
>   'In uncouth rhymes,
> 'Fir'd at the simple, artless lays
>   'Of other times.
>
>   (95)

The development of the poet, who was thus marked out at birth, is presented through a series of examples of his heightened sensitivities: to the powerful and threatening aspects of nature, to the warm and flourishing "gen'ral mirth" (96) of springtime, to the pensive sadness of autumn, and to the throes of "*youthful love*, warm-blushing, strong" (96). Further, the poet has lived under a special moral dispensation which hallowed even his emotional excesses:

> 'I saw thy pulse's maddening play,
> 'Wild-send thee Pleasure's devious way,
> 'Misled by Fancy's *meteor-ray*,

'By Passion driven;
'But yet the *light* that led astray,
'Was *light* from Heaven.'
(97)

In the penultimate stanza Coila summarizes her advice to the poet:

'To give my counsels all in one,
'Thy *tuneful flame* still careful fan;
'Preserve the *dignity of Man*,
　　'With Soul erect,
'And trust, the UNIVERSAL PLAN
　　'Will all protect.'
(98)

Ten years after the first publication of these lines, Burns was dead, in circumstances that did little either to enhance the dignity of man or to illustrate providential benevolence.

We have abundant evidence that Wordsworth was moved by the pathetic contrast between Burns's vision and his destiny. In 1842 he began the last of his published commemorative poems with these lines:

Too frail to keep the lofty vow
That must have followed when his brow
Was wreathed—"The Vision" tells us how—
　　With holly spray,
He faultered, drifted to and fro,
　　And passed away.
(*PW* 3:67; 1–6)

An earlier response is preserved in lines Wordsworth added to his poem "To the Sons of Burns" in 1827, where he suggests which of their father's qualities should be emulated and which shunned:

His judgment with benignant ray
Shall guide, his fancy cheer, your way;
But ne'er to a seductive lay
　　Let faith be given;

> Nor deem that "light which leads astray
> "Is light from Heaven."
>   (*PW* 3:70; 37–42)

Coila's advice was sadly ill–considered. In Wordsworth's three com-memorative poems and his prose defense, he attempts to come to terms with the paradox of Burns—the vigor and the frailty, the joy and despondency, the wisdom and the folly. It may be, though, that in "The Leech-Gatherer" and "Resolution and Independence" we find both his earliest and most significant attempts to address these problems.

"The Vision" is a striking example of one central phenomenon of the poetry of sensibility, the rebirth of the muse. The most interest-ing thing about the muse Burns has created is that she is not needed to inspire poetry. The poet is seen as a natural, gifted by song from his birth and indeed cursed by his inability to do anything except sing. Consequently the muse is necessary not to inspire him but to protect and preserve him while he sings. The poem creates a polar opposition between the life of the poet and the life of men, "getting and spending" as it were, and casts its lot with the former, whose haplessness is both fortunate and foreordained, and provided for in the universal plan. If we consider "The Leech-Gatherer" as a revision-ary poem about the muse, its strategy seems straightforward: it par-allels "The Vision" closely in its depiction of the poet's dilemma, only to deviate sharply at the point of its visionary encounter, offer-ing in place of Burns' lively, graceful, and beautiful overseer a com-monplace figure who could objectify his worst fears of age. Thus considered, the old man becomes a substitute muse chosen from among those "grave livers" of Scotland for whom Burns felt such disdain. In both cases the poet is rescued from his despair by an external figure, who gives him human counsel. "Resolution and In-dependence" works differently, insisting that the poet's despondency is itself an imaginative creation which can be cured only by further and stronger imaginative activity. The counsel of the "muse" is com-pressed and its role diminished. Here the aged figure sets the poetic mind into motion, giving it an object outside the self, and it is what the poet can make of the man before him which frees him from his anxieties. Something is still given, but something more must be created. The old man in "Resolution and Independence" serves far more crucially to inspire poetic creation than he did in "The Leech-Gatherer," and Wordsworth's revision takes him past the conventions of the muse of sensibility into more time-honored considerations of the relationship between poetic inspiration and poetic creation.

"Resolution and Independence" does not parodically reduce Coleridge's Verse Letter so bluntly as "The Leech-Gatherer" had done. Still, it is evasive. By eliminating any mention of the old man's domestic losses, Wordsworth has erased all reflections of Coleridge's chronicling of his marital discontents. Coleridge had presented a poem based on two kinds of loss, which he had insisted were intimately connected. One proceeded from the misfortunes of his married life, as his ties to one woman made another forever inaccessible. The other came from what he perceived as his failing poetic imagination. The two kinds of loss were together indicative of his loss of joy, which alone could sustain him as a man and a poet. In "Resolution and Independence" Wordsworth has brushed aside half the problem and inverted the other. Coleridge's failure of imagination becomes Wordsworth's excess of imagination, a power so great that it can disable unless it pays close attention to the actual state of things in nature and human life.

There is no more evidence that Coleridge was satisfied with Wordsworth's response to his poem than that Wordsworth himself expected him to be. Coleridge's work on the Verse Letter will continue in one way or another for most of the remainder of his life. Both the wife of fact and the mistress of the heart will ultimately vanish from Coleridge's poem, but the steady refinement of the poem will insist that there are problems so deep and so intense that a fortuitous stroll on the moors cannot resolve them.

Coleridge's "Dejection,"

Morning Post, 4 October 1802

"LATE, late yestreen I saw the New Moon
"With the Old Moon in her arms;
"And I fear, I fear, my master dear,
"We shall have a deadly storm."
     BALLAD OF SIR PATRICK SPENCE

DEJECTION.
AN ODE, WRITTEN APRIL 4, 1802
WELL! if the Bard was weather-wise, who made
  The grand Old Ballad of Sir PATRICK SPENCE,
  This night, so tranquil now, will not go hence
Unrous'd by winds, that ply a busier trade
Than those, which mould yon clouds in lazy flakes,   [5]
Or this dull sobbing draft, that drones and rakes
Upon the strings of this Œolian lute,
Which better far were mute.
For lo! the New Moon, winter-bright!

And overspread with phantom light,   [10]
(With swimming phantom light o'erspread,
But rimm'd and circled by a silver thread)
I see the Old Moon in her lap, foretelling
    The coming on of rain and squally blast:
And O! that even now the gust were swelling,   [15]
    And the slant night-show'r driving loud and fast!
Those sounds which oft have rais'd me, while they aw'd
And sent my soul abroad,
Might now perhaps their wonted impulse give,
Might startle this dull pain, and make it move and live! [20]

II.

A grief without a pang, void, dark, and drear,
    A stifled, drowsy, unimpassion'd grief,
    Which finds no nat'ral outlet, no relief
In word, or sigh, or tear——
O EDMUND! in this wan and heartless mood,   [25]
To other thoughts by yonder throstle woo'd,
All this long eve, so balmy and serene,
    Have I been gazing on the Western sky,
And its peculiar tint of yellow-green:
    And still I gaze—and with how blank an eye!   [30]
And those thin clouds above, in flakes and bars,
That give away their motion to the stars;
Those stars, that glide behind them, or between,
Now sparkling, now bedimm'd, but always seen;
Yon crescent moon, as fix'd as if it grew,   [35]
In its own cloudless, starless lake of blue,
A boat becalm'd! a lovely sky-canoe!
I see them all, so excellently fair—
I *see*, not *feel*, how beautiful they are!

III.

    My genial spirits fail,   [40]
    And what can these avail,

To lift the smoth'ring weight from off my breast?
   It were a vain endeavour,
   Tho' I should gaze for ever
On that green light that lingers in the west;   [45]
I may not hope from outward forms to win
The passion and the life, whose fountains are within!

IV.

O EDMUND! we receive but what we give,
And in *our* life alone does Nature live:
Ours is her wedding-garment, ours her shroud!   [50]
And would we aught behold, of higher worth,
Than that inanimate cold world, *allow'd*
To the poor loveless ever-anxious crowd,
Ah from the soul itself must issue forth,
A light, a glory, a fair luminous cloud   [55]
Enveloping the earth—
And from the soul itself must there be sent
A sweet and potent voice, of its own birth,
Of all sweet sounds the life and element!
O pure of heart! Thou need'st not ask of me   [60]
What this strong music in the soul may be?
What, and wherein it doth exist,
This light, this glory, this fair luminous mist,
This beautiful and beauty-making pow'r?
JOY, virtuous EDMUND! joy that ne'er was given,   [65]
Save to the pure, and in their purest hour,
Joy, EDMUND! is the spirit and the pow'r
Which wedding Nature to us gives in dow'r
   A new earth and new Heaven,
Undream'd of by the sensual and the proud—   [70]
JOY is the sweet voice, JOY the luminous cloud—
   We, we ourselves rejoice!
And thence flows all that charms or ear or light,
All melodies the echoes of that voice
All colours a suffusion from that light.   [75]

V.

Yes, dearest EDMUND, yes!
   There was a time when tho' my path was rough,
      This joy within me dallied with distress,
   And all misfortunes were but as the stuff
      Whence fancy made me dreams of happiness: [80]
For hope grew round me like the twining vine,
And fruits and foliage, not my own, seem'd mine.
But now afflictions bow me down to earth:
Nor care I, that they rob me of my mirth,
   But O! each visitation   [85]
Suspends what nature gave me at my birth,
   My shaping spirit of imagination.

[The sixth and seventh Stanzas omitted; so indicated in *MP* text.]

. . . .

VIII.

O wherefore did I let it haunt my mind,
   This dark distressful dream?
I turn from it, and listen to the wind   [90]
   Which long has rav'd unnotic'd. What a scream
Of agony, by torture, lengthen'd out,
That lute sent forth! O wind, that rav'st without,
   Bare crag, or mountain tairn,* or blasted tree,
Or pine-grove, whither woodman never clomb,   [95]
Or lonely house, long held the witches' home,
   Methinks were fitter instruments for thee,
Mad Lutanist! who, in this month of show'rs,
Of dark-brown gardens, and of peeping flow'rs,
Mak'st devil's yule, with worse than wintry song,   [100]

*Tairn, a small lake, generally, if not always, applied to the lakes up in the mountains, and which are the feeders of those in the vallies. This address to the wind will not seem extravagant to those who have heard it at night, in a mountainous country [Coleridge's note in *MP*].

The blossoms, buds, and tim'rous leaves among.
   Thou Actor, perfect in all tragic sounds!
      Thou mighty Poet, ev'n to frenzy bold!
What tell'st thou now about?
'Tis of the rushing of an host in rout,   [105]
   With many groans of men with smarting wounds—
      At once they groan with pain and shudder with the cold!
But hush! there is a pause of deepest silence!
   And all that noise, as of a rushing crowd,
      With groans and tremulous shudderings—all is over! [110]
   It tells another tale, with sounds less deep and loud—
      A tale of less affright,
      And temper'd with delight,
   As Edmund's self had fram'd the tender lay—
      'Tis of a little child,   [115]
      Upon a lonesome wild,
Not far from home; but she has lost her way—
And now moans low, in utter grief and fear,
And now screams loud, and hopes to make her mother *hear*!

                              IX.
'Tis midnight, and small thoughts have I of sleep;   [120]
Full seldom may my friend such vigils keep!
Visit him, gentle Sleep, with wings of healing,
   And may this storm be but a mountain birth,
May all the stars hang bright above his dwelling,
   Silent as tho' they *watch'd* the sleeping earth!   [125]
      With light heart may he rise
      Gay fancy, cheerful eyes,
And sing his lofty song, and teach me to rejoice!
O Edmund, friend of my devoutest choice,
O rais'd from anxious dread and busy care,   [130]
By the immenseness of the good and fair
Which thou see'st ev'ry where,
Joy lifts thy spirit, joy attunes thy voice,
To thee do all things live from pole to pole,
Their life the eddying of thy living soul!   [135]

O simple spirit, guided from above,
O lofty Poet, full of life and love,
Brother and Friend of my devoutest choice,
Thus may thou ever evermore rejoice!
                                  ΕΣΤΗΣΕ.

*L*IKE ITS WRITER, the reader of this book has struggled with
one hypothetical text, one dated holograph manuscript of dubious provenance, one mutilated transcription of certain provenance,
and one transcription retranscribed at a remove of a little over a year.
It should be a relief to come at last upon a poem in print, accessible
to anyone curious about things as they were first published. Oddly
enough, the version of "Dejection" published in *The Morning Post* has
received less scholarly and critical attention than any other text in
this cycle. It has been overshadowed both by the notoriety of the
Verse Letter which was its origin and by the canonical sanctification
of "Dejection: an Ode," as found in *Sibylline Leaves* and after, a work
upon which a goodly portion of Coleridge's claim to poetic greatness
has sometimes been made to rest. Despite its self-evident historical
importance, the 1802 text of "Dejection" has suffered from an endemic critical neglect of all things medial. Spurred by the growing
availability of appropriate texts and reliable intellectual and biographical data, especially that supplied through Kathleen Coburn's
editions of the Notebooks, study of Coleridge has only recently been
seized by the developmental fervor which has gripped study of
Wordsworth, for good and ill, since the publication in 1926 of the
1805 version of *The Prelude*.[1]
      Having said this much, I confess that this chapter will not provide
a full reading of the poem, because my primary interest is in the role
the work plays within the intertextual cycle we have been following.
Besides, much of the work has been read in the chapter devoted to
the Verse Letter, and it would require a more thoroughgoing formalism than mine to insist that every revision changes all things utterly.
I will attend primarily to the way in which the first published version

of "Dejection" responds to Wordsworth's "The Leech-Gatherer" and "Resolution and Independence," which have already been presented largely as responses to the Verse Letter. It is most important, though, to recognize that the Verse Letter does not become "Dejection" easily and quickly, and that the paper trail through which we hesitantly follow its emergence has fascinating twists and turns. The published "Dejection" must be approached through three clusters of documentary evidence which seem strangely assorted but are all elements of one body of intertextual dialogue: Coleridge's early revisions of the Verse Letter; the records of his solitary rock-scrambling tour of early August 1802; and his verse publications in *The Morning Post* which lead up to "Dejection."

Our first preserved evidence of Coleridge's continuing work on the Verse Letter is found in a letter to William Sotheby, dated 19 July 1802. It postdates, then, "Resolution and Independence," which Dorothy had transcribed for Coleridge on 5 July (*DWJ* 145), and it follows by a week Wordsworth's and Dorothy's departure on the journey which was to take them to France. Sotheby was an ideal recipient for the revisions of the Verse Letter. He was a recent acquaintance of some intellectual and artistic achievement, and he was relatively unconnected with the Wordsworth-Coleridge network of relationships, although through Coleridge he had met Wordsworth briefly. In writing to Sotheby, Coleridge is consequently able to make and remake his work and himself more freely than he could with his more established and intimate friends. Coleridge's recasting of his continuing autobiography actually begins in his first letter to Sotheby, written the previous week, reflecting upon the circumstances of their meeting and his concerns about the impression he might have made:

> . . . after I had left you on the Road between Ambleside & Grasmere, I was dejected by the apprehension, that I had been unpardonably loquacious, and had oppressed you, & still more Mrs Sotheby, with my many words so impetuously uttered. But in simple truth you were yourselves in part the innocent causes of it / for the meeting with you; the manner of the meeting; your kind attentions to me; the deep & healthful delight, which every impressive & beautiful object seemed to pour out upon you; kindred

opinions, kindred pursuits, kindred feelings, in persons whose Habits & as it were *Walk* of Life, have been so different from my own—; these, and more than these which I would but cannot say, all flowed in upon me with unusually strong Impulses of Pleasure / and Pleasure, in a body & soul such as I happen to possess, 'intoxicates more than strong Wine.'—However, *I promise to be a much more subdued creature—when you next meet me* / for I had but just recovered from a state of extreme dejection brought on in part by Ill-health, partly by other circumstances / and Solitude and solitary Musings do of themselves impregnate our Thoughts perhaps with more Life & Sensation, than will leave the Balance quite even. (*STCL* 2:808–9)

What is most interesting here is Coleridge's veiled description of his "state of extreme dejection" and its causes, combined with his confident pronouncement of his own recovery. When Coleridge cites a week later revised passages from the Verse Letter, he will elaborate that tale of dejection and recovery.

Within the letter of 19 July, the Verse Letter arises as a subject through reflection on the nature of poetry. Coleridge reports to Sotheby that he has finished translating "the first Book of the Erste Schiffer [of Salomon Gessner]; it consists of about 530 Lines—the second Book will be a 100 lines less" (*STCL* 2:813).[2] He claims that he has translated the work for two reasons: "because I could not endure to appear *irresolute & capricious* to you" and

because I wished to force myself out of metaphysical trains of Thought—which, when I trusted myself to my own Ideas, came upon me uncalled—& when I wished to write a poem, beat up Game of far other kind—instead of a Covey of poetic Partridges with whirring wings of music, or wild Ducks *shaping* their rapid flight in forms always regular (a still better image of Verse) up came a metaphysical Bustard, urging it's slow, heavy, laborious, earth-skimming Flight, over dreary & level Wastes. To have done with poetical Prose (which is a very vile Olio) Sickness & some other & worse afflictions, first forced me into *downright metaphysics* / for I believe that by nature I have more of the Poet in me / In a poem written during that dejection to Wordsworth, & the greater part of a private nature—I thus expressed the thought—in language more forcible than harmonious. (814–15)

What follows immediately in the letter is a revision and compression of lines 231–71 of the Verse letter. Coleridge's notations of ellipsis mark the exclusion of much that was indeed "of a private nature": those portions of the original which speak so revealingly of Coleridge's unhappiness in his marriage (243–64):

> Yes, dearest Poet, yes!
> There was a time when tho' my Path was rough,
> The Joy within me dallied with Distress,
> And all Misfortunes were but as the Stuff
> Whence Fancy made me Dreams of Happiness:
> For Hope grew round me, like the climbing Vine,
> And Fruit and Foliage, not my own, seem'd mine.
> But now Afflictions bow me down to Earth—
> Nor car'd I, that they rob me of my Mirth;
> But O! each Visitation
> Suspends what Nature gave me at my Birth,
> My shaping Spirit of Imagination!
>
> . . . .
>
> For not to think of what I needs must feel,
> But to be still & patient all I can;
> And haply by abstruse research to steal
> From my own Nature all the natural Man;
> This was my sole Resource, my wisest Plan—
> And that which suits a part infects the whole,
> And now is almost grown the Temper of my Soul!
>
> (815)

Coleridge's revisions in this passage seem almost wholly shaped to fit the self he is creating for his newly found audience, or at least his construction of that audience.

Coleridge probably found Sotheby appealing because he was a man at home in several worlds: he was a poet and intellectual, though not oppressively accomplished in either sphere; he was a sufficiently

contented family man to have been traveling with his wife for pleasure; and as a former army officer, he was a man of substance in the
world of affairs. He seems in short to have been the sort of person to
whom, in his frequent fits of heroizing those who appear to lead fuller
lives, Coleridge felt compelled to present and explain himself. If
Coleridge in their first meeting seemed mercurial, the causes lay both
in his sensibility and his immediate circumstances, especially "that
dejection" from which he had recently recovered. To present himself
to such a man as unhappily married and hopelessly in love with another woman would not do. Consequently, Coleridge readdresses the
passage to Wordsworth, converting what had been an erotic crisis
into an obliquely aesthetic crisis. The "Ill Tidings" (238) which had
bowed him down in the Verse Letter (apparently news of Sara's response to his mysterious "complaining Scroll" [115]) become the
more general "Afflictions" of the passage sent to Sotheby. The habits
of "abstruse research," which in the Verse Letter had been a strategy
for withdrawal from feeling caused by his unhappy marriage, now
become as much a cause in themselves as a failed anodyne. The
"Natural Man" of the Verse Letter (268), so clearly the man of erotic
feeling who had to be self-neutered, now becomes in some way the
man of poetic feeling. If the total picture Coleridge presents in the
passage doesn't quite come together, his indications of ellipsis explain
that something of a merely "private nature" has been omitted. Most
importantly, though, the crisis is over, erased as thoroughly as the
private matter has been. Coleridge's change from the present to the
past tense ("Nor car'd I" for "Nor care I" [239]), attempts to write
even his analysis into the past, and immediately after the extract he
exclaims, "Thank Heaven! my better mind has returned to me—and
I trust, I shall go on rejoicing" (815). As a whole the letter is a mixed
bid for sympathy and admiration—sympathy for his sufferings, and
admiration both for the depth of his feelings and for his having regained command of them.

Presenting them rhetorically as an afterthought, Coleridge then
transcribes for Sotheby five continuous stanzas adapted from the
Verse Letter: "As I have nothing better to fill the blank space of this
Sheet with, I will transcribe the introduction of that Poem to you,
that being of a sufficiently general nature to be interesting to you"

(815). Coleridge transcribes nothing like "the introduction" of the
Verse Letter. The first three stanzas in the extract, through line 51,
do follow the original closely except for the substitution of Wordsworth for Sara as their addressee. The two remaining stanzas,
though, take up the Verse Letter at line 296, revising its penultimate
stanza, beginning "O Sara! we receive but what we give," primarily
by the continued substitution of Wordsworth as addressee. It is in
the final stanza of the extract, sharply compressed from the corresponding lines of the Verse Letter (324–40), that this version breaks
something like new ground:

> Calm stedfast Spirit, guided from above,
> O Wordsworth! friend of my devoutest choice,
> Great Son of Genius! full of Light & Love!
>   Thus, thus dost thou rejoice.
> To thee do all things live from pole to pole,
> Their Life the Eddying of thy living Soul!
> Brother & Friend of my devoutest choice,
> Thus may'st thou ever, ever more rejoice!
>   (817–18)

Not only does Wordsworth replace Sara, the qualities singled out for
praise in the stanza are also sharply altered. The power of Sara had
come from innocence, emotion, and her freedom from oppressive
concerns:

> Thou being innocent & full of love,
> And nested with the Darlings of thy Love,
> And feeling in thy Soul, Heart, Lips, & Arms
> Even what the conjugal & mother Dove
> That Borrows genial Warmth from those, she warms,
> Feels in her thrill'd wings, blessedly outspread—
> Thou free'd awhile from Cares & human Dread
> By the Immenseness of the Good & Fair
>   Which thou see'st every where—
> Thus, thus should'st thou rejoice!
>   (VL 325–34)

In the version offered to Sotheby, the redeeming virtues of innocence
and tenderness have been supplanted by the virtue of strength, which
is in part generated by Wordsworth's freedom from Sara's feminine
susceptibilities. What is praised in not quasi-conjugal and maternal
feeling but the "Calm stedfast Spirit, guided from above." To hail
Wordsworth as the "Great Son of Genius!" is to reread the poem's
earlier depiction of the failure of the poet's "genial spirits," which in
the Verse Letter had been contrasted to Sara's capacity to borrow
"genial Warmth, from those, she warms." For Coleridge "genial" is
always a slippery, polysemous term, but the weight of emphasis in
the extracts for Sotheby has shifted from connotations of generative-
ness and geniality to artistic and intellectual genius alone.

The poem patched together for Sotheby is a masterpiece of disguise. It has buried its erotic origins, converted its opening and closing stanzas from depictions of a crisis of passional feeling to a crisis
stemming from a poet's inability to connect his intellectual understandings with his emotional responses to the natural world, and it
has discovered its hero in a poet who has retained this power: "To
thee *do* all things live from pole to pole" (emphasis added). For those
who insist upon reading "Dejection" as a poem of affirmation, the
Sotheby version might well be the text of choice. It circumscribes its
crisis as an aesthetic crisis, and it pays its tribute to a poet who shows
that the crisis can be overcome. It manages this feat, of course, at
the cost of eliminating altogether or keeping outside its borders stanzas which are among its most disturbing and problematical. They
hover like ghosts about the continuous text imbedded in the letter,
uneasy spirits which can neither be assimilated nor rejected—the
opening passage already cited on the diseases of imagination, and the
passage which Coleridge goes on to append: "I have selected from
the Poem which was a very long one, & truly written only for 'the
solace of sweet Song,' all that could be interesting or even pleasing
to you—except indeed, perhaps, I may annex as a *fragment* a few
Lines on the Eolian Lute, it having been introduced in its Dronings
in the 1st Stanza" (818). Coleridge then includes an adaptation of
lines 184–215 of the Verse Letter, the stanza exorcizing the "dark
distressful Dream" (185). In keeping with his rhetorical presentation
of a recovered self, Coleridge apologizes for "troubling" Sotheby

"with such a long verse-cramm'd Letter," and wishes instead that he could

> but send to you the Image now before my eyes—Over Bassen-
> thwaite the Sun is setting, in a glorious rich *brassy* Light—on the
> top of Skiddaw, & one third adown it, is a huge enormous Moun-
> tain of Cloud, with the outlines of a mountain——this is of a
> starchy Grey—but floating fast along it, & upon it, are various
> Patches of sack-like Clouds, bags & woolsacks, of a shade lighter
> than the brassy Light of the clouds that hide the setting Sun—a
> fine yellow-red somewhat more than sandy Light—and these the
> highest on this mountain-shaped cloud, & these the farthest from
> the Sun, are suffused with the darkness of a stormy Color. Marvel-
> lous creatures! how they pass along! (819)

Another day, another sunset. The Coleridge of *this* letter feels as well
as sees, and to the recovered poet rehearsing his powers for the benefit
of Sotheby, once more "do all things live from pole to pole."

Not so for the Coleridge who writes to Robert Southey ten days
later. His letter has a mock festivity, bubbling with spirits and boil-
ing over with projects: ". . . if any Bookseller will take the risque, I
shall in a few weeks, possibly, send to the Press a small Volume under
the Title of 'Letters to the British Critic concerning Grenville Sharp's
Remarks on the uses of the Definitive article in the Greek Text of the
new Testament, & the Revd C. Wordsworth's Six Letters to G. Sharp
Esq. in confirmation of the same / together with a Review of the
Controversy between Horsley & Priestly respecting the faith of the
Primitive Christians' " (*STCL* 2:829). And: "I purpose afterwards to
publish a Book—Concerning Tythes & Church Establishment—for
I conceit, that I can throw great Light on the Subject" (829). And:
"Concerning Poetry, & the characteristic Merits of the Poets, our
Contemporaries—one Volume Essays, the second Selections / the
essays are on Bloomfield, Burns, Bowles, Cowper, Campbell, Dar-
win, Hayley, Rogers, C. Smith, Southey, Woolcot, Wordsworth—
the Selections from every one, who has written at all, any way above
the rank of mere Scribblers—Pye & his Dative Case Plural, Pybus,
Cottle &c &c" (829). Coleridge makes a running joke of the projective

fecundity with which he spins forth ideas for works (in prose, let it be noted), and Southey responds in kind. Poetry, though, is a different matter:

> As to myself, all my poetic Genius, if ever I really possessed any *Genius*, & it was not rather a mere general *aptitude* of Talent, & quickness in Imitation / is gone—and I have been fool enough to suffer deeply in my mind, regretting the loss—which I attribute to my long & exceedingly severe Metaphysical Investigations— & these partly to Ill-health, and partly to private afflictions which rendered any subject, immediately connected with Feeling, a source of pain & disquiet to me. (831)

Immediately in the letter he inserts the lines on the suspension of his power of imagination and his abstruse researches, much as they had been sent to Sotheby, except that he provides no explanation at all of their original context, and the address to the "dearest Poet" is omitted. At the point of elision in the earlier text, Coleridge inserts this parenthetical remark: "Here follow a dozen Lines that would give you no pleasure" (831). A dozen is a conservative estimate. Coleridge this time makes no attempt to disguise the conjugal import of the passage on his abstruse researches: "Having written these Lines, I rejoice for you as well as myself, that I am able to inform you, that now for a long time there has been more Love & Concord in my House, than I have known for years before" (832). As he goes on to describe the nature of the truce achieved between himself and Mrs. Coleridge, neither we nor Southey would be likely to overlook the comparative "more" of his general description or to overestimate the precise degree of his marital bliss.

My study's doubts about the possibility of reconstituting a writer's state of mind from his written records are justified by Coleridge's surviving writings of July 1802. Coleridge's letters are always rhetorical performances, and those of this period are intensely so. But we can describe his verbal behavior with some accuracy. He is determined to present himself as a man who has come through a crisis, and who is attempting to find what happiness he can in circumstances he cannot change. Even his letter to Sara Hutchinson of 27 July 1802 overflows with playful good spirits (*STCL* 2:825–28).

He writes like a man who has made resolutions and is determined to live by them, perhaps in no respect more fully than in his response to his natural surroundings. He begins his letter to Sara:

> If the weather be with you what it is here, our dear Friends [William and Dorothy] must have had a miserable Day yesterday. It rained almost incessantly at Keswick; till the late Evening, when it fell a deep Calm, & even the Leaves, the very topmost Leaves, of the Poplars & Aspens had Holiday, & like an overworked Boy, consumed it in sound Sleep. The whole Vale presented a curious Spectacle / the Clouds were scattered by the wind & rain in all shapes & heights, above the mountains, on their sides, & low down to their Bases—some masses in the middle of the valley— when the wind & rain dropt down, & died—and for two hours all the Clouds, white & fleecy all of them, remained without motion, forming an appearance not very unlike the Moon as seen thro' a telescope. On the Mountains directly opposite to our House (in Stoddart's Tobacco-juice Picture) the Clouds lay in two ridges _ _ _ _ _ _ with a broad, strait *road* between them, they being the *walls* of the Road. Blessings on the mountains! to the Eye & Ear they are always faithful. I have often thought of writing a set of *Play-bills* for the vale of Keswick—for every day in the Year—announcing each Day the Performances, by his Supreme Majesty's Servants, Clouds, Waters, Sun, Moon, Stars, &c. (825)

Having doubted in the Verse Letter the restorative power of "These Mountains, too, these Vales, these Woods, these Lakes, / . . . Where all my Life I fondly hop'd to live" (290, 292), he now seems determined to respond to them emotionally. Some such resolution seems to underlie Coleridge's nine-day solitary tour of the neighboring lakes and mountains at the beginning of August, recorded so minutely in his notebook, and memorialized dramatically in his journal letters to Sara Hutchinson covering his adventures of the first six days. Perhaps he could not "hope from outward Forms to win / The Passion & the Life, whose Fountains are within" (*VL* 50–51), but he would give them their day.

It is difficult to determine any particular motivation for Coleridge's journey. On 27 July he wrote breezily to Sara, "I wait only for a truly

fine Day to walk off to St Bees. Best compliments to the River Bee,
& if he have any commands to the Saint, his Relation, I shall be
happy to communicate the same" (*STCL* 2:825). Two days later he
wrote Southey, mentioning a library "at St Bees—whither I mean to
walk tomorrow, & spend 5 or 6 days, for Bathing—it is four miles
from Whitehaven by the Sea side" (*STCL* 2:834). As it turned out,
he left on 1 August, but St. Bees was only an intermediate destination, and the remainder of his nine-day absence was not spent at the
shore. Most memorably, his travels took him to the top of Scafell,
some twenty miles to the southeast of St. Bees, and down its steep
face in a mad descent which is the dramatic center of his account
to Sara.

Coleridge's letter to Sara begins the story of his descent of Scafell
with a presentation of one of his traits of personality:

> There is one sort of Gambling, to which I am much addicted;
> and that not of the least criminal kind for a man who has children
> & a Concern.—It is this. When I find it convenient to descend
> from a mountain, I am too confident & too indolent to look round
> about & wind about 'till I find a track or other symptom of safety;
> but I wander on, & where it is first *possible* to descend, there I
> go—relying upon fortune for how far down this possibility will
> continue. (*STCL* 2:841)

I hope it is not impossible for others to hear within Coleridge's depiction of his situation and proclivities faint echoes of both the confidence and indolence depicted at the beginning of "Resolution and
Independence":

> Even such a happy Child of earth am I,
> Even as these happy creatures do I fare;
> Far from the world I walk & from all care;
>   (31–33)

And:

> My whole life I have liv'd in pleasant thought
> As if life's business were a summer mood,

And they who liv'd in genial faith found nought
That grew more willingly than genial good.

(36–39)

Certainly Coleridge's mounting high ("O my God! what enormous
Mountains these are close by me, & yet below the Hill I stand on"
[840]) leads to a perilous sinking low—but not this time to a sinking
into dejection:

. . . the first place I came to, that was not direct Rock, I slipped
down, & went on for a while with tolerable ease—but now I came
(it was midway down) to a smooth perpendicular Rock about 7 feet
high—this was nothing—I put my hands on the Ledge, &
dropp'd down / in a few yards came just such another / I *dropped*
that too / and yet another, seemed not higher—I would not stand
for a trifle / so I dropped that too / but the stretching of the
muscle[s] of my hands & arms, & the jolt of the Fall on my Feet,
put my whole Limbs in a *Tremble*, and I paused, & looking down,
saw that I had little else to encounter but a succession of these
little Precipices—it was in truth a Path that in a very hard Rain
is, no doubt, the channel of a most splendid Waterfall.—So I
began to suspect that I ought not to go on / but then unfortunately
tho' I could with ease drop down a smooth Rock 7 feet high, I
could not *climb* it / so go on I must / and on I went / the next 3
drops were not half a Foot, at least not a foot more than my own
height / but every Drop increased the Palsy of my Limbs—I shook
all over, Heaven knows without the least influence of Fear / and
now I had only two more to drop down / to return was impossible—but of these two the first was tremendous / it was twice my
own height, & the Ledge at the bottom was [so] exceedingly narrow, that if I dropt down upon it I must of necessity have fallen
backwards & of course killed myself. My Limbs were all in a
tremble—I lay upon my Back to rest myself, & was beginning
according to my Custom to laugh at myself for a Madman, when
the sight of the Crags above me on each side, & the impetuous
Clouds just over them, posting so luridly & so rapidly northward,
overawed me / I lay in a state of almost prophetic Trance & Delight—& blessed God aloud. . . . (841–42)

Coleridge's blessing comes as a startling rhetorical turn in the letter, and not the least of its surprises is what he blesses God for: "the powers of Reason & the Will, which remaining no Danger can overpower us! O God, I exclaimed aloud—how calm, how blessed am I now / I know not how to proceed, how to return / but I am calm & fearless & confident" (842). He then opposes his conscious, waking reaction to such dire perils to what his response might have been in a dream, using language that recalls dark passages of the Verse Letter: "if this Reality were a Dream, if I were asleep, what agonies had I suffered! what screams!—When the Reason & Will are away, what remain to us but Darkness & Dimness & a bewildering Shame, and Pain that is utterly Lord over us, or fantastic Pleasure, that draws the Soul along swimming through the air in many shapes, even as a flight of Starlings in a Wind" (842). Coleridge arises, and begins to exercise his powers of observation and analysis: ". . . I glanced my eye to my left, & observed that the Rock was rent from top to bottom—I measured the breadth of the Rent, and found that there was no danger of my being *wedged* in / so I put my Knap-sack round to my side, & slipped down as between two walls, without any danger or difficulty" (842).

Coleridge's letter to Sara may well be a literal recreation of his journey. It reads, though, like an allegory which is set simultaneously against the Verse Letter and "Resolution and Independence." It presents a daytime Coleridge who is conscious, rational, and self-possessed, and who in the face of a genuine crisis, rather than a fancied one, is capable of calm decisive action. Indeed, the Coleridge of this journey seems to have assimilated some of the characteristics of the leech-gatherer: "From Pond to Pond he roam'd from Moor to Moor, / Housing with God's good help by choice or chance" (117–18). On this solitary trek, "with many hardships to endure" (116), having apparently informed no one of his hazardous itinerary— even then that must have been the First Law of Mountaineering— Coleridge shows himself to be both Resolute and Independent. Nor is the "happy child of earth," the gambler and risk-taker, utterly confuted. Without his impetuous and careless descent of the mountain, heedless of the claims of "children & a Concern," there could

have been no "state of almost prophetic Trance & Delight," no revelation of the blessings of Reason and the Will.

Some such understanding about the allegorical meaning of Coleridge's journey is necessary to come to terms with the role it plays in
two important poems published in *The Morning Post* in the month
preceding "Dejection": "The Picture, Or the Lover's Resolution,"
6 September 1802, and "Chamouny; The Hour Before Sun-rise. A
Hymn," 11 September 1802.[3] Between them, the two poems may
help to explain the somber, cryptic note in Coleridge's hand found
on a stray sheet of paper pinned into the notebook in which he recorded his trek: "Love to all the Passions & Faculties, as Music to all
the varieties of Sound" (*CNB* 2 : 1229).

The idea for "The Picture" dates from the ominous period of the
composition of the Verse Letter. In the notebook entries between
13 March and 16 April 1802 the following item appears: "A Poem
on the endeavor to emancipate the soul from day-dreams & note the
different attempts & the vain ones" (*CNB* 2 : 1153).[4] As published in
The Morning Post, "The Picture" begins with the purposeful energies
of a quest, which is quickly revealed to be a flight instead (or perhaps
a flight as well):

> THROUGH weeds and thorns, and matted underwood,
> I force my way; now climb, and now descend
> O'er rocks, or bare or mossy, with blind foot
> Crushing the purple whorts; while oft unseen,
> Hurrying along the drifted forest leaves,
> The scar'd snake rustles. Onward still I toil,
> I know not, ask not whither. A new joy
> Lovely as light, sudden as summer gust,
> And gladsome as the first-born of the spring,
> Beckons me on, or follows from behind,
> Playmate or guide. The master-passion quell'd,
> I feel that I am free.

Several features of Coleridge's opening scene are suggestive: the nature into which he has ventured at first seems far removed from that
of pastoral convention. Tangles of "weeds and thorns, and matted

underwood" impede human effort. The scene is not without the beauty of late flowers, but they are ground down by the "blind foot" of the pilgrim. The "drifted forest leaves" identify an autumnal setting, as do the figures for the "new joy" which moves him, "sudden as summer gust" and "gladsome as the first-born of the spring." In the beginning, at least, the poem is set against its setting, proceeding from an unseasonal accession of joy that is, in another figure hauntingly reminiscent of the cycle of poems from which it emerges, "Lovely as light." The new joy which has quelled the "master-passion" is an ambiguous force: the speaker cannot tell whether it leads him or follows him.

What little the poem's subtitle may leave unclear about the nature of the "master-passion" is settled in its second stanza:

> No myrtle-walks are here! These are no groves
> For Love to dwell in; the low stumps would gore
> His dainty feet; the briar and the thorn
> Make his plumes haggard; till, like a wounded bird,
> Easily caught, the dusty Dryades,
> With prickles sharper than his darts, would mock
> His little Godship, making him per force
> Creep thro' a thorn bush on yon hedgehog's back.

The rugged, spartan setting is an erotic anodyne, an earnestly sought antipastoral realm deadly to the claims of Eros, "His little Godship," who is too tender and delicate to survive as its lord. By implication, the man who has made his way into and through this wild is also superior to erotic impulses, which he has put behind him in both space and time. The irony of the poem's antipastoralism is that its early descriptions, while remaining suited to Coleridge's recent mountain ramble, are freely adapted from Salomon Gessner's "Der Veste Vorsaz," itself one of the *Idyllen* of the writer known to England as the German Theocritus.[5] Coleridge has knowingly chosen his antipastoral imagery from within the canon of a writer who is among the most steadfast and unreflective promulgators of the pastoral ideal, in effect almost guaranteeing the failure of his narrator's resolution. Coleridge proclaims:

> This is my hour of triumph! I can now
> With my own fancies play the merry fool,
> And laugh away worse folly, being free.

A removal outside the domain of Eros brings freedom, and the claims of Eros in this barren setting are diminished to fancies and follies. Coleridge's laughing them away recalls equally Gessner's prose poem ("*und die Liebe verlachen*"),[6] Wordsworth's laughing himself to scorn at the conclusion of "Resolution and Independence," and Coleridge's laughing at himself as a madman in his letter on the descent of Scafell.

The elemental setting, "As safe and sacred from the step of man / As an invisible world," offers such security that the speaker can play indulgently with old love themes, including that wind which had vexed him in the Verse Letter:

> This breeze, that visits me,
> Was never Love's accomplice, never rais'd
> The tendril ringlets from the maiden's brow,
> And the blue, delicate veins above her cheek;
> Ne'er played the wanton—never half disclos'd
> The maiden's snowy bosom, scatt'ring thence
> Eye-poisons for some love-distemper'd youth,
> Who ne'er, henceforth, may see an aspen-grove
> Shiver in sun-shine, but his feeble heart
> Shall flow away, like a dissolving thing.

This wind lifts only "the feathers of the robin's breast." The presence of the robin also recalls the Verse Letter ("tho' my Robin may have ceas'd to sing" [87]), as does the sound of "bees, that in the neighb'ring trunk / Make honey-hoards" (compare *VL* 88–91).

In an even more remarkable engagement with erotic topics of the Verse Letter, the poet proclaims that no "pool" of the "desart stream" by which he sits

> Did e'er reflect the stately virgin's robe,
> The face, the form divine, her downcast look

> Contemplative, her cheek upon her palm
> Supported, the white arm and elbow rest
> On the bare branch of half uprooted tree,
> That leans towards its mirror!

The passage above is an elaborate displacement of one of the central scenes of the Verse Letter, which recollects "that happy night" (99) with Mary and Sara:

> Dear Mary! on her Lap my head she lay'd—
>   Her hand was on my Brow,
>   Even as my own is now;
> And on my Cheek I felt thy eye-lash play.
>   (104–7)

The memory of the evening with Mary and Sara is worked into a conventionalized portrait of an idealized maiden, bending narcissistically to view herself in the reflecting stream. The love-struck youth, who cannot bring himself to look directly upon the maiden, "Worships the wat'ry idol, dreaming hopes / Delicious to the soul, but fleeting, vain." The maiden ("sportive tyrant") destroys the vision by plucking flowers and throwing them on the water:

>   Then all the charm
> Is broken—all that phantom-world so fair
> Vanishes, and a thousand circlets spread,
> And each mis-shapes the other.

The pool once more "becomes a mirror," the elements of nature reflected in it reunite, but the maiden has vanished forever. The poet scornfully directs the "Ill-fated youth" to

> Go, day by day, and waste thy manly prime
> In mad love-gazing by the vacant brook,
> Till sickly thoughts bewitch thine eyes, and thou
> Behold'st her shadow still abiding there,
> The Naiad of the Mirror!

Coleridge's account here is a powerfully revisionary tale, rewriting the innocent Sara of the Verse Letter into the Naiad of the Mirror, who has carelessly destroyed the love she has inspired, leaving the youth who has fallen for a shadow to pine hopelessly until he deludes himself that he has recreated his vision.

For the speaker of this poem, that is a story of other climes: "Not to thee, / O wild and desart stream! belongs this tale." He is situated beyond the pathos of erotic longing:

> This be my chosen haunt—emancipate
> From Passion's dreams, a freeman, and alone,
> I rise and trace its devious course.

The poem's echo of the Verse Letter—"the weather-fended Wood, / Thy lov'd haunt" (80–81)—is surely intentional. And Coleridge is clearly in control of the procedures through which the poem ceaselessly undercuts its narrator's proclamations. Every effort made to proclaim the scene secure from the ravages of erotic impulse ends in erotic revery. The "devious course" of the stream leads to an island, around which its "disparted waves / Dart off asunder with an angry sound, / How soon to reunite!" The waves "join / In deep embrace" and "Lie calm and smooth," becoming a figure for "the delicious hour / Of deep enjoyment, foll'wing Love's brief quarrels."

The poem's pattern is to proclaim a region free from the disturbances of passion, only to relapse into erotic renderings of its features, which it then denies. The devious course of the lover's hermetic retreat has led only to the haunts of the beloved and the accidental discovery of a picture

> Sketch'd on a strip of pinky-silver skin,
> Peel'd from the birchen bark!—Divinest maid—
> Yon bark her canvass, and these purple berries
> Her pencil!—See—the juice is scarcely dried
> On the fine skin! She has been newly here,
> And lo! Yon patch of heath has been her couch—
> The pressure still remains!

The "fine skin" of the birch has an eerily anthropomorphic quality, and the juice of the berries is the color of blood. Isabel the beloved, "More beautiful" than Sappho, "The Lesbian woman of immortal song," is at hand. Like the Sara of the Verse Letter, she is described as "full of love to all, save only one, / And not ungentle ev'n to me" (cf. *VL* 325–30). The steadfast spirit gives way to erotic imaginings and self-delusions.[7] His beloved is alone. Her picture, "Dropp'd unawares, no doubt," must be returned. To keep it would "but idly feed" his consuming "passion." He has a sound reason now for pursuing her: "She cannot blame me, that I follow'd her: / And I may be her guide the long wood through!" The poem discovers that the most secluded landscape cannot be kept "safe and sacred from the step of man" or, more accurately, woman.

Michael J. Kelly, who has studied "The Picture" more closely than any other commentator, calls it "a remarkable performance." I agree, but my reasons differ from Kelly's. The poem is an allegorization of Coleridge's tour of the lakes, discussed above, supplying retroactively a motivation missing from Coleridge's accounts of the journey: to immerse himself in the grand and noble aspects of nature, as Wordsworth might have put it, away from all temptations to erotic despair. Like the journal letters to Sara, the greater part of the poem is an exercise in self-congratulation on the success of his efforts, as the narrator is able to project and mock the "love-distempered youth" he has almost persuaded himself that he has left behind. The network of allusions to the Verse Letter parades the speaker's present superiority to them, and yet the poem has little affective power beyond that of its erotic constructions of landscape, negatively stated. The poem's breeze "was never Love's accomplice"; its stream never reflected the image of the "stately virgin's robe"; its "steep banks" harbor "no loves" other than those of the birds; and so forth. The strenuous attempt to create and inhabit an anti-erotic landscape is only the other side of erotic longing, and when the narrator and love-distempered youth once more coalesce at the conclusion of the poem, all the heroic exertions of Coleridge's recent months are called into question. In the circumstances in which it was published, "The Picture" becomes both a psychoanalytically deconstructive reading of

the tour of the lakes and a return to the mode of Verse Letter. Its
intimate audiences would have looked directly through its surface
playfulness and wry self-mockery, and they could hardly have delighted in the narrator's headlong resumption of his quest for the
divine Isabella.

The Coleridge canon is filled with sudden detours, but none may
be sharper than the turn from "The Picture" to "Chamouny," which
appears in the *Morning Post* on 11 September, five days later. I will
circumnavigate the poem warily, because it has always been a black
hole of Coleridge commentary, capable of absorbing considerable
scholarly energy without returning any discernible light of its own.
Even the dizzying letter to Sotheby announcing and describing the
poem, the day before its publication, could serve as the central text
for a monograph on Coleridge.[8] It is hard to know where to enter
this letter, because it is difficult to tell when one topic ends and
another begins. Perhaps we may begin with Coleridge's resuming a
theme he announced in his first letter to Sotheby (13 July 1802) on
the indispensability of passion in poetry. Once more he cites William
Lisle Bowles, this time concentrating on his

. . . trick of *moralizing* every thing—which is very well, occasionally—but never to see or describe any interesting appearance in
nature, without connecting it by dim analogies with the moral
world, proves faintness of Impression. Nature has her proper interest; & he will know what it is, who believes & feels, that every
Thing has a Life of it's own, & that we are all *one Life*. A Poet's
Heart & Intellect should be *combined, intimately* combined & *unified*,
with the great appearances in Nature—& not merely held in solution & loose mixture with them, in the shape of formal Similes.
I do not mean to *exclude* these formal Similes—there are moods of
mind, in which they are natural—pleasing moods of mind, & such
as a Poet will often have, & sometimes express; but they are not
his highest, & most appropriate moods. They are 'Sermoni pro-
piora' which I once translated—'*Properer for a Sermon.*' The truth
is—Bowles has indeed the *sensibility* of a Poet; but he has not the
Passion of a great Poet. His latter Writings all want *native* Passion—
Milton here & there supplies him with an appearance of it—but

he has no native Passion, because he is not a Thinker—& has probably weakened his Intellect by the haunting Fear of becoming extravagant. (*SCTL* 2:864)

This is a junction passage in Coleridge, equally retrospective and
prospective. Its criticism of Bowles is an oblique revision of Coleridge's own poetic career, and it is highly disingenuous, because
Sotheby has no way of knowing how thoroughly Coleridge had been
in thrall to Bowles. Indeed, the proclaimed disregard for connecting
nature to the moral life is an extreme reversal, a judgment which
jeopardizes much not just of Wordsworth's but of Coleridge's own
poetry, and much of his best at that. It may be worth remarking that
a central category of Wordsworth's 1807 volume, incorporating many
of his shorter lyrics of 1802, would be called *Moods of My Own Mind.*
Coleridge's passage looks forward to a fully articulated discrimination
of imagination and fancy, sketched later in the letter, although at
this point the seductive opposite to the unity of heart and intellect
provided by an apprehension of the *one Life* is not fancy but sensibility, the predominant faculty of the Verse Letter, the ink of which
has been dry a full four months, and of "The Picture" as well, to
which Coleridge does *not* direct Sotheby's attention.

All this becomes a backdrop to Coleridge's introduction of his
forthcoming poem. He frames it by quoting lines taken from "To
Matilda Betham from a Stranger," apparently written for and included in a letter to her the day before:

> Poetic Feelings, like the flexuous Boughs
> Of mighty Oaks, yield homage to the Gale,
> Toss in strong winds, drive before the Gust,
> Themselves one giddy storm of fluttering Leaves;
> Yet all the while, self-limited, remain
> Equally near the fix'd and parent Trunk
> Of Truth & Nature, in the howling Blast
> As in the Calm that stills the Aspen Grove.
>
> (864)

We should remember that Coleridge had sent Sotheby on 19 July the
stanzas from the Verse Letter which use the wind harp as a model for

poetic creation, or at least as an ironic counterpoint to the poet's lack of creative resources. Coleridge plucked the figure from Bowles, among others.⁹ That letter had brought the figure forward within a rhetorical context that treated it as a product of his recent bout of dejection. The oak tree of this letter is an alternative model, which appropriates the responsiveness of the harp (oaks in the wind become "one giddy storm of fluttering leaves"), without resigning itself to the passivity and characterlessness of that instrument. The test of genuine poetic feelings is that they remain, in the storm as in the calm, near the "parent Trunk / Of Truth & Nature."

That such an understanding of poetic creation, fluidly responsive while intensely itself, "is deep in our Nature," Coleridge goes on,

> . . . I felt when I was on Sca'fell—. I involuntarily poured forth a Hymn in the manner of the *Psalms*, tho' afterwards I thought the Ideas &c disproportionate to our humble mountains—& accidentally lighting on a short Note in some swiss Poems, concerning the Vale of Chamouny, & it's Mountains, I transferred myself thither, in the Spirit, & adapted my former feelings to these grander external objects. You will soon see it in the Morning Post—& I should be glad to know whether & how far it has pleased you. (864–65)

Coleridge's summary of the inspiration, provenance, and compositional strategies of "Chamouny" sets up one of the most historically important passages in any of his letters, in which he first articulates the distinction between Fancy and Imagination to which he will dedicate much of his subsequent philosophical and critical career.¹⁰ Reflecting upon the Psalms in the light of syncretic interpretations of Greek and Hebraic religion and culture, Coleridge observes:

> It must occur to every Reader that the Greeks in their religious poems always address the Numina Loci, the Genii, the Dryads, the Naiads, &c &c—All natural objects were *dead*—mere hollow Statues—but there was a Godkin or Goddessling *included* in each— In the Hebrew Poetry you will find nothing of this poor Stuff— as poor in genuine Imagination, as it is mean in Intellect— / At best, it is but Fancy, or the aggregating Faculty of the mind—not

Imagination, or the *modifying*, and *co-adunating* Faculty. This the
Hebrew Poets appear to me to have possessed beyond all others—
& next to them the English. In the Hebrew Poets each Thing has
a Life of it's own, & yet they are all one Life. In God they move &
live, & *have* their Being—not *had*, as the cold System of New-
tonian Theology represents / but *have*. (865–66)

So much has been made of the later repercussions of this passage that
commentary has seldom attended to its immediate context.[11] Its rhetorical purpose is to reinforce the claim that "Chamouny" is a break-
through poem by appropriating biblical and Miltonic models for its
imaginative procedures. The passage casts more than the work of
Bowles into the unproductive mode of the fancy: its most recent
quarrel would seem to be with Coleridge's poem of the previous
week, "The Picture," with its half-parodic reverie of the "Naiad of
the Mirror." Under the pressure of such a reading, any locale-
hauntedness becomes weakly fanciful rather than strongly imaginative, and it is the very displacement practiced in "Chamouny," its
stripping the experience atop Scafell of all experiential particulars,
and its transference of its devotions to a situation amidst the "grander
external objects" of the Swiss Alps created in the poem, which is the
mark of its high imagination. Coleridge has found a way to retain
his praise of Wordsworth, to whom "all things live from pole to
pole," but also a way around Wordsworth's characteristic mode of
rejoicing. True genius is not the genius of place. Wordsworth is
here distanced if not displaced by the examples of Milton and the
Psalmist.

"Chamouny" is the first published poem Coleridge called a hymn.[12]
Because of this, and because he did not go on to make a career of the
form, we can only speculate on its place in his taxonomy and hierar-
chy of the lyric genres. Paul Fry has meditated the differences between the ode and the hymn more seriously than most other critics,
in the face of potential embarrassments posed by some promiscuous
and playful naming practices among the poets themselves. "The
ode," Fry says, "is never a hymn. . . . Like the hymn, the ode or
'hymn extempore' longs for participation in the divine, but it never

participates communally, never willingly supplies a congregation with common prayer because it is bent on recovering a priestly role that is not pastoral but hermetic." He observes that "in the considerable odes of every era, a burden of doubt subverts the assertion of knowledge. Only the hymn speaks from knowledge, while the ode always hopes for knowledge."[13] However provisional, the distinction is sound and useful. Hymns are to be sung by congregations as acts of devotion; whatever their archaic communal origins, odes have in modern practice become monodies, or if they contain multiple voices, those voices as frequently clash as harmonize, and any ultimate harmonies they express must be won rather than presupposed.

The letter to Sotheby suggests that for Coleridge the movement to a hymn is a movement to a higher form. Certainly he plays the trump of biblical precedent with authority. Insofar as he is imitating Psalms in "Chamouny," he is doing so very selectively. His version of a hymn does not praise God for helping its singer and his people to bash their enemies, nor is its praise for the divine commingled with reprobation of the unrighteous. It simply, if that is the word, calls the creation to testify to the glory of God. Perhaps it is as close to Psalm 148, which Reeve Parker mentions as a possible model, as to any other:[14]

> Praise ye the Lord. Praise ye the Lord from the heavens: praise
>   him in the heights.
> Praise ye him, all his angels: praise ye him, all his hosts.
> Praise ye him, sun and moon: praise ye him all ye stars of light.
> Praise him, ye heaven of heavens, and ye waters that be above the
>   heavens.
> Let them praise the name of the Lord: for he commanded, and
>   they were created.
>
>   (Psalms 148.1–5)

Not all the Psalms are wholly free of some burden of self-examination, but 148 is, and so is Coleridge's "Chamouny." I find only two movements of the self depicted within the poem: the first is a minute readjustment, from an initial perception that the mountain is invading its celestial setting to a realization that the two exist in harmony:

Deep is the sky, and black: transpicuous, deep,
An ebon mass! Methinks, thou piercest it
As with a wedge! But when I look again,
It seems thy own calm home, thy crystal shrine,
Thy habitation from eternity.

The second is an even easier shift, from rapt and silent adoration to voluntary praise:

O dread and silent form! I gaz'd upon thee,
Till thou, still present to my bodily eye,
Did'st vanish from my thought. Entranc'd in pray'r,
I worshipp'd the INVISIBLE alone.
Yet thou, meantime, wast working on my soul,
E'en like some deep enchanting melody,
So sweet, we know not, we are list'ning to it.
But I awake, and with a busier mind,
And active will self-conscious, offer now
Not, as before, involuntary pray'r
And passive adoration!—
Hand and voice, Awake, awake! and thou, my heart, awake!

Considered from the perspective afforded by accustomed turns of the confessional lyric, as practiced by either Wordsworth or Coleridge, such shifts are not the stuff of high drama. Nor, if I read Coleridge's purposes correctly, should they be.

As Coleridge is envisioning the power of the imagination at this time, its union of passion and intellect is anything but a *discordia concors.* Certainly the landscape he creates before his eyes itself consists of the stuff of paradox: the silent mountain has at its base rivers which "Rave ceaselessly"; its "sunless pillars" jar against its "countenance" filled with "rosy light"; its "five wild torrents" issue from still and silent glaciers. In one of the poem's most astonishing touches, the torrents are imagined as preceding their glacial origins: "And who commanded, and the silence came— / 'Here shall the billows stiffen, and have rest?' " But the speaker of the poem is located firmly outside any perplexities that such a landscape might in other circumstances generate. He is able from the outset of the poem to contain its apparent contradictions, because all its elements "Utter forth GOD! and fill the hills with praise!"

The art of appreciating such a poem may be as lost as the kind of art which created it. Coleridge here employs arts of invention, of disposition, of variation. Above all he becomes a master of the art of epithet. To transform Mont Blanc from "Companion of the morning star at dawn" to "Earth's rosy star, and of the dawn / Co-herald" is to do some remarkable things. Among others, it is to transgress fixed boundaries by reading a light received as a light conferred. Thinking ahead to "To William Wordsworth" (". . . power streamed from thee, and thy soul received / The light reflected as a light bestowed" [*CPW* 1:405; 18–19]), we are almost ready to read Mont Blanc, with Parker, as an obscure allegory of the power of his friend. But by virtue of the severe terms under which it is created, "Chamouny" cannot stage its passionate thought as a discovery. To allegorize it as Parker does is to convert it into a kind of displaced quest-romance, the very form it is strenuously attempting to transcend. No other major lyric by a major poet of the age remains so wholly devoid of any sense of its speaker's temporal situation, or so steadfastly avoids narrative line.

The Coleridge who creates himself in his writings from mid-July through mid-September 1802 is a creature of fits and starts. His writing is filled with self-representations of recovery. He adapts the Verse Letter for Sotheby, treating its depiction of dejection as a relic of the past, from which he has arisen. He sharpens and exercises his immediate perceptions of nature, glorying in surroundings which he had declared could no longer inspire him. He undertakes a physically exhausting and hazardous tour of the mountains, which demonstrates both his renewed appreciation for nature and his self-possession. He follows this phase of his recovery with the publication of a poem, "The Picture," which represents such attempts to leave passional concerns behind as inevitably vain. His argument with himself continues in "Chamouny," a poem which leaves personal concerns so far behind that we can hardly locate its speaker in its landscape. He develops a theory of imagination which gives biblical warrant to the mode of "Chamouny" as part of a running argument with his predominant literary influences, Bowles and Wordsworth. Figuring somehow in all this turmoil of self-creation is the fact that the two major poems published in September are unacknowledged adaptations of German originals.

My purpose in this extended prologue to a discussion of the version of "Dejection" published in 1802 is to demonstrate two things: First, the issues of the Verse Letter and Wordsworth's related poems, the fragmentary Ode, "The Leech-Gatherer," and "Resolution and Independence," were enormously important to Coleridge during the months leading up to Wordsworth's wedding. Coleridge's decision to publish "Dejection" could not have been lightly made, however pressed he was by his obligations to *The Morning Post*. Second, because Coleridge's writings of the preceding months have acted out the oscillating cycles of despair and recovery so much a part of the texture of the Verse Letter, the closest possible study of them cannot reveal what the poem meant to him or what he wanted through its publication to say to its intimate audiences. In exploring the situational meaning of the poem, David Erdman has echoed and intensified the reading offered by Parker: "The 'Dejection' triumphs, not only over his own dejection but over his envy, and the version published on Wordsworth's wedding day and the anniversary of his own, constitutes, as Reeve Parker suggests, 'an epithalamic gesture' of tremendous sincerity." [15] While accepting both Parker's "gesture" and Erdman's "sincerity," I am uncertain of the nature of the gesture.

My third chapter discussed at some length the generic relationship between Wordsworth's Ode and Coleridge's Verse Letter, suggesting that Coleridge's response might be read as a gesture of humility. He responds to the "higher" with a "lower" form, implicitly resigning the realm of elevated lyric utterance to his friend. Coleridge's decision to revise his erotic epistle into an ode, then, would have to be seen as an act of reassertion in which he not only rises from the extreme personalism of the Verse Letter to an utterance more nearly in keeping with the goals announced in the letter on "Chamouny," but does so through a kind of alchemical transmutation of the matter of the Verse Letter into a purer substance. Where "The Picture," "Chamouny," and the Scafell writings deal with the Verse Letter through indirection and dislocation, "Dejection" confronts its predecessor poem directly. Most previous critics have interpreted Coleridge's movement in this way, even those few who have in the end preferred the Verse Letter. In this they are following what seems to be Coleridge's clear rhetorical intention.

Whether the poem fully achieves its rhetorical intention is another matter, one which requires an investigation of Coleridge's revisionary strategies. My next several paragraphs track the surprisingly small changes Coleridge makes in turning his epistle into an ode and reflect on the generic tensions which result from these revisions. His alterations begin with his borrowed motto and his retitling of the work. Coleridge's four-line quotation from the "Ballad of Sir Patrick Spence" is a new addition, supplementing the allusion retained from the two opening lines of the Verse Letter. To begin any literary work with a quoted epigraph is to foreground its literariness, its attachment to prior traditions of writing. The literariness of any ode is beyond serious question, as the form has never attempted to provide an illusion of spontaneity or naturalness. To head an ode with a snatch of an anonymous folk ballad, though, is surely to juxtapose kinds and levels of poetic discourse. Even the difference between a verse epistle and an ode is largely a matter of elevation within two varieties of expressive discourse. The pure narrative logic of the ballad quotation (if this, then that) jars against the absence of "story" in Coleridge's poem.[16] This is the first time Coleridge called his poem an ode: in the extracts sent to Sotheby and Southey it was never so designated.

Any ode which takes its title from an emotional state or quality, or which addresses an abstract emotional phenomenon, is by the early nineteenth century inextricably associated with the work of William Collins, whose stark emotional power Coleridge had recognized in a letter to John Thelwall, 17 December 1796. Coleridge's praise was not unmixed: "Now Collins' Ode on the poetical character—that part of it, I should say, beginning with—'The Band (as faery Legends say) Was wove on that creating Day,' has inspired & whirled *me* along with greater agitations of enthusiasm than any the most *impassioned* scene in Schiller or Shakespeare—using 'impassioned' in it's confined sense for writings in which the the human passions of Pity, Fear, Anger, Revenge, Jealousy, or Love are brought into view with their workings" (*STCL* 1:279). Coleridge goes on to say that the writings of Schiller and Shakespeare are nevertheless "more valuable" because they give "*more general* pleasure."

The practice of Collins made it clear that odes can deal with more or less firmly embodied abstractions in two ways: they may describe the abstraction they name in the title ("Ode on the Poetical Character," "The Manners. An Ode," "The Passions. An Ode for Music"), or they may address the abstraction directly ("Ode to Pity," "Ode to Fear," "Ode to Mercy"). The distinction is later to be generally honored in the odes of Keats ("Ode on Melancholy," "Ode to Psyche"). In an ode *to*, the titular subject and addressee coincide; in an ode *on*, they need not coincide. In "The Manners," for example, Collins's ultimate address is to "Nature," the source of the writer's knowledge of human behavior; in "The Passions" the address is to "Music," which in "this laggard age" no longer expresses directly the elemental passions. Coleridge's title, in which a full stop also separates his subject from his generic designation, leaves oblique the poem's relationship between subject and addressee.[17]

Even Coleridge's choice of the emotional state of his title, "Dejection," requires reflection. The word did not appear in the Verse Letter, nor is it used in this or any later version of the ode. Here Coleridge clearly steps outside the path charted by Collins, the centers of whose odes are generally their title words, which are subject within the poems to simple repetition, periphrasis, personification, and elaborate epithetic substitutions. Indeed, the concordance to Coleridge's poetry marks no other occurrences of the word *dejection* anywhere in his verse.[18] Because the word was not a poetic favorite of Wordsworth's either (his only prior use of it in a published poem was in "The Convict" [1798]),[19] we must assume that Coleridge has borrowed his title itself from central lines in "The Leech-Gatherer" and "Resolution and Independence": "As high as we have mounted in delight / In our dejection do we sink as low." As we have seen, these poems of Wordsworth's lie directly behind Coleridge's running discourse on the topic of dejection in his letters and notebooks of the summer and early autumn of 1802. In both of Wordsworth's poems written in response to the Verse letter, dejection is presented as a product of excessive volatility of the spirits, something which afflicts the careless mind which has too much leisure to dwell on its own internal activities. Coleridge's ode takes on Wordsworth's naming of the problem but attempts to provide a substantially different analysis of the sources and consequences of the emotional state. It also, of course, attempts to disentangle the Verse Letter's "joy" from Wordsworth's "delight."

From a generic perspective, Coleridge's dating of his poem within the subtitle is perplexing. He appropriates the date he habitually assigned to the Verse Letter—a date which must have been burned into the memories of his closest friends. While odes are traditionally occasional poems, the version of "Dejection" which appears in *The Morning Post* simultaneously flourishes its date of "composition" and hides the occasion for either its composition or publication. It appears six months to the day after the stipulated date of its writing: October 4 is the date both of Wordsworth's wedding and Coleridge's anniversary—facts which any intimate of the circle would know—but they no more than the casual reader could be guided by this knowledge to a certain understanding of the poem's relevance to these occasions. Here we have yet another transgression of generic expectations: odes celebrate events outside themselves—victories in chariot races, Cromwell's military successes in Ireland, the birth of Christ, weddings, and funerals—but not their own writing. When Collins entitles his single dated poem in the form "Ode. Written in the Beginning of the Year 1746" ("How sleep the brave"), he expects his reader to think immediately of the battle of Falkirk, not of himself as he is composing the poem. Indeed, only a few literary genres are scrupulous about the dates of their composition, whether genuine or fictive, the most relevant of which is the epistle, from which Coleridge's ode descends.

The opening of the poem provides no greater generic comfort. The colloquial offhandedness of "WELL!" as its first word has frequently been remarked. A coinage such as "weather-wise" and a metaphor based in commerce, winds "that ply a busier trade," also grate against the level of diction traditionally associated with the higher ode. Sounding unlike a conventional ode, I hasten to add, is not necessarily a bad thing. But given Cyrus Hamlin's recent claim that "Dejection" marks the beginning of the English romantic ode, it is worth remarking that Coleridge's choice of an opening level of

diction finds no counterpart in the works of his most distinguished
Romantic successors, Shelley and Keats. The language borrowed
from the Verse Letter creates just another of this ode's generic anoma-
lies. The detail and circumstantiality of the visual descriptions in
stanzas I and II also run against prevailing generic tendencies. Despite both Coleridge's strong sense of traditional genre and his substantial previous experience with the form, he makes few efforts to
obscure the vestigial marks of his ode's epistolary origins.

His larger revisionary strategy parallels and intensifies that employed in selecting the extracts he sent to Sotheby on 19 July, which
had amounted to 138 lines culled and adapted from the 340 lines of
the Verse Letter. The 139 lines of "Dejection" incorporate lightly
emended versions of 131 of the lines sent to Sotheby, and the overall
outline of the ode follows the continuous core of 87 lines Coleridge
earlier described as the poem's "introduction." But "Dejection" is
marked by substantial changes as well. In approximate order of their
occurrence in the revised poem, Coleridge adds four newly composed
lines, strikes three passages of five, six, and four lines from the continuous core, reincorporates selected parts of the overflow material
transcribed for Sotheby (eliminating entirely seven of these lines),
and revives from the Verse Letter eleven lines not included in the
July letter. Revisions of such different character inevitably have more
than one consequence, but in discussing them in order I will suggest
their overall effect on the poem.

Coleridge's fresh composition for "Dejection" comes first, four
lines which are added to the Verse Letter's opening stanza of sixteen
lines. The lines project a possible result of the "coming on of rain
and squally blast" (14), for which he longs:

> Those sounds which oft have rais'd me, while they aw'd
> And sent my soul abroad,
> Might now perhaps their wonted impulse give,
> Might startle this dull pain, and make it move and live.
>
> (17–20)

These lines accomplish two tasks within the poem. They credit external phenomena with a potential power over the human spirit, and

they provide the poem's first renaming of the emotional state in its title. The sounds of the "gust" and "night-show'r" are grounded in the speaker's past experiences. They "oft" have "rais'd" and "aw'd" him, and they have alleviated his self-absorption, by sending his "soul abroad." One need not dwell on the positive nature of such effects within a narrowly Coleridgean scheme, because they are generally laudable effects within Western culture. All are routes to transcendence of narrow personal concerns: elevation, humility, and other-centeredness. The lines proceed to undercut these potentially positive effects, though. If the wind and rain were to give their "wonted impulse," the result in the speaker's current situation would not be transcendence of personal suffering but an alteration, even an intensification of it. The sounds of the storm "Might startle this dull pain, and make it move and live." The reader is forced to imagine the gravity of "this dull pain" by envisioning a state in which a moving and living pain would actually be preferable. The coming of the storm may portend emotional change, but not emotional relief.[20]

"This dull pain" is Coleridge's first renaming of the state he calls "dejection." Stanza II continues this renaming in lines carried over nearly intact from the Verse Letter:

> A grief without a pang, void, dark, and drear,
>   A stifled, drowsy, unimpassion'd grief,
>   Which finds no nat'ral outlet, no relief
> In word, or sigh, or tear—
>
>   (21–24)

In this stanza we see the remarkable effects Coleridge has achieved through his simple retitling of the work. Accepting the conventions of the descriptive ode, the reader supplies "dejection" as the reference for these lines, construing them as attempts at definition, or at least a narrowing of specification. They then seem to have an analytical, even clinical, detachment absent in the Verse Letter, where, lacking the reference, the reader can only look forward to the poem's revelation of the causes for the state it is circuitously describing.

Coleridge's deletions are substantial in this stanza. Its nineteen lines are taken from a continuous section of twenty-seven lines in the

Verse Letter. The primary effect of the omissions is to obscure the
erotic charge of this section of the earlier text. The following lines
from the Verse Letter,

> In word, or sigh, or tear—
> This, Sara! well thou know'st,
> Is that sore Evil, which I dread the most,
> And oft'nest suffer! In this heartless Mood,
> To other thoughts by yonder Throstle woo'd,
> That pipes within the Larch-tree, not unseen,
> (The Larch, which pushes out in tassels green
> It's bundled Leafits) woo'd to mild Delights
> By all the tender Sounds & gentle Sights
> Of this sweet Primrose-month—& *vainly* woo'd
> O dearest Sara! in this heartless Mood,
> All this long Eve . . .
>
> (20–31)

are reduced to the following in "Dejection":

> In word, or sigh, or tear——
> O EDMUND! in this wan and heartless mood,
> To other thoughts by yonder throstle
>   woo'd,
> All this long eve . . .
>
> (24–27)

While the verb *woo* necessarily retains its erotic connotation in the
revised passage, it is not insistently foregrounded by a triple use and
can here slip by as merely poetic diction. The song of the thrush
remains, but as a general beckoning sign from the external world,
not as one of several elements of explicitly erotic invitation. The
elimination of the larch tree removes connotations of vegetative renewal and fertility, as does the removal of the more inclusive "tender
Sounds & gentle Sights / Of this sweet Primrose-month." With this
taming of the erotic landscape, "unimpassion'd grief" no longer plays
so strongly against *impassioned* nature.

Deletions from the Verse Letter in the ensuing stanza of "Dejection" continue the pattern observed above. Except in matters of capi-

talization and punctuation, the poems coincide in the following lines, which constitute all of stanza III of the published work:

> My genial spirits fail,
>   And what can these avail,
> To lift the smoth'ring weight from off my breast?
>   It were a vain endeavour,
>   Tho' I should gaze for ever
> On that green light that lingers in the west;
> I may not hope from outward forms to win
> The passion and the life, whose fountains are within.
>   (39–46; VL 44–51)

These lines are followed in the Verse Letter, though, by a failed attempt to respond to the external world by means of erotic association:

> These lifeless Shapes, around, below, Above,
>   O what can they impart?
> When ev'n the gentle Thought, that thou, my Love!
>   Art gazing now, like me,
>   And see'st the Heaven, I see—
> Sweet Thought it is—yet feebly stirs my Heart!
>   (VL 52–57)

And in the Verse Letter, we recall, *feebly* is the key word which triggers Coleridge's nostalgic reverie of his age of presexual adolescent innocence.

Like the extract in the letter to Sotheby, stanza IV of "Dejection" takes up the Verse Letter at line 296, beginning the section of the poem which has always been most fruitful for traditional Coleridgean commentary. Luther Tyler has recently observed that the beginning formulation, "O Edmund! we receive but what we give, / And in *our* life alone does Nature live" (47–48), reflects Coleridge's love of aphorism and "readily offers itself as what Coleridge called a 'philosopheme.'"[21] While in the Verse Letter the line "Ours is her Wedding Garment, ours her Shroud" (*VL* 298) had seemed a grim coda to Coleridge's account of his marital woes, in "Dejection" (49) it seems just to borrow resonances from similar biblical formulations of the soul's relationship to joy. Inclusion of aphoristic, gnomic wisdom is characteristic of the higher ode, and Coleridge's turn to proverbial formulation is signaled here by a shift from the first-person singular to the plural pronoun. In the twenty-seven lines of stanzas II and III the words *I* and *my* had appeared eight times, and the plural form had not been used. In stanza IV, *we, us, our, ours,* and *ourselves* appear nine times in twenty-three lines, and *me* appears once. After stanza IV, the first-person plural disappears from the poem.

The wisdom Coleridge proffers here differs very little from that provided in lines 296–323 of the Verse Letter. The major change is in the quality of the addressee to whom Joy is accessible. Like Sara in the Verse Letter, "Edmund" in "Dejection" is addressed "O pure of heart!" (60; *VL* 308). But in the earlier poem Joy "ne'er was given / Save to the Pure, & in their purest Hour" (313–14). In "Dejection," though, Edmund is not "innocent" (*VL* 313) but "virtuous" (65). This change in the necessary condition for Joy accounts for much of the less negative effect of "Dejection." *Innocence* and *purity* are spiritual attributes culturally associated with avoidance of erotic experience. They can never be regained once they have been lost. *Virtue,* though, is characterized by more than the negative attribute of not having fallen; it can be maintained in the course of ordinary events (including physical as well as metaphysical marriage), and it can be reattained. The monism of the stanza is still uncompromising:

> Joy is the sweet voice, Joy the luminous cloud—
>   We, we ourselves rejoice!
> And thence flows all that charms or ear or light,
> All melodies the echoes of that voice,
> All colours a suffusion from that light.
>
> (72–75)

But the moral distance between speaker and addressee in "Dejection" is bridgeable in a way it had not been in the Verse Letter.

If stanza IV is the philosophical core of "Dejection," as it has existed in Coleridgean commentary, stanza V is an infrequently acknowledged crux of the poem, beset by problems at both ends. It is developed from the following address from the Verse Letter:

> Yes, dearest Sara! Yes!
> There was a time when tho' my path was rough,
> The Joy within me dallied with [?Di]stress;
> And all Misfortunes were but as the Stuff
> Whence Fancy made me Dreams of Happiness:
> For Hope grew round me, like the climbing Vine,
> And Leaves & Fruitage, not my own, seem'd mine!
> But now Ill Tidings bow me down to earth—
> Nor care I, that they rob me of my Mirth—
> But oh! each Visitation
> Suspends what Nature gave me at my Birth,
> My shaping Spirit of Imagination!
> (VL 231–42)

Because this passage from the Verse Letter had directly followed a description of the poet as no longer "bouyant," no longer able to bear "all things . . . as if I nothing bore" (*VL* 228–30), the "Yes" with which he proclaimed his golden time made rhetorical sense in that context. It does not in "Dejection," and it never will in any succeeding version. The burden of the passage within the Verse Letter had been the impact of "Ill Tidings" of the afflictions of others, not "afflictions" of his own, which replace them in "Dejection" (83). Now, "each visitation" of an affliction "Suspends what nature gave me at my birth, / My shaping spirit of imagination" (85–87). *Imagination* is not for Coleridge at this time the full-grown conjure word it was to become. Here it hangs at the end of a truncated stanza: nothing has prepared for its enunciation, and nothing follows from it within the poem. Is *imagination* a name for the "light," the "glory," the "fair luminous cloud," the "sweet and potent voice," and the "strong music in the soul" (55–61)? If so, why has stanza IV so strenuously named them *joy*? Are *joy* and *imagination* identical? Are they consanguinous? Is one the effect of the other? If imagination is a birthright, does it take priority over joy? Anachronistic explications of the 1802 "Dejection" might be able to smooth over these questions by reference to later systems, but neither the poem as published in *The Morning Post* nor Coleridge's thinking about imagination up to this time does much to satisfy them. It would also take a brave commentator to make strong claims that this stanza discriminates the "fancy" (80) from the imagination. They appear to be used synonymously: it is the suspension of the "shaping spirit of imagination" that makes the fancy unable to make from misfortunes "dreams of happiness."

Stanza V leaves more hanging than a clear conception of the imagination. The passage incorporated into Coleridge's letter to Sotheby had provided an ellipsis between the loss of the imagination and the poet's habits of "abstruse research," but the letter itself had argued a connection between them: "Sickness & some other & worse afflictions, first forced me into *downright metaphysics* / for I believe that by nature I have more of the Poet in me" (*STCL* 2:814). The *Morning Post* version of "Dejection" eliminates entirely the latter part of the passage, which has been crucial both to many readings of the poem and to biography's general construction of Coleridge's character:

> For not to think of what I needs must feel,
> But to be still & patient all I can;
> And haply by abstruse research to steal
> From my own Nature all the natural Man;
> This was my sole Resource, my wisest Plan—
> And that which suits a part infects the whole,
> And now is almost grown the Temper of my Soul!
> (*STCL* 2:815)

I can only speculate on Coleridge's motivation for leaving out this passage, which he was almost immediately to send to various correspondents as a supplement to "Dejection." My guess is that the research program is so thoroughly implicated in the erotic discontents of the Verse Letter, where abstruse research is a cure for love, that the passage still seems too private to be printed.

Indeed, rather than print this section or any of the materials associated with it, Coleridge deliberately prints the poem as a fragment. Immediately following Stanza V in the newspaper text is the statement "The sixth and seventh Stanzas omitted." Now it just may be that in the course of his revisions Coleridge had written two more stanzas for "Dejection" (which he sent or showed to none of his correspondents, so far as extant documents reveal), and that he decided to omit them. I will be happy to pursue that hypothesis when some enterprising archivist comes up with the hundred-page chapter on imagination and fancy withheld from *Biographia Literaria* or even the 530 lines translated from Salomon Gessner. Until then, a more likely hypothesis is that the fragmentation of the poem is a rhetorical strategy pure and simple, though complex in its effects on the poem's intended audiences. For the general reader, the claim of omissions absolves the poem from any tests of continuity, consistency, or completeness. Problems in comprehending it (such as I have just exhibited) can always be referred to the hole in its middle. For Coleridge's intimate audience, the omission carries a double message. It reminds them just how far he has come in regaining control of his emotions. They know very well what has been left out of the poem in this crucial place: his account of the plagues of his marriage. But the documented omission also reminds his intimates of what could be put back into the poem, the erotic center which has been laid aside but not destroyed. The omission would have seemed to Coleridge's intimates a kind of veiled threat—something of the way you feel around an alcoholic who ostentatiously declines a public drink. It would be more reassuring if a show had not been made of the virtue.

Coleridge's indicated elision solves one enormous structural problem of "Dejection," though: the transition from the credal center of the poem to the beginning of what is called stanza VIII:

> O wherefore did I let it haunt my mind,
>   This dark distressful dream?
> I turn from it, and listen to the wind
>   Which long has rav'd unnotic'd. What a scream
> Of agony, by torture, lengthen'd out,
> That lute sent forth!
>
>   (88–93)

We recall from the Verse Letter that the "dark distressful Dream" (*VL* 185) had followed Coleridge's vow of voluntary exile from the charmed Wordsworth circle. Its substance had been a vision of Sara pining "in body or in mind" (171), "weak & worn with pain" (177), and Coleridge unable to comfort her:

> . . . O! to mourn for thee, & to forsake
> All power, all hope of giving comfort to thee—
> To know that Thou art weak & worn with pain,
> And not to hear thee, Sara! not to view thee—
>   Not sit beside thy Bed,
>   Not press thy aching Head,
>   Not bring thee Health again—
>   At least to hope, to try.
>
> (VL 175–182)

Coleridge's problems in reintegrating the exorcism of the dark dream into "Dejection" have been foreshadowed by its treatment in the letter to Sotheby, where it was simply appended to the continuous "introduction." The stanza as published in "Dejection" contains enough minor changes to suggest that Coleridge has worked carefully over it, but it seems at this time that he is able neither to integrate nor omit it. He has not yet hit upon his ultimate structural expedient of converting his immersion in abstruse researches into the dream itself. In its *Morning Post* incarnation the stanza serves mainly to provide some point for the opening description of the eolian harp by bringing the topic of poetic creation into the poem.

Coleridge brings "Dejection" to a close by welding together two highly revised segments of the Verse Letter (216–26 and 324–40) into stanza IX. The first movement of the stanza is adapted from a prayer for Sara:

> 'Tis midnight, and small thoughts have I of sleep;
> Full seldom may my friend such vigils keep!
> Visit him, gentle Sleep, with wings of healing,
>   And may this storm be but a mountain birth,
> May all the stars hang bright above his dwelling,
>   Silent as tho' they *watch'd* the sleeping earth!
>   With light heart may he rise
>   Gay fancy, cheerful eyes,
> And sing his lofty song, and teach me to rejoice!
>
> (120–28)

The Edmund of this prayer, of course, is wished a poetically rejuvenative sleep, so that he will awaken with "Gay fancy, cheerful eyes" (not "clear & cheerful eyes" [*VL* 224]), and "sing his lofty song, and teach me to rejoice" (not send "good Tidings" of his health and spirits [*VL* 226]).

The concluding address to Edmund is an enumeration of his attributes as a poet:

> O EDMUND, friend of my devoutest choice,
> O rais'd from anxious dread and busy care,
> By the immenseness of the good and fair
>   Which thou see'st everywhere,
> Joy lifts thy spirit, joy attunes thy voice,
> To thee do all things live from pole to pole,
> Their life the eddying of thy living soul!
> O simple Spirit, guided from above,
> O lofty Poet, full of life and love,
> Brother and Friend of my devoutest choice,
> Thus may thou ever, evermore rejoice!
>   (129–39)

The qualities of Edmund are a mix of the qualities of the Wordsworth of the letter to Sotheby and the Sara of the Verse Letter. The Wordsworth of the Sotheby version was an overwhelming, austerely elevated poet, addressed in language that verges on idolatry: "Calm stedfast Spirit, guided from above, / . . . / Great Son of Genius, full of Light & Love" (*STCL* 2:817). The less godlike Edmund of "Dejection" is not addressed so abjectly: "O simple Spirit, guided from above, / O lofty Poet, full of life and love" (136–37). And like Sara's in the Verse Letter, Edmund's gift of joy is conditional rather than absolute, sustained by the circumstances of his life. Coleridge's closing address to Sara had stressed the paradoxical generativity of her maiden state, in which she is both "innocent" and "full of love" (*VL* 325). When Coleridge addresses her as

> . . . free'd awhile from Cares & human Dread
> By the Immenseness of the Good & Fair
>   Which thou see'st every where
>   (331–33),

he is alluding to her lack of particular conjugal attachments like those which cripple him. She can be "mother Dove" to all because she is in fact wife and mother to none. When the lines are adapted for application to Edmund, the dread becomes "anxious" rather than simply "human," and cares become "busy cares" rather than all cares. The alterations subtly adjust the poem to its epithalamic occasion, for which the earlier poem's concentration on purity would be absurd.

How, then, does "Dejection" finally relate to its former self, the Verse Letter, and to Wordsworth's intervening poems on the leech-gatherer? "Dejection" is marked by a thorough purgation of its erotic associations. The most obvious changes result from the deletion of that material of a "private nature," but the revisions affect figures and imagery as well. The landscape of the poem is cleansed of its erotic connotations to such an extent that it is almost impossible to glimpse the conventions of spring elegy that underlie it. Wordsworth's poems on the leech-gatherer locate the source of the poet-narrator's ills in excessive indulgence of volatile spirits and excessive morbid imagination, pitting dejection against delight and seeing one as the inevitable consequence of the other. "Dejection" methodically suppresses the matter of delight, omitting all scenes of remembered pleasure. It insists that dejection is a chronic problem, just as Wordsworth-Edmund's joy is an enduring gift. It strips away the self-indulgence of the prior poem, without altering in the least its assessment of the severity of the problem. Even without Sara Hutchinson, it argues, and without a disastrously unhappy marriage, elemental problems would remain. As a part of the poetic dialogue, "Dejection" displays a force of pure resistance, unwilling to be easily cajoled out of its assessment of the poet's situation. Blake said opposition was true friendship. In large part opposition is Coleridge's greatest gift when Wordsworth comes to reconfront and complete his own fragmentary ode.

7

Time Passes

HE first completed version of the Ode which Wordsworth
had begun in March 1802 appears in MS. M of *The Prelude*
(DC MS. 44). Completed by mid-March 1804 (*CMY* 254–56), this
compilation of Wordsworth's writings was prepared for Coleridge on
the occasion of his departure for Malta. The manuscript reveals illuminating patterns in furnishing a fairly complete retrospective of
Wordsworth's poetic activity over the past two years. Its contents
may be broken down into four distinct chronological categories, although—given the fuzziness of our dating of several of the shorter
pieces—some overlap is inevitable.

The first category would be records of unfinished business, transcriptions of longer poems Wordsworth had long been working at,
"The Ruined Cottage" and *Peter Bell*. The manuscript of the latter
poem is dated 21 February 1802. The second category consists of
shorter poems, probably written between late winter of 1802 and the
conclusion of the first period of intensive work on the cycle of major
lyrics we have been tracing, which ended for Wordsworth on 5 July
1802, when his revised poem on the leech-gatherer, "Resolution and
Independence," was copied for Coleridge. The third category contains Wordsworth's efforts as a sonneteer, which began 21 May 1802,
when Dorothy read Milton's sonnets to him and he quickly composed

two sonnets on Bonaparte (*DWJ* 127). The sonnets continue through-out the remainder of the period of work covered in MS M. Finally, the fourth category is work of early 1804 itself, primarily the first five books of *The Prelude*, in a state close to that we know as the 1805 poem, apparently composed and transcribed shortly after Words-worth abandoned the notion of a five-book poem.[1] The shorter poems in this grouping are "To H. C.," "Ode to Duty" (untitled), "She was a phantom of delight," and the version of the Ode which begins the next chapter. Only two poems of note lie outside the categories sug-gested: untitled versions of "The Highland Girl" and "Yarrow Un-visited, " which are products of the tour of Scotland in 1803.

Within the literary context established by this manuscript, it is altogether too tempting to scorn the sonnet, or at least to see the work of the third period, between the summer of 1802 and early 1804, as a fallow span between the highly experimental lyric pro-duction which preceded it and the recovery and extension of that work a year and a half later. However, the particular series of public sonnets Wordsworth began in August 1802 casts an intriguing light on the work which preceded it and creates a new context for the work which will follow.

On 9 July, a few days after transcribing "Resolution and Indepen-dence" for Coleridge, Wordsworth and Dorothy began a journey which would keep them away from Grasmere for three months. Mary Moorman covers admirably both their itinerary and motivations.[2] Wordsworth was entering into the final stage of preparations for his marriage to Mary Hutchinson, and in their travels he and Dorothy were to touch the lives of almost all of those who were closest to them. They stayed three days at Keswick with the Coleridges, two more at Eusemere with the Clarksons, and on 16 July arrived at Gallow Hill for ten days with the Hutchinsons. Their ultimate des-tination was France, where they were to meet Annette and Caroline Vallon in Calais. Although the emotional turmoil both of the journey and of the month in Calais are easy enough to guess, they have had to be imagined because they surface hardly at all in the nine sonnets Wordsworth wrote between his departure from and return to Gras-mere. Only one reflects personal concerns even indirectly. In "It is a beauteous Evening" Wordsworth turns to address someone we iden-tify as his daughter Caroline:

Dear Child! dear Girl! that walkest with me here,
If thou appear'st untouch'd by solemn thought,
Thy nature is not therefore less divine:
Thou liest in Abraham's bosom all the year;
And worshipp'st at the Temple's inner shrine,
God being with thee when we know it not.

(P2V 151)

Wordsworth has left the French location of the scene unspecified and his relationship to the girl oblique. Those sonnets which do specify their locales and dates avoid any of the private anxieties which must have preoccupied the Wordsworths in France.

In the first of the *Sonnets Dedicated to Liberty*, entitled "Composed by the Sea-side, Near Calais, August, 1802," the poet looks to the west, concerned for the future of his nation: "I, with many a fear / For my dear Country, many heartfelt sighs, / Among Men who do not love her linger here" *(P2V 155)*. Other sonnets lament the character of France ("Shame on you, feeble Heads, to slavery prone!" [156]), the joylessness of the Napoleonic regime (156–57), the hollowness of the pomp and ceremony of Bonaparte's proclamation as Consul for life (158–59), and other issues reflecting the state of hostilities, dormant but far from dead, between England and France.

Although it would be wrong to underestimate either Wordsworth's patriotism or his concern over his country's affairs with France, it must still seem odd to find this particular sequence of poems coming from this set of personal circumstances. Wordsworth's sonnets owe more to Milton's than just versification and tone. Their public stance excludes private concerns, suppressing similarly the amatory origins of the Renaissance sonnet. For Wordsworth, the sonnet offered the virtues of both restriction and impersonality. The "Prefatory Sonnet" published in 1807, probably written late in 1802 *(CMY 32)*, explores the value of limitation:

In truth, the prison, unto which we doom
Ourselves, no prison is: and hence to me,
In sundry moods, 'twas pastime to be bound
Within the Sonnet's scanty plot of ground:
Pleas'd if some Souls (for such there needs must be)

Who have felt the weight of too much liberty,
Should find short solace there, as I have found.
                              (*P2V* 133)

As the narrow room is to the nun, the cell to the hermit, the pensive citadel to the student, the prison to the voluntary inmate (and the grave to the corpse?), so is the sonnet to the poet. It is a place of retirement, of abstinence, which defends against excessive personal liberty or, perhaps, excessive engagement with difficult personal themes. Wordsworth would later make more extravagant claims for the sonnet ("with this key / Shakespeare unlocked his heart" [*PW* 3:20]), but the form seems in 1802 to have served more as a barrier than an opening.

In setting the lyrics of the spring and summer of 1802 against the sonnets which followed them, I am not invoking a dialectic between originality and convention. My discussions of all the major lyrics of the earlier period have stressed their conventionalities, but the conventions are diametrically opposed. The conventions which govern the earlier works come from literary presentations of an unstable self, expressing its own uncertainties. Because the great storehouse of such themes is the tradition of erotic poetry, Wordsworth borrowed heavily from its figures and commonplaces. The political sonnets have no use for such materials. They seek above all else to establish a stable self, whose anxieties are generated from without by the great or degrading national and international events it is witnessing and meditating. When Wordsworth arranges these and later sonnets into the *Sonnets Dedicated to Liberty* in the edition of 1807, he is not encouraging the reader to observe the vacillations of a soul, or even the growth of a political consciousness, but rather the current of events as they are registered by a sensitive, concerned, but consistent commentator. He is uneasy in France not because of some flaw in his inner being, but because of what he sees there; he breathes with relief upon his return to England simply because it is England, and if "Europe is yet in bonds" (*P2V* 163), his native land remains free. The vexed and self-vexing voices of the Ode and "Resolution and Independence" are antithetical to a poetry which pursues the purposes of the sonnets.[3]

But by writing the political sonnets, and especially by allowing several of them to be published in the *Morning Post*, Wordsworth had become a different poet, with an altered relationship to his audience, when he resumed work on the great Ode. Because so much has been written about Wordsworth's political sympathies, we must remind ourselves that he had not written an explicitly political poem, which is to say a poem taking a stand on a current issue, since "The Old Cumberland Beggar" of the spring of 1798 (*CEY* 32). That poem had been withheld from the first edition of *Lyrical Ballads*. When it appeared in 1800, it was prefaced by a headnote which attempted to make its objections to the campaign against mendicity all but nostalgic: "The class of Beggars to which the old man here described belongs will probably soon be extinct. It consisted of poor, and, mostly, old and infirm persons, who confined themselves to a stated round in their neighbourhood. . . ." (*LB* 205).[4] The sonnets begun in 1802, then, present Wordsworth publicly in an unaccustomed role, as a consciously Miltonic activist political commentator, the stern moral conscience of his country. In the 1807 volume such efforts ring oddly against the self-exploratory work with which he had most recently been involved. Not the least of the strains within the *Poems in Two Volumes* is its play of two voices, the self-searching of "Resolution and Independence" and the Ode alongside the elevated certitude of a sonnet like "London, 1802":

> Milton! thou should'st be living at this hour:
> England hath need of thee: she is a fen
> Of stagnant waters: altar, sword, pen,
> Fireside, the heroic wealth of hall and bower,
> Have forfeited their ancient English dower
> Of inward happiness. We are selfish men;
> Oh! raise us up, return to us again;
> And give us manners, virtue, freedom, power.
> (*P2V* 165)

Wordsworth's sonnets mark his decision to become a public figure in England, to become the Milton of his age. Awareness of the new role he had taken on added to the pressures he faced when he turned in

1804 to the completion of his fragmentary Ode. In 1802 he could explore fluctuations of the spirit in relative freedom; by 1804 he had openly declared his stable maturity.

Aside from the date of the manuscript in which it appears, existing records give little hint of exactly when Wordsworth returned to the Ode. No more do they suggest why he took it up again at this time. The immediate cause for Wordsworth's decision was probably a protracted visit to Grasmere by Coleridge, accompanied by his son Derwent, which began 20 December 1803. Coleridge's visit was a farewell, as he was embarking on his scheme to seek a warmer climate to improve his health. The visit portended an indefinite separation of the friends, and if Coleridge's correspondence and notebook entries around this time are accurate indicators, it rang repeatedly many of the themes of the spring of 1802. During the visit Coleridge variously wrote of his absorption in metaphysical speculation: "I am bound to trace the Ministery of the Lowest to the Highest, of all things to Good / and the presence of a certain Abstract . . . or Generical Idea, in the Top, Bottom, & Middle of each Genus" (*CNB* 1:1827); of his unhappiness in his marriage: "Mrs C. is to me all *strange*, & the Terra incognita always lies near to or under the frozen Poles" (*CNB* 1:1816); of his love for Sara Hutchinson: "Derwent asleep in the other Bed, God love little dear Heart—& Dorothy in the Parlour, dear Dorothy—& O dear Sara Hutchinson" (*CNB* 1:1820); and of the genius of his friend: "Mental space constituent of Genius, Wordsworth's genius illustrates" (*CNB* 1:1823). Always and everywhere there is Coleridge's illness. Indeed, his sickness prolonged his stay in Grasmere from a projected single day to nearly a month (*STCL* 2:535).

Mixed blessing that it must usually have been, Coleridge's presence set Wordsworth to work. Coleridge's letter to Richard Sharp, written the day after his departure from Grasmere, suggests that he has left a poet who is once more at the height of his powers and hard at work on projects of cardinal significance: "I dare affirm that he will be hereafter admitted as the first & greatest philosophical Poet. . . . I prophesy immortality to his *Recluse*, as the first & finest philosophical Poem, if only it be (as it undoubtedly will be) a Faithful Transcript of his own most august & innocent Life, of his own habitual

Feelings & Modes of seeing and hearing" (*STCL* 2:1034). From these remarks we can be nearly certain that Wordsworth was working on *The Prelude* during the visit, because that portion of the projected masterwork was rapidly becoming just such an account.

Of the Ode itself we get only one tantalizing and possibly misleading glimpse. In a notebook entry c. 9 January, Coleridge asks:

> Is more gained by repeating to a beloved Housemate your Poem or Work, passage by passage, that is, by repeating each night after supper the work of the Day?—Or by storing it up a week or fortnight?—Till the whole Poem, if it be Ode or Tale / or a whole Book, if a long Work / or a complete Part, or Section, if in a Prose Work?—Ask William & Dorothy—
>
> —Dorothy thinks that it would be better to wait till some thing was finished, that could be repeated as a whole, Ode or single Book, or Chapter— (*CNB* 1:1830)

Is this jealousy on Coleridge's Part?

It is intriguing that Coleridge twice specifies an Ode as one form of a work which might be in progress, because Wordsworth could have been working on only two such poems at this time, the Immortality Ode and the "Ode to Duty." He had written no odes before the former and attempted no others until the latter. The notebook entry strongly suggests that the "work of the Day" was not being read every evening to at least one "beloved Housemate." Dorothy's response to Coleridge's theoretical inquiry is most easily construed as a defense of the status quo against Coleridge's indirect appeal that he be brought more intimately into the processes of his friend's composition. Even if this is pure conjecture, the notebook entry should deter anyone from imagining that in January of 1804 Coleridge was peering over Wordsworth's shoulder at *The Prelude* or the Ode, steering his pencil. Given the latter poem's associations with the painful subject of the Verse Letter, combined with the reappearance in Coleridge's notebooks and letters of the woes he had lamented there, Wordsworth's reticence would be both understandable and admirable. Coleridge's recuperative program lay directly before him, and no worthwhile purpose could be served by dishing up daily reminders of his earlier pains.

In the eighteen months which separated "Resolution and Independence" from the completion of the Ode, it had in fact been Coleridge who had kept the topics of the poetic cycle alive. In addition to heavily revised extracts from the Verse Letter—now addressed to Wordsworth—sent to Sotheby on 19 July 1802 (*STCL* 2:815–19); the much smaller extract sent to Southey ten days later, with no description of their larger context (*SCTL* 2:831–32); and the passage on his abstruse researches sent to Tom Wedgwood on 20 October 1802 to supplement the *Morning Post* version of "Dejection" (*STCL* 2:875), Coleridge continued to quote snatches of the poem to explain himself to his correspondents. Writing to Thomas Poole on 17 December 1802, he quoted his sneering attack on his wife ("two unequal minds," etc.) while simultaneously declaring that their relations had improved (*STCL* 2:901). Because Coleridge quotes the lines as though Poole should be familiar with them, we may conjecture that he had sent Poole a copy of some version of the Verse Letter, which he had earlier described on 7 May in this way: " . . . on the 4th of April last I wrote you a letter in verse; but I thought it dull & doleful—& did not send it" (*STCL* 2:801). On 13 August 1803 he followed a transcription of "Resolution and Independence" for Sir George Beaumont with a partial transcription of "Dejection," breaking off at the loss of his "Shaping Spirit of Imagination" (*STCL* 2:966–73. On 2 October 1803 he repeated for George Coleridge the passage on his abstruse researches omitted from the published poem (*STCL* 2:1008); and on 10 March 1804, shortly before he left for Malta, he wrote to Sara Hutchinson, repeating lines of his blessing to her from the Verse Letter (*STCL* 2:1083). For Coleridge, "Dejection" and its companion poems had remained living presences which were not to be put by.

One brief episode may suggest the ways in which the cycle of lyrics shaped the behavior and attitudes of both the writers and their companions. On 15 August 1803, just two days after Coleridge had posted his transcriptions of "Resolution and Independence" and "Dejection" to the Beaumonts, he, Dorothy, and Wordsworth left Keswick for a tour of Scotland. The tour laid bare dissonances of personality almost from its outset, and Coleridge broke away after two weeks to return home. His notebook entry on the day of his

departure commented, "Here I left W(ordsworth) & D," an inscrip-
tion followed by a later insertion in Latin, "would that I had never
seen [them]" (*CNB* 1:1471, 1471n). To his entry of the next day,
noting that he must travel alone to Edinburgh, he later added, "O
Esteesee! that thou hadst from thy 22nd year indeed made *thy own
way & alone!*" (*CNB* 1:1472). Wordsworth would later attribute
Coleridge's precipitate departure to his being "somewhat too much
in love with his own dejection,"[5] a remark which suggests the extent to which Coleridge's poem had shaped his intimates' perception
of him.

Surely no single cause lay behind Coleridge's depression on the
Scottish tour, but his spirits could not have been lifted by the early
itinerary, which featured a sentimental pilgrimage to the Burns
country. One incident recollected by Dorothy overflows with implications both for the relationships among the friends and for the sequence of major lyrics:

> I cannot take leave of the country which we passed through to-
> day, without mentioning that we saw the Cumberland mountains
> within half a mile of Ellisland, Burns's house, the last view we had
> of them. . . . We talked of Burns, and of the prospect he must
> have had, perhaps from his own door, of Skiddaw and his compan-
> ions, indulging ourselves in the fancy that we *might* have been
> personally known to each other, and he have looked upon those
> objects with more pleasure for our sakes. We talked of Coleridge's
> children and family, then at the foot of Skiddaw, and our own new-
> born John a few miles behind it; while the grave of Burns's son,
> which we had just seen by the side of his father, and some stories
> respecting the dangers his surviving sons were exposed to, filled us
> with a kind of melancholy concern, which had a kind of connection
> with ourselves.[6]

Coleridge was not present at this incident. He had absented himself
from the visit to Burns's house and grave earlier in the day. But
considering the equation drawn between himself and Burns in "Resolution and Independence"—a poem fresh in his mind—he must occasionally on these days have felt himself a participant in a later
memorial tour of his own pathetic life. Kathleen Coburn notes that

at this time "Coleridge was trying to leave off opium, and the withdrawal-symptoms . . . became gradually more evident." She comments astutely: "If the Wordsworths tried at this time to stiffen his resolution by talking of his family responsibilities, they could hardly have chosen a moment more inopportune" (*CNB* 1:1436n). Coleridge's journal entry for the evening of the visit to Burns's house reflects upon "how little there was in this World that could compensate for the loss or diminishment of the Love of such as truly love us" (*CNB* 1:1436). If Wordsworth and Dorothy were attempting once more to treat Coleridge with a dose of Burns, their strategy was no more effective than it had been in the summer of 1802.

I have attended at such length to Coleridge's self-quotations of "Dejection" and to the tensions of the Scottish tour because such phenomena help us to understand the poem to which Wordsworth returned in 1804. It is as impossible to step into the same poem twice as it is the same river. The Ode had become a different work, even if, as I have speculated, hardly a word had been changed. As innocent and conventional as its first four stanzas had been, they had provoked Coleridge's Verse Letter and "Dejection," a poem he had virtually fashioned into his signature. The Verse Letter had in its turn provoked "The Leech-Gatherer" and "Resolution and Independence," which had attempted ineffectually to divert or counteract Coleridge's despair. When Wordsworth turned back to the Ode, its original stanzas had become burdened by a complex of emotional associations at least as powerful as any that had appeared in its lines. In completing the poem Wordsworth was forced at the same time to be true to what he had written and, so far as it might be possible, to acknowledge and address those powerful issues which its lines had occasioned. His efforts result in a poem far greater than any he might have envisioned when he began it.

8

Wordsworth's Ode of 1804

There was a time when meadow grove and stream
The earth and every common sight
    To me did seem
    Apparel'd in celestial light
The glory and the freshness of a dream   [5]
It is not now as it has been of yore
Turn wheresoe'er I may
    By night or day
The things which I have seen I see them now no more

    The Rainbow comes and goes   [10]
And lovely is the rose
The Moon doth with delight
Look round her when the heavens are bare
    Waters on a starry night
Are beautiful and fair   [15]
    The sunshine is a glorious birth
But yet I know where'er I go
That there hath pass'd away a glory from the earth

Now while the Birds thus sing a joyous song
   And while the young lambs bound   [20]
      As to the tabor's sound
To me alone there came a thought of grief
A timely utterance gave that thought relief
   And I again am strong
The cataracts blow their trumpets from the steep   [25]
No more shall grief of mine the season wrong
I hear the echoes from the fields of sleep
   And all the earth is gay
      Land and sea   [30]
   Give themselves up to jollity
   And with the heart of May
Doth every Beast keep holiday
   Thou Child of joy
Shout round me, let me hear thy shouts thou happy
                    Shepherd boy   [35]

Ye blessed Creatures I have heard the call
Ye to each other make: I see
The heavens laugh with you in your jubilee
   My heart is at your festival
   My head hath its coronal   [40]
Even yet more gladness I can hold it all
   O evil day if I were sullen
While the earth herself is adorning
   This sweet May morning
And the Children are pulling   [45]
     On every side
In a thousand Vallies far and wide
   Fresh flowers: while the sun shines warm
And the Babe leaps up in his Mother's arm
   I hear I hear with joy I hear——   [50]
But there's a tree of many one
A single field which I have look'd upon
Both of them speak of something that is gone

The pansy at my feet
Doth the same tale repeat [55]
Whither is fled the visionary gleam
Where is it gone the glory and the dream

Our Birth is but a sleep and a forgetting
The Soul that rises with us our life's star
Hath had elsewhere its setting [60]
And cometh from afar
Not in entire forgetfulness
And not in utter nakedness
But trailing clouds of glory do we come
From God who is our home. [65]
Heaven lies about us in our infancy
Shades of the prison-house begin to close
Upon the growing Boy
But he beholds the light and whence it flows
He sees it in his joy [70]
The Youth who daily farther from the East
Must travel, still is Nature's Priest
And by the Vision splendid
Is on his way attended
At length the Man beholds it die away [75]
And fade into the light of common day

Earth fills her lap with pleasure of her own
Yearnings she hath in her own natural kind
And even with something of a Mother's mind
And no unworthy aim [80]
The homely nurse doth all she can
To make her foster Child her Inmate Man
Forget the glories he hath known
And that imperial palace whence he came

Behold the Child among his new-born blisses, [85]
A four year's darling of a pigmy size,

See where mid work of his own hand he lies,
Fretted by sallies of his Mother's kisses
With light upon him from his Father's eyes
   See at his feet some little plan or chart   [90]
Some fragment from his dream of human life
Shaped by himself with newly learned art
     A wedding or a festival
     A mourning or a funeral
   And this hath now his heart   [95]
   And unto this he frames his song
    Then will he fit his tongue
To dialogues of business love or strife
    But it will not be long
   E're this be thrown aside   [100]
   And with new joy and pride
The little actor cons another part
   Filling from time to time his humourous stage
   With all the persons down to palsied age
   That Life brings with her in her Equipage   [105]
     As if his whole vocation
    Were endless imitation

O Thou whose outward seeming doth belie
    Thy Soul's immensity
  Thou best philosopher who yet dost keep   [110]
  Thy heritage thou eye among the blind
That deaf and silent read'st the eternal deep
   Haunted for ever by the eternal mind
  Thou mighty Prophet Seer blest
On whom those truths do rest   [115]
Which we are toiling all our lives to find
  O Thou on whom thy immortality
  Broods like the day a Master o'er a Slave
  A presence which is not to be put by
    Thou unto whom the Grave   [120]
Is but a lonely bed without the sense or sight
    Of day or the warm light

A living place where we in waiting lie
Why with such earnest pains dost thou provoke
   The years to bring the inevitable yoke   [125]
   Thus blindly with thy blessedness at strife
Full soon thy soul shall have her earthly freight
And custom lie upon thee with a weight
Heavy as frost and deep almost as life.

   O joy that in our embers   [130]
   Is something that doth live
   That nature yet remembers
   What was so fugitive
The thought of our past years in me doth breed
Perpetual benedictions; not indeed   [135]
For that which is most worthy to be blest
Delight and liberty the simple creed
Of childhood whether fluttering or at rest
With new-born hope for ever in his breast
   Not for these I raise   [140]
   The song of thanks and praise
But for those blank misgivings of a Creature
Moving about in worlds not realized
High instincts before which our mortal nature
Did tremble like a guilty thing surprized   [145]
   But for those first affections
   Those shadowy recollections
   Which be they what they may
Are yet the fountain-light of all our day
Are yet the master light of all our seeing   [150]
   Uphold us cherish us and make
Our noisy years seem moments in the being
Of the eternal silence truths that wake
   To perish never
   Which neither listlessness nor mad endeavour   [155]
   Nor man nor Boy,
  Nor all that is at enmity with joy
  Can utterly abolish or destroy.

Hence in a season of calm weather
  Though inland far we be   [160]
 Our souls have sight of that immortal sea
   Which brought us hither
  Can in a moment travel thither
And see the children sport upon the shore
And hear the mighty waters rolling evermore [165]

Then sing ye Birds sing sing a joyous song
  And let the young lambs bound
   As to the Tabor's sound!
We in thought will join your throng
   Ye that pipe and ye that play   [170]
  Ye that through your hearts to day
  Feel the gladness of the May.
What though it be past the hour
Of splendour in the grass, of glory in the flower,
   We will grieve not, rather find   [175]
 Strength in what remains behind;
 In the soothing thoughts that spring
  Out of human suffering;
  In the faith that looks through death;
In years that bring the philosophic mind.   [180]

And Oh! ye fountains meadows fields & groves
 Think not of any severing of our loves
Yet in my heart of hearts I feel your might
 I only have relinquished one delight
 To live beneath your more habitual sway [185]
I love the brooks that down their channels fre[t?]
 Even more than when I tripped lightly as the[y?]
 The innocent brightness of a new-born day
   Is lovely yet
The clouds that gather round the setting sun [190]
Do take a sober colouring from an eye
That hath kept watch o'er mans mortality:
Another race hath been, and other palms are w[on?]
Thanks to the human heart by which we live

Thanks to its tenderness its joys and fears [195]
To me the meanest flower that blows can give
Thoughts that do often lie too deep for tears.

ORDSWORTH'S first step toward completing the Ode reflects the heightened stakes of the poem by 1804. However conventional it may have been, the experience of loss recorded
in the stanzas of 1802 was presented as wholly personal, singular to
the point of idiosyncrasy. Such a presentation was wholly consonant
with the erotic underpinnings of the fragment, because the cardinal
privilege of all erotic lamentation is to believe itself unique. As critics
have long observed, the "I" of stanzas I—IV shifts into a "we" which
governs the remainder of the work. The earlier stanzas were marked
by a first-person singular formation which repeated almost obses-
sively, even within individual lines: "The things which I have seen I
see them now no more" (9); "But yet I know where'er I go" (17). The
first word of stanza V is "Our." The singular form makes only two
brief, almost neutral appearances in stanzas V—X ("The thought of
our past years in me doth breed / Perpetual benedictions" [134—35];
"Not for these I raise / The song of thanks and praise" [140—41]),
before reassuming its central place in the final stanza. What had been
perceived as isolated experience—"to me alone" [22]—becomes the
experience of all. Further, this corporate experience is wrapped in
mythic trappings which proclaim its divine ordination.

Wordsworth's movement from individual to mythic experience has
traditionally been read as the turn and the crux of the Ode. Within
generic conventions, however, the turn presents no problems. One
of Pindar's favorite techniques was to parallel the achievements of his
contemporary victors with the actions of a hero or god, and Wordsworth could easily have seen the device at work in Abraham Cowley's
versions of either "The Second Olympique Ode" or "The First Ne-
meaen Ode," the works which begin his famous volume of *Pindarique
Odes*. In the first poem Pindar elevates Theron's victory in the chariot
race by comparing it to his forefathers' founding of Agrigentum, an
event which in turn is set into the context of the mythical descent of

the house from the line of Oedipus. In the second poem Pindar begins in praise of the young charioteer Chromius, discovers (or forces, or creates) an analogy between the victor and Hercules, and concludes with what Cowley terms "a Digression of Hercules, and his slaying of the two Serpents in his Cradle."[1] Cowley's adaptations smoothed the abrupt disjunctions in Pindar by providing transitions between contemporary and mythic narratives. Consequently, Wordsworth's sudden turn from individual experience to a myth of the species is more fully Pindaric than we normally find in Pindar's first great popularizer.

Wordsworth's mythic account of human existence has a number of potential sources, many of which have received exhaustive commentary, and a few of which will be exhausted even more fully in the course of this chapter. No external source for Wordsworth's myth, though, is more important than the four stanzas he had written in 1802. Indeed, stanza V may best be understood as an interpretive narrative overlay, designed to extract as much meaning as possible from the deeply ambiguous, disturbingly imprecise, but richly evocative lines written in 1802. The new narrative takes the form of an etiological myth, which explains the causes of the perplexing phenomena of stanzas I–IV. Such a myth necessarily works with a dual force: from one perspective it is an explanation of puzzling phenomena; from the other it is an allegory of existence which, because of its teleological claims, is capable of generating anxieties even deeper than those caused by the phenomena it explains. For example, the account of the Fall in Genesis 3 is meant to explain the origins of the pain of childbirth and the necessity of tillage of the soil. However, the larger theological implications of the myth for human existence—the kind of God it presupposes and his relationship to man and woman—have dominated speculation about the episode. In treating Wordsworth's myth I shift among three inseparably interrelated concerns: its etiological mission, its possible sources and intertextual resonances, and its allegorical adequacy.

The myth begins:

> Our Birth is but a sleep and a forgetting
> The Soul that rises with us our life's star

> Hath had elsewhere its setting
> And cometh from afar
> Not in entire forgetfulness
> And not in utter nakedness
> But trailing clouds of glory do we come
> From God who is our home.
>
> (58–65)

The fragment of 1802 was not specific about the time of glory it celebrated. In the Verse Letter Coleridge could without undue distortion assign its time of joy to a period as late as the stage of sentimental adolescent love. Now Wordsworth specifies his golden age on earth, tracing it back to the moment of birth. In so doing he cleanses the age of the elaborate network of erotic associations that have grown in the course of the poetic cycle.[2] By naming earliest childhood as the time of the "visionary gleam" he also suppresses any possible volitional causes either for his having perceived the gleam or for its fading. An infant cannot have perceived the "celestial light" because he believed or behaved in certain ways, nor could he have lost his ability because of ill circumstances or human error. He beheld and lost the light equally because he was born. Consequently, the light can hardly be associated with the poetic imagination, and its diminution cannot cause or coincide with the death of poetry, as it so clearly does in Coleridge's contributions to this cycle.

The details of Wordsworth's myth are assembled from suggestions in the poem's first four stanzas. The paradoxical assertion that birth is a "sleep and a forgetting" is justified by a literal reading of the earlier description of the celestial light as bearing the "glory and the freshness of a dream" (5). Metaphor is literalized in the recourse to birth itself, which derives from a cluster of associations: "The sunshine is a glorious birth" (16); the implied fertility of the idealized May landscape; and the "Babe [who] leaps up in his Mother's arm" (49). The selection of a star image for the soul is on the one hand conventional and on the other hand a recognition of images which had dominated stanzas I and II: the "celestial light" (4) and the catalogue of lights which prove the loss in stanza II, encompassing stars, moon, and sun. The journey of the star-soul itself, "which cometh from afar," has no source in the opening stanzas. This addition comes from the imposition of a narrative pattern as an interpretive grid for lines which had had no narrative patterning at all, only a two-pole temporal discrimination between then and now, golden age and diminished present. Finally, the clothing of the star-soul, equated with memory, elaborates a single observation of stanza I, that every common sight at one time seemed "Apparel'd in celestial light" (4).

Wordsworth's myth is a highly selective reading and interpretation of his original stanzas that suppresses as much as it explains. The Ode of 1802 had recorded two kinds of loss, the chronic loss of the celestial light and the acute anxiety, the "thought of grief" (22), that plagues the speaker in the present scene. This latter anxiety and its partial recovery preoccupy most of stanzas III and IV, and the earlier stanzas did nothing to explain the connections between the two kinds of loss. The explanatory myth avoids entirely this crux of the earlier stanzas. It addresses only the problem of chronic loss, evading acute anxieties as thoroughly as "The Leech-Gatherer" and "Resolution and Independence" had evaded questions of chronic despair. Consequently, nothing in the remainder of the Ode will ever help to unravel the obscurities of the two stanzas which record those surface disturbances or to resolve the interpretive disputes which have grown around the "thought of grief" (22), the "timely utterance" (23), or the winds which come "from the fields of sleep" (28).[3] The myth elaborated in stanza V amounts to a rhetorical revision of stanzas I–IV. It elevates to crucial importance portions of the earlier discourse which might have seemed merely decorative; it diminishes other lengthy and elaborate portions by its silence about them. Its reading of earlier "Wordsworth" is almost as reductive and redactive as Blake's annotations of the poems.

After having specified both the time of the celestial light as infancy and the source of the light as vestigial traces of a prior being with God, Wordsworth sketches the outlines of the soul's sojourn on earth:

> Heaven lies about us in our infancy
> Shades of the prison-house begin to close
> Upon the growing Boy
>   But he beholds the light and whence it flows
>   He sees it in his joy

> The Youth who daily farther from the East
> > Must travel, still is Nature's Priest
> And by the Vision splendid
> > Is on his way attended
> At length the Man beholds it die away
> And fade into the light of common day.
>
> > (66–76)

This narrative makes the journey of the soul on earth continuous with its descent from God, smoothing over for the moment the ontological break between the two realms of existence. The clouds which surround the infant at his birth are suggested in part by the opening descriptions of Coleridge's Verse Letter and "Dejection," and by Coleridge's insistence that "from the soul itself must issue forth, / A light, a glory, a fair luminous cloud / Enveloping the earth" ("Dejection" 53–55). Wordsworth's clouds are like Coleridge's in that they reveal rather than obscure, making visible the light which has already been lost at birth, at least in its immediacy. As the infant gives way to the boy, and in turn to the youth and the man, the celestial light fades "into the light of common day." Here human life has been figured in the commonplace of a solar day, from the sun's rising in the east to its setting in the west. Not only is none of this necessary to explain the phenomena which had generated the Ode of 1802, the new narrative profoundly alters the emotional terms of the earlier fragment. What had been presented and written as a sudden break— or a suddenly apprehended break—has now been read, rewritten, and represented as part of a gradual process, in which, almost imperceptibly, light has faded into light. The discontinuities of stanzas I–IV now become isolated points on a graduated scale, which were disturbing because the pattern uniting them had not been apprehended. Peter Manning observes that Wordsworth's "deterministic myth, with its generalized picture of decline from infancy to manhood, . . . comes into being as a consoling formulation. The lament contains a comfort: it places the vision safely in the past and represents its dissolution as an inevitability rather than a matter of individual fallibility."[4] The terms of the myth, though, make its consolatory power as precarious and fleeting as the celestial light itself.

Problems within the myth begin in its opening stanza, the narrative of which introduces one element which had not been apparent
in stanzas I–IV, an explicit devaluation of mundane experience. The
original stanzas had lamented not a world of earthly things but the
speaker's inability to see them as he once had: "meadow grove and
stream / The earth and every common sight" (1–2) no longer are
clothed in celestial light; "there hath pass'd away a glory from the
earth" (18); and the single tree, field, and daisy "speak of something
that is gone" (53). When Wordsworth figures earth as a "prison-
house" whose "Shades . . . begin to close / Upon the growing Boy"
(67–68), he sharply revises the values of his original stanzas, which
had not fully differentiated the things seen from the light enveloping
them. Wordsworth's etiological myth does its work by extracting a
dualism from his earlier record of perceptual change. The myth is
able to value earth only by positing an intermediate entity between
earth and the soul—Nature. "The Youth who daily farther from the
East / Must travel, still is Nature's Priest / And by the vision splendid / Is on his way attended" (71–74). For the purposes of the myth,
nature is earth appareled in celestial light; with the fading of the
light, nature dies into earth.

Commentary has never known just what to make of Wordsworth's
myth, which manages to explain (or at least to contain) the anxieties
of stanzas I–IV only by recourse to an uncharacteristic dualism. Because such questions bear heavily on the function of the myth within
the finished poem, I will bring forward the response of George
McLean Harper, who voices his perplexity more clearly and firmly
than most subsequent critics. "What," Harper asks,

> is the subsidiary idea, which the Fenwick note unduly emphasizes,
> upon which commentators have spent themselves, and which, to
> be sure, is elaborately indicated in the title of the ode? It is a
> surmise, nothing more, that the excellence of childhood may be
> an inheritance from a previous and presumably superior state of
> existence. This is not . . . original with Wordsworth, in the only
> senses in which any such thought can be original—that is to say,
> either inborn or something conquered and assimilated. It was al-
> together derivative, extrinsic, and novel to him. It is connected
> with no other of his writings. It is alien to his mind. He habitually

poeticizes the facts of nature and human experience, shunning equally the cloudland of metaphysics and the light mists of fancy.[5]

Harper goes on to blame Coleridge for Wordsworth's unfortunate conceit. Harper's common-sense outrage helps to focus certain issues implicit in Wordsworth's presentation of his myth. Despite Harper, Wordsworth's poetry is no stranger to surmise. The poet who could invite his sister for a walk on the first mild day of March, venturing that "One moment now may give us more / Than fifty years of reason" (*LB* 59; 25–26), is at home with outlandish speculation. What is missing in the Ode is that crucial "may," which would condition its overstatements, identifying its myth as conjecture. Here we have no apologetic formula, no "If this / Be but a vain belief," an equivocation which conditions a conjecture inherently less treacherous in "Tintern Abbey" (*LB* 115; 50–51). Wordsworth unfolds the ode's myth as calmly and firmly as if it were an account of creation, authorized by common consent, handed down from the beginning of time.

Although Wordsworth always seemed shocked at the ease with which his conceptions could shock the conventionally pious, he could hardly have expected his explanatory myth to pass unremarked and unquestioned. Why, then, did he offer it in such a scriptural manner? One answer would be that the myth does answer definitively the questions left dangling at the end of his earlier fragment, "Whither is fled the visionary gleam / Where is it now the glory and the dream" (56–57). The problem is not that the myth doesn't accomplish its task but that it is more than adequate to its occasion. It explains more than has been asked and raises other perplexing questions in the process of its own unfolding. Why call upon the awesome power of a myth of origins, bearing deeply upon the very essence of being, in order to address a question of changing appearances? Wordsworth had dealt with analogous changes in "Tintern Abbey," in shorter lyrics of 1802 like "To the Cuckoo," and he was working simultaneously on the expanded *Prelude*. None of these works engages the power of myth so immediately or so unequivocally. Without underestimating the latent power of Wordsworth's first four stanzas, I find nothing in them which necessitates his recourse to etiological myth. Indeed, our considerations might better be reversed, so that we may observe the effect the myth has upon those first four stanzas.

The radical severity of Wordsworth's "cure" works rhetorically to accentuate the malady which his earlier stanzas had described. Cowley's Pindaric example is useful, when he underlines the victory of a youthful charioteer by likening his struggles to those of the infant Hercules. Coleridge's agonized responses to those four stanzas of 1802 must have persuaded Wordsworth of their potential power and importance. His turn to etiological myth in 1804 acknowledges the power they have gained through the rich poetic dialogue in which they have become enmeshed. By 1804 the first four stanzas, which I described earlier as a symptomatology in search of a disease, have come instead to serve as a faint, veiled allegory of the experience of the myth.

Outside the opening stanzas of the Ode itself, the most crucial sources for Wordsworth's myth are Coleridge's Verse Letter and "Dejection." Coleridge's various cloud figures helped to furnish the clothing for Wordsworth's new-born soul, and enabled him to conflate sunrise and sunset. But it is at the conceptual rather than the figurative level that Wordsworth most fully engages Coleridge's companion poems. In both poems Coleridge insists strenuously that the sources of both strength and loss lie within, and no future revision will ever give up this point. The Verse Letter establishes its position in the second stanza:

> I may not hope from outward forms to win
> The Passion & the Life whose Fountains are within!
> These lifeless Shapes, around, below, Above,
>   O what can they impart?
>
>   (VL 50–53)

The identical position is underlined in the poem's concluding movement:

> O Sara! we receive but what we give,
> And in *our* Life alone does Nature live.
> Our's is her Wedding Garment, our's her Shroud—
> And would we aught behold of higher Worth

Than that inanimate cold World allow'd
To the poor loveless ever-anxious Crowd,
Ah! from the Soul itself must issue forth
A Light, a Glory, and a luminous Cloud
Enveloping the Earth!
                              (295–303)

Wordsworth's myth adapts the passage above through radical inversion. It admits the existence of an "inanimate cold World," which it calls "earth" or the "prison-house," and it holds that its sterility becomes living "Nature" only through the mediation of "clouds," "light," and "vision." These agreements pass for naught, however, because Wordsworth's myth locates his light as wholly outside the self as Coleridge had buried it within.

One of the truths commentary cherishes is that Wordsworth was attempting in the Ode to counteract the despair of Coleridge's Verse Letter, and that his primary instrument for this mission was the myth of pre-existence. It remains to be seen whether this was either the intention or the effect of the myth, because by the end of stanza V Wordsworth has inverted Coleridge's metaphysics without offering any consolation. In both Wordsworth's myth and Coleridge's poems something of paramount value has been lost, and under the terms Wordsworth has proposed to this point the self is powerless to do anything about its situation. Coleridge is impotent because the source of his light, his inner joy, has vanished, Wordsworth because he is caught in a divinely ordained pattern of existence which has determined the fate of all mankind. Coleridge's extreme interiority and Wordsworth's steadfast exteriority meet in stunning agreement. If Coleridge has been undone by circumstances and faulty choices, and Wordsworth by an inevitable pattern of mortality, both are still essentially powerless. Or rather, like Coleridge's Hamlet, their only power lies in their ability to analyze their hopeless situations, to mark and tally the failings and fates that have brought them to this pass.

Because I will be arguing that Wordsworth's myth is not a significant instrument of recuperation in the Ode, it is especially important to note its traces in the two writers' earlier works. Both Wordsworth and Coleridge had flirted with the notion of pre-existence, Coleridge the more seriously of the two. In discussing the influence of Coleridge on Wordsworth's Ode, John D. Rea called attention to a sonnet Coleridge had written in 1796 upon hearing of the birth of his son Hartley:

> Oft *of some unknown Past* such Fancies roll
> Swift o'er my brain, as make the Present seem,
> For a brief moment, like a most strange dream
> When, not unconscious that she dreamt, the Soul
> Questions herself in sleep! and Some have said
> We liv'd ere yet this *fleshly* robe we wore.
> O my sweet Baby! when I reach my door,
> If heavy Looks should tell me, thou wert dead
> (As sometimes thro' excess of Hope, I fear)
> I think, that I should struggle to believe,
> Thou wert a Spirit to this nether sphere
> Sentenc'd, for some more venial crime to grieve—
> Didst scream, then spring to meet Heaven's quick Reprieve;
> While we wept idly o'er thy little Bier![6]

Convinced that Wordsworth had written stanzas V–VIII of the Ode in 1802, Rea went on to suggest that this was the poem sent to Wordsworth in a packet of materials on 6 May 1802, when Dorothy's journal records the receipt of "verses to Hartley" (207). Rea points out that Coleridge had appended a note to the poem: "Almost all the followers of Fénelon believe that men are degraded intelligences who had once existed in a paradisiacal or perhaps heavenly state" (206).

Our more detailed understanding of Wordsworth's texts makes it difficult to credit the scenario of influence that Rea assembles: that on 10 June 1802 Coleridge brought in a "sack full of books" (207), which were readings in neo-Platonic philosophy, including a brief compendium in Latin by Marsilio Ficino he had requested of John Thelwall on 19 November 1796 (*STCL* 1:262). But it is clear that Coleridge's sonnet prefigures many elements of Wordsworth's myth. Both play heavily upon dreaming, and both distinguish realms of existence through the the figure of garmentry: "this fleshly robe," "apparel'd in celestial light," and "not in utter nakedness." Wordsworth's "prison-house" may echo Coleridge's sentence for "some more venial crime." What is clearest, though, is how thoroughly Coleridge conditions his conjectures. The idea of pre-existence is suggested by nameless authorities ("and Some have said"), and if needed to underpin a faith in the afterlife would require a "struggle to believe." The Ode's development of the myth stands in stark contrast to such equivocations.

Wordsworth's other uses of the explanatory myth, whether contemporary with the Ode or antedating it, are as slippery as Coleridge's. Lucy Newlyn has made an impressive effort to reestablish "To H. C., Six Years Old," as a work of 1802 rather than winter 1804, which Reed finds more probable (*CMY* 180–181).[7] In "To H. C." (the version in MS. M which I follow does not indicate an age for the child) Hartley's "fancies . . . from afar are brought," and he makes of his words "a mock apparel." The poem's imagery is clearly reminiscent of the myth of the Ode, as is its sense of the disjunction between its two realms of being:

> What hast thou to do with sorrow
> Or the injuries of tomorrow?
> Thou art a Dew-drop which the morn brings forth
> Not doom'd to jostle with untimely shocks
> Or to be trail'd along the soiling earth
> A gem that glitters while it lives
> And no forewarning gives
> But at the touch of wrong without a strife
> Slips in a moment out of life.
>
> (MS. M)

Our dating of "To H. C." is shaky enough for multiple conjectures: that it was written in 1802, and that the myth of the Ode formalizes conceptual suggestions in its imagery; that it was written simultaneously with the Ode, perhaps even put together from overflow materials from that poem; or that it was composed after the Ode was finished and reflects in its imagery the conceptual foundations of that poem.

In some ways, though, the differences between "To H. C." and the Ode are more striking than their similarities. "To H. C." puts its suggestions of a prior existence to work for purposes of cosmic/ comic hyperbole. It addresses a single, particular, and peculiar child, whose alien nature perplexes adults. The poet's fears for the child's future, "of times when pain might be thy guest" or "grief uneasy Lover! never rest / But when she sate within the touch of thee," are brushed aside as products of "too industrious folly" and "vain and causeless melancholy!" Hartley is so different, his perceptions and behavior so foreign to adult modes, that only two fates seem possible, sudden extinction or perpetual childhood:

> Nature will either end thee quite
> Or lengthening out thy season of delight
> Preserve for thee by individual right
> A young lamb's heart among the full-grown flocks.
>
> (MS. M)

Whatever may in fact have become of Hartley, and Newlyn traces his future life grimly, it is difficult to read this poem as a brooding projection. It can afford to entertain the dire pole of its prophecy, early death, only because its mood is so self-evidently playful. "To H. C." does little to prepare a reader for the authority with which stanza V of the Ode articulates its myth of pre-existence. There destiny makes no allowances for "individual right," because its laws are not subject to suspension.

Wordsworth makes one other extended use of pre-existence, this time in a work we are much more certain is contemporaneous with the Ode, Book the Fifth of what was to become *The Prelude*. Here the problems with its appearance are rhetorical rather than tonal. Wordsworth is writing of the influence of books on his early development, praising especially the literature of fantasy:

> Dumb yearnings, hidden appetites are ours,
> And they must have their food; our childhood sits,
> Our simple childhood sits upon a throne
> That hath more power than all the elements.
> I guess not what this tells of Being past,
> Nor what it augurs of the life to come;
> But so it is: and in that dubious hour,
> That twilight when we first begin to see

This dawning earth, to recognise, expect;
And in the long probation that ensues,
The time of trial, ere we learn to live
In reconcilement with our stinted powers,
To endure that state of meagre vassalage;
Unwilling to forego, confess, submit
Uneasy and unsettled; yoke fellows
To custom, mettlesome, and not yet tam'd
And humbled down; Oh! Then we feel, we feel,
We know when we have friends, Ye Dreamers, then,
Impostors, Drivellers, Dotards, as the ape
Philosophy will call you; then we feel
With what and how great might ye are in league,
Who make our wish our power, our thought a Deed
An Empire, a Possession; Ye whom Time,
And Seasons serve, all faculties, to whom
Earth crouches, th'elements are potter's clay,
Space like a Heaven fill'd up with Northern lights,
Here, no where, there, and every where at once.
   It might demand a more impassion'd strain
To tell of later pleasures link'd to these,
A tract of the same isthmus which we cross
In progress from our native continent
To earth and human life.

                     (MS. M)

This enormously important passage simultaneously advances and evades the central claim of the myth of the Ode, according an equal privilege to the powers of childhood while declining to speculate about "Being past" or "the life to come." Its resonances with the Ode are of course remarkable: "That twilight when we first begin to see / This dawning earth" is a "dubious hour." Maturation brings "stinted powers" and a state of "meagre vassalage." To grow is to be forced to "forego, confess, submit," to become one of the "yoke fellows / To custom." On the other hand, the passage offers a consolation that appears nowhere in the Ode, because the child is neither alone nor beset solely by fallen, alien adults. He has "friends," writers of the fantastic "Who make our wish our power, our thought a Deed / An Empire, a Possession." Here one kind of literature at least transcends the sway of earth; time and the seasons bend to its will, and "Earth crouches." This potent Miltonism, borrowed from the account of the Fall, is staggeringly audacious when applied to the power of such writers as those of "The Tales that charm away the wakeful night in Araby" (MS. M).

Here Wordsworth has energized just enough of the concept of preexistence to lend force to his arguments for the native powers of childhood, against the evils of forcefed, precocious maturation, and in praise of the liberating force of fantasy. His declaration of war on "the ape / Philosophy" has been traced to numerous sources, including Godwinianism, the infamous Wedgwood proposal for childrearing, and the stiffly Rousseauist educational proposals of the French Directorate.[8] It is likely, though, that Wordsworth would have known that he was also rebutting the attack on poets in Plato's *Republic*, and doing so through recourse to a myth invariably considered Platonic in its origins. I will return to this issue after discussing stanzas VI–VIII of the Ode, which present the human consequences of the myth of origins from divergent perspectives. It is enough for now to note that in this contemporaneous passage from *The Prelude* the myth itself is subsidiary to the poet's intentions and is presented hesitantly. Its concluding lines on the "isthmus which we cross / In progress from our native continent / To earth and human life" develop from a context of polemical hyperbole which allows them to be read as decoratively metaphoric.

Stanzas VI–VIII of the Ode do not modify the stark outlines of the myth. They give it human dimension by presenting the passage through life from different viewpoints. Stanza VI explores the role earth plays in the pilgrimage of the human soul:

> Earth fills her lap with pleasures of her own
>   Yearnings she hath in her own natural kind
> And even with something of a Mother's mind
>   And no unworthy aim
> The homely nurse doth all she can
>   To make her foster Child her Inmate Man
>   Forget the glories he hath known
> And that imperial palace whence he came.
>
>   (77–84)

Concentrating on the role played by earth casts the myth into a relatively benign light. As Carl Woodring has pointed out, Wordsworth borrows upon the stuff of fairy-tales in this passage, suggesting that the child be viewed as a foundling prince, fallen among good-hearted rustics who do their limited best to raise him.[9] Barren herself, the "homely nurse" yearns for true maternity and "even," the poem grudgingly allows, has "something of a mother's mind." Her kindly act of comfort, of course, distracts the alien being from memory of his former glories. The tale implied is easily finished. Foundling princes discover their true identities, resume their rightful inheritances, and fittingly reward their well-meaning foster-parents, who are in fact unworthy in everything except their intentions. Blood tells. The only sign that the stanza's condescension masks a deeper hostility—a "Woman I know thee not"—is its jarring apposition of "foster Child" and "Inmate Man," with the latter phrase pointing directly back to the "Shades of the prison-house" (67). Stanza VI maintains its mild, amused detachment by directing its attention toward the foster-mother, who here represents material reality rather than humankind. It is not the translation from an "imperial palace" to a hut that calls forth the poem's deepest anxieties, nor is it the fall into the flesh that inflicts the greatest damage on the soul, but its immersion in human society.

The following stanza begins on the lightest of notes, viewing the young child surrounded by his immediate human family:

> Behold the Child among his new-born blisses,
> A four-year's darling of a pigmy size,
> See where mid work of his own hand he lies,
> Fretted by sallies of his Mother's kisses
> With light upon him from his Father's eyes.
> (85–89)

The child's newly discovered blisses are not reminiscences of his imperial abode but those humbler pleasures with which earth fills her lap, leading the child to forget his previous joys. On the whole the initial scene is warm and reassuring, recalling Wordsworth's depiction of the infant's human bonding first sketched in the *Two-Part Prelude* of 1797–98. Both the bonding passage and the passage from

Book the Fifth just examined are complexly interrelated in ways crucial to the procedures of the Ode:

> Bless'd the infant babe
> (For with my best conjectures I would trace,
> The progress of our being), blest the Babe
> Nurs'd in his Mother's arms, the Babe who sleeps
> Upon his Mother's breast who when his soul
> Claims manifest kindred with an earthly soul
> Doth gather passion from his Mother's eye
> Such feelings pass into his torpid life
> Like an awakening breeze, and hence his mind
> Even in the first trial of its powers
> Is prompt and watchful, eager to combine
> In one appearance all the elements
> And parts of the same object, else detach'd
> And loth to coalesce. Thus day by day
> Subjected to the discipline of love
> His organs and recipient faculties
> Are quick'ned are more vigorous; his mind spr[eads?]
> Tenacious of the forms which it receives,
> In one beloved presence, nay and more
> In that most apprehensive habitude
> And those sensations which have been deriv[ed?]
> From this beloved presence, there exists
> A virtue which irradiates and exalts
> All objects through all intercourse of sense.
> No outcast he, bewilder'd and depress'd;
> Along his infant veins are interfus'd
> The gravitation and the filial bond
> Of nature that connect him with the world.
> Emphatically such a being lives
> An inmate of the *active* universe;
> From nature largely he receives nor so
> Is satisfied, but largely gives again,
> For feeling has to him imparted strength;
> And powerful in all sentiments of grief
> Or exultation fear and joy his mind
> Even as an agent of the one great mind

Creates, creator and receiver both
Working but in alliance with the works
Which it beholds.—Such verily is the first
Poetic spirit of our human life
By uniform controul of after years
In most abated and suppress'd, in some
Through every change of growth or of decay
Preeminent till death.

(MS. M)

Of the slightly different versions of these lines which appear in the poems of 1799 and 1805, the editors of the Norton *Prelude* remark: "In 1799, when these lines were written, Wordsworth sees this force as the 'filial bond' of child and mother, which establishes the larger bond of man and Nature; for a very different position see *Intimations Ode*, 67–84, of spring 1804." [10] The note implies that Wordsworth had modified or rejected his earlier views by the time he repeated the lines in 1804 and 1805, a view in keeping with the edition's attempts to privilege the earliest version of the poem. I wonder. Both the central myth of the Ode and its embellishments in stanzas VI–VIII appear to be dark, partial readings of this earlier passage.

For the passage which Wordsworth began in 1799, the child arrives as an alien creature, who must be attached to this world, whose soul must *claim* "manifest kindred with an earthly soul." If he is not an outcast, "bewilder'd and depress'd," it is only because his mother is able to precipitate "The gravitation and the filial bond / Of nature that connect him with the world." Stanzas VII–VIII of the Ode and the passage I have been discussing describe the crossing of the same isthmus, but they face in different directions. Ignoring the realm the infant soul has left, the passage begun in 1799 observes the process through which it becomes an "earthly soul." It sees a miracle of human love, growth, and adaptation. Stanzas VII and VIII of the Ode watch the identical process with a mounting outrage at what is lost in human growth, an outrage which sinks at last into despair. From their perspective the watchful, loving, and hopeful parents are, like earth itself, no better than foster-parents. Even in the opening lines of the stanza troubling undercurrents are suggested. The "pigmy size" of the four-year-old hints as much at alien being as diminutive stature. In the line, "See where mid work of his own hand he lies," the verb carries a double charge which suggests that the child is being led to falsify his being. His induction into the world of human emotion is also problematical, as he is "Fretted by sallies of his Mother's kisses," her actions carrying connotations of a sudden military onslaught. And the light beaming from his father's eyes is an integral part of that light of common day, under the glare of which the celestial light will disappear.

As the stanza broadens beyond the family circle, it sees socialization as a process in which the soul loses itself in a cycle of unending imitation:

> See at his feet some little plan or chart
> Some fragment from his dream of human life
> Shaped by himself with newly learned art
>   A wedding or a festival
>   A mourning or a funeral
> And this hath now his heart
> And unto this he frames his song.
>
>   (90–96)

While it is possible to read these lines as a protest against premature socialization, against education that will not let children be children, they carry no such limitation. The child of this stanza is not the monstrous prodigy of Book the Fifth of *The Prelude*, nor is he necessarily Hartley Coleridge, who is widely assumed to have been its model.[11] He is any child, playing and learning to adapt to his social environment by trying on adult roles. He makes up (and makes) human life, which is now to him only a "fragment" of a "dream." In the passage of *The Prelude* drafted in 1799 Wordsworth had claimed that the child's reciprocal perception of the world, grounded in his bond with his mother, his receiving and creating sensations, is "verily is the first / Poetic spirit of our human life" (MS. M). Here in the Ode we see an extension of that same poetic spirit, and what the child is framing from the materials of social life is a "song." The materials of his new art, "A wedding or a festival / A mourning or a funeral," are hardly degrading. Indeed, what he is doing is reminis-

cent of Wordsworth's depiction of his younger self in "Michael,"
where the tale of the shepherd and his son had led him

> on to feel
> For passions that were not my own, and think
> At random and imperfectly indeed
> On man; the heart of man and human life.
>   (*LB* 227; 30–33)

He goes on to declare that he is relating the tale of Michael and Luke
partially to assure the continuation of the same imitative cycle, "for
the sake / Of youthful Poets, who among these Hills / Will be my
second self when I am gone" (37–39).

By this point of Wordsworth's elaboration of the consequences of
his myth, the reader must struggle to share a perspective from which
its value judgments may be understood. What kind of philosophy
can lament the trafficking of the soul in such profound and moving
human rites as weddings and funerals and deplore the fall into maturity as it is evidenced in the creation of *song*? The answer has to be
an inhuman, even antihuman perspective. Stanza VII views human
life from the eye of eternity, in which all mortal concerns and accom-
plishments can seem equally trivial and contemptible. The celestial
light has an enormous leveling power. It scorns the process through
which the child fits "his tongue / To dialogues of business love or
strife" (97–98), as though all talk were one, and equally futile. In
his fertile imitativeness, the child tries on all the successive ages of
mankind:

> But it will not be long
> E're this be thrown aside
> And with new joy and pride
> The little actor cons another part
> Filling from time to time his humorous stage
> With all the persons down to palsied age
> That Life brings with her in her Equipage
> As if his whole vocation
> Were endless imitation.
>   (99–107)

Helen Darbishire notes that Wordsworth's account of human life as imitation draws the phrase "humorous stage" from Samuel Daniel's introductory sonnet to *Musophilus*.[12] It draws its power, though, from its conceptual echo of the chillingly bitter speech of Jaques on the seven ages of man: "All the world's a stage, / And all the men and women merely players."[13] To Jaques the "infant, / Mewling and puking in the nurse's arms" (143–44), has no inherent privilege, and the Ode can elide the roles "down to palsied age," which for Jaques is "second childhood and mere oblivion, / Sans teeth, sans eyes, sans every thing" (165–66), because all are equally banal. It is ironically but wholly appropriate that the divine perspective of Stanza VII invokes the spirit of the most fully secular cynic in English literature. The stanza's attitude toward the merely human was determined when Wordsworth stipulated his myth of origins. If the joy of childhood is to be attributed to a prior and higher life of the soul, and if every acquisition of earthly knowledge damages the soul's communion with its supernatural heritage, then nothing in human life is worthy of attention. Even the poetry which sings its joys and sorrows is wasted breath.

Stanza VIII attempts a recovery through yet another shift in perspective. If viewing the child in his familial context discloses only too vividly the accelerating process through which he clothes and masks his blessed essence, perhaps concentration on the child as he is in himself will provide relief. The voice of this stanza no longer approaches the child from above, from the prospect of eternity, but from the humility of a supplicant. The stanza begins as an extended apostrophe to the child, elaborately calling him forth in all his glory and paradoxical power:

> O Thou whose outward seeming doth belie
>   Thy Soul's immensity
> Thou best philosopher who yet dost keep
> Thy heritage thou eye among the blind
> That deaf and silent read'st the eternal deep
>   Haunted for ever by the eternal mind
> Thou mighty Prophet Seer blest
> On whom those truths do rest
> Which we are toiling all our lives to find

> O Thou on whom thy immortality
> Broods like the day a Master o'er a Slave
> A presence which is not to be put by
> Thou unto whom the Grave
> Is but a lonely bed without the sense or sight
> Of day or the warm light
> A living place where we in waiting lie.
>
> (108–23)

The poet invokes the child as though he were a god to whom he is ritually appealing by praising his attributes.[14] The stanza begins as a prayer of praise, which by both by generic rhythm and by the rhetorical dictates of the poet's situation should become a prayer of petition, as the child is asked to intercede on behalf of the supplicant adult. "Our Father who art in Heaven . . . give us this day our daily bread." Any churchgoer would know the formula, and any poet would know its literary adaptations, which range from the devout to the blasphemous, from "Ave Maria" to "Holy Willie's Prayer."

In Wordsworth's prayer of praise, the soul of the child is immense. As long as he is true to his heritage of eternity, he is the "best philosopher" in the root sense of the term, a lover of truth because a liver of truth. Possessing the visionary capacity of a prophet, he is an "eye among the blind." The passage's play upon the topic of language is as intricate as its play upon vision. The child lacks either understanding or articulation of human language, which has already been shown to be a primary mechanism and manifestation of the fall into maturity. Still, he is able to "read" the language of eternity. He has by divine gift truths inaccessible to the world of adult striving, and by the very terms of its myth, the poem must privilege possession over effort, "rest" over "toiling." The child's immortality is wholly unconscious and inescapable. It "Broods" over him "like the day a Master o'er a Slave." Wordsworth's composite image here comes close to reversing the child's blessing into a curse. The more closely they are described, the more problematical these blessings appear. The solar day had measured human development's recession from the soul's perfection, and marked its journey into the prison-house. The eternal day of the celestial light has connotations of another and improgressive mode of bondage, a blessed "presence," but one which is "not to be put by." Is it a benefit to see the grave as just "a lonely bed without the sense or sight / Of day and the warm light / A living place where we in waiting lie?" [15] The child's attributes grow increasingly questionable as they are enumerated, but all are consequences of the myth of origins. Genuine knowledge is prelinguistic and incommunicable; prophecy is mute; the best philosopher can read but not write; full knowledge of immortality precludes awareness of mortality. [16]

Just as the prayer reaches what would be its turn to petition, after the intercessor has been called forth and his attributes praised, nothing can be asked. The childgod has been distanced so thoroughly from the human condition that human language cannot bridge the gap. Because of the conditions established by the myth and reiterated in the invocation, the deity can neither comprehend nor respond. The anticipated petition is suspended, and the stanza ends not in a supplication but in a question. The question has to be rhetorical, because the logic of the myth holds that if the child were able to answer, he would no longer know the answer:

> Why with such earnest pains dost thou provoke
> The years to bring the inevitable yoke
> Thus blindly with thy blessedness at strife
> Full soon thy soul shall have her earthly freight
> And custom lie upon thee with a weight
> Heavy as frost and deep almost as life.
>
> (124–29)

The address to the child in essence has become contaminated by a recollection of the child in action, eagerly trying out the roles of adult life, acquiring language so that he can speak, but losing the message that he alone has been able to read: to learn to talk is to have nothing to say. Human society itself is figured as a grave in which the soul acquires its "earthly freight" and "custom" presses upon it "with a weight / Heavy as frost and deep almost as life." The final effect of Wordsworth's myth is not to triumph over the grave but to entomb life, turning it into a terminal utterance more chilling than death. I doubt that any reader has failed to start at the final line of this stanza. The tenor of its closing simile, "deep," establishes an alliterative potential which should inevitably end in "death." The rule of rhyme in the final quatrain, though (that "strife" which calls forth "life),'" is as inflexible as the law established by the governing myth. Death would be too easy an answer when life has been made to seem something more fearful yet.

Any reader who finds his burdens lifted at the close of stanza VIII would not need Dr. Pangloss to unfold for him the providential blessings of the Lisbon earthquake. In recent years commentary has chipped away at the troubling consequences of Wordsworth's myth without coming to full terms with its function in the poem. Building upon Lionel Trilling's analysis of the Ode, Harold Bloom laid out twenty-five years ago the rudiments of the argument I am pursuing, but did not follow his insight further: "Discursive logic can demonstrate an adequate relationship between the poem's first and second movements, and a more complicated one between the first and third, but nothing to link together the second and third. The poem's initial four stanzas state the problem; the next four embody a negative reaction to it; the final three a positive."[17] Jerome Christensen and Peter Manning provide compelling psychodynamic readings of the myth grounded in what the former calls "the potential for tragedy in the relations of child and father" (Christensen 53). In both essays the child's turn from the light of his divinely paternal origins to pursue human maturity has inescapable Oedipal resonances which create striking psychological tensions in the myth. The disturbances they discern are surely present, but the reading I offer places the problematical elements of the myth under more conscious control of the poet, as part of his rhetorical movement.

As I stated earlier, stanzas V–VIII of the Ode provide a mythic overlay for the personal experience presented in I–IV. Their function is repetitive rather than developmental. By selectively incorporating the phenomena of the earlier stanzas into a myth of origins, in which human loss is divinely, systematically, and irreversibly determined, stanzas V–VIII intensify the despair which had closed the poem in 1802. Each of the stanzas ends in a downward turn that echoes more and more ominously the crisis expressed two years before. Stanza V establishes the journey through life which ends in the loss of the celestial light. Stanza VI determines the complicity of earth in the process of loss. Stanza VII trivializes the adult world into which the child educates himself. And stanza VIII, having placed all its hopes in the child himself, finds the child a distant and inadequate intercessory figure. The myth has converted a difficulty into an impossibility, creating a nadir of despondency lower than any Coleridge reaches in the Verse Letter and "Dejection." In Coleridge's poems human circumstances and human error have combined to extinguish an inner light. The situation is grim but potentially reversible, and it is singular rather than universal. Wordsworth's myth has created an understanding of the human condition which seems to offer no way out. If "The Leech-Gatherer" and "Resolution and Independence" had attempted to counter Coleridge's despair by trivializing it, the Ode attempts the more remarkable task of countering it by intensifying it. The myth attempts the darkest possible reading of the Ode's early stanzas. It does not hasten recovery but impedes it, and finally makes that recovery the more significant by increasing the enormity of the obstacles that have been overcome.

With Coleridge's sonnet of 1796, Wordsworth's work on *The Prelude* through 1804, and his own opening stanzas of 1802, we have gathered more than enough "sources" to explain the elaboration of the poem in 1804. One need not hypothesize a Wordsworth who undertook a crash course in Plato, Origen, Plotinus, Porphyry, Proclus, Ficino, Henry More, Joseph Glanvil, Henry Vaughan, and Thomas Taylor the Platonist in order to discover the intellectual resources for the completion of his poem. On the other hand, in articulating his myth Wordsworth was entering an extended and perplexed tradition of discourse on the relations of the body and the soul. We cannot begin to assess the precise function of the myth in the Ode without some basic understanding of its place in cultural history. Belief in the pre-existence of the soul is a piece of heterodoxy which by Wordsworth's time had survived numerous attempts to suppress it. Because both the appeals of the doctrine and its consequences are curiously static, entering into the discourse at one cultural moment is very much like entering at any other. I will explore only two of its important historical manifestations, which range between the improbable and probable as Wordsworthian sources, but are illuminating as revelations of the terms of this discursive tradition.

The version of pre-existence which Wordsworth offers does not come down from ancient times. While it smacks of the metempsychotic beliefs of archaic and largely Eastern religions, it differs from them in limiting the soul's journey to a single cycle. The soul comes from afar, enters into the body, and (implicitly) returns somewhere upon the body's death. Wordsworth's version is the most Westernized, most Christianized form of the doctrine. The conflict between East and West is already apparent in Plato's *Phaedo*, in which the pre-existence of the soul is established dialectically and is then used as the basis for arguing for the survival of the soul after death. The dialogue ends with a wholly poetic and wholly undemonstrated myth of the metempsychotic travails of the soul, which, unless it has perfected itself in its most recent incarnation, will have to be scrubbed up and sent back for another attempt. That which is philosophical in the *Phaedo*, that which has been demonstrated to serve as the basis for further argumentation, is an ideal pre-existence for the individual soul. The dialogue's further speculations on metempsychosis are cultural baggage provided by Pythagorean beliefs and Orphic mystery cults, and they have the same relationship to systematic philosophy as Pindaric myths—none. We need not bow before dialectic, but we should acknowledge that Plato confers ontological privilege upon the pre-existence alone, and that this privilege governs further manifestations of the myth in the Christian West.

The myth Wordsworth presents was first articulated by Origen (c. 185–253). Thus it is not only coincident with Christianity, it is also crucial to the formation of Christian belief during one of the most vital ages of the development of its doctrines, the third century. At Alexandria in the time of Origen, Christianity began its complex, occasionally treacherous, but enormously productive encounter with Greek speculation. According to Johannes Quasten, the intellectual currents of Hellenism, mixed with Oriental, Egyptian, and Jewish cultures, created an appropriate cradle for systematic theology: "When Christianity entered the city at the end of the first century it came in close contact with all of these elements. As a result there sprang up that strong interest in problems of an abstract nature that led to the foundation of a theological school. . . . The environment in which it developed gave it its distinctive characteristics, predominant interest in the metaphysical investigation of the content of the faith, a leaning to the philosophy of Plato, and the allegorical interpretation of Sacred Scripture."[18] If the interests of Alexandria sound like those of Coleridge, it is no accident: Thomas McFarland places Coleridge theologically "in the counter-tradition of Origen" rather than the mainstream of western theology articulated by St. Augustine.[19]

Origen's most important surviving writings on the soul are found in *First Principles*, written at Alexandria between 220 and 230, known to us almost entirely through a free adaptation in Latin by Rufinus (c. 345–410). Quasten calls it "the first Christian system of theology and the first manual of dogma" (57). Origen's project is nothing less than the reconciliation of two kinds of truth, the truth of biblical text and the truth available through the highest mode of intellectual inquiry, which was to him Platonic dialectic. Origen posits, obliquely and hesitantly in Rufino's adaptation, that human souls are fallen angelic souls. The clearly observable differences in humankind are attributable to the kind and degree of error in their prior angelic existences. Those celestial beings who fell too far for incarnation in human form became devils and demons:

> . . . certain beings who fell away from that one beginning of which we have spoken, have sunk to such a depth of unworthiness and wickedness as may be deemed altogether undeserving of that training and instruction by which the human race, while in the flesh, are trained and instructed with the assistance of the heavenly powers; and continue, on the contrary, in a state of enmity and opposition to those who are receiving this instruction and teaching. And hence it is that the whole of this mortal life is full of struggles and trials, caused by the opposition and enmity of those who fell from a better condition without at all looking back, and who are called the devil and his angels, and the other orders of evil, which the apostle classed among the opposing powers.[20]

For Origen the arc of universal history is a fall from primal unity into diversity, which will ultimately be recuperated in a return to unity.

The theological, social, and ethical consequences of Origen's system are readily deduced. Human history and the flesh are devalued so completely that he is finally generous toward error. His vision of the Apokatastasis foresees the "universal restoration of all things in their original, purely spiritual state. . . . Origen does not know any eternal fire or punishment of hell. All sinners will be saved, even the demons and Satan himself will be purified by the Logos. When this has been achieved, Christ's second coming and the resurrection of all men, not in material, but in spiritual bodies, will follow, and God will be all in all."[21] The final optimism of Origen's system is combined with the fierce asceticism characteristic of any philosophy which considers the soul's presence in the flesh to be the result of a cosmic blunder. Origen's most eloquent testimony to his contempt for the flesh is the single act by which he has become best known, his self-emasculation early in his teaching career. His self-mutilation became the cause, or at least the pretext, for successive ecclesiastical calamities: his excommunication from the church of Alexandria and the deprivation of his priesthood.[22]

To an extraordinary degree Origen's contribution to Christian doctrine has been negative, which seems fully appropriate for such a thoroughgoing apostle of the negative way. His assimilation of Christianity and Platonism established an early pole of theoretical symmetry against which the religion has reacted, as Gnosticism and Montanism have repeatedly restaged their perpetual conflict. Although Origen's reputation has been thoroughly rehabilitated in the last century, the controversies surrounding him began virtually at the outset of his teaching career and climaxed with the anathematization of his teachings by the Synod of Constantinople in 543, which holds as the first of its fifteen articles: "If anyone maintains the legendary pre-existence of souls and the fanciful apocastasis (restitution of all things), let him be anathema."[23] In the wake of the anathematization of Origen's teachings came the loss of most of his prolific works, which survive in patches and fragments, primarily through quotations in the writings of others.

My purpose here has not been to suggest that because the early church had discredited pre-existence, Wordsworth could not have credited it. Rather, I have wanted to bring forward tensions in the doctrine's initial formulation which we have already seen at work in Wordsworth's Ode. The belief is inevitably hostile to the flesh, the senses, and to the material creation. It engenders a religion of withdrawal, asceticism, and contemplation, severely limited in its ability to value the human life lived in time. The doctrine of pre-existence is the product of a hunger for absolutes that threatens always to extinguish the present. If we push Origen's system one step further, the entire history of humankind, including the advent of Christ, becomes little more than a stain on the white radiance of eternity.

Two elements of Wordsworth's myth clearly missing in Origen are a sense of the soul's yearning for its individual past existence with God and a wholly non-Platonic conferral of privilege upon childhood. These feelings are at the center of the experience of the Cambridge Platonists, the group of religious writers with whom Wordsworth's Ode has most often been associated.[24] Henry Vaughan may stand for the school as its greatest poet, and as a writer with whom Wordsworth was almost certainly acquainted. "The Retreate" is the poem closest to the myth of Wordsworth's Ode:

> Happy those early dayes! when I
> Shin'd in my Angell-infancy.
> Before I understood this place
> Appointed for my second race,
> Or taught my soul to fancy ought
> But a white, Celestiall thought.[25]

Vaughan too conceives life as a journey, during the early stages of which the "bright-face" of God can still be glimpsed and nature has a profound fascination: "on some *gilded Cloud*, or *flowre* / My gazing soul would dwell an houre" (11–12). In childhood the "weaker glories" of natural phenomena still reflect "Some shadows of eternity" (14). Like Wordsworth, Vaughan praises the time "Before I taught my tongue to wound / My Conscience with a sinfull sound" (15–16), although it is not clear whether he condemns language itself or only its misuse. Vaughan differs profoundly from Wordsworth in the resolution of his poem, with its longing "to travell back / And tread again that ancient track" (21–22): the way out is for Vaughan the way back:

> Some men a forward motion love,
> But I by backward steps would move,
> And when this dust falls to the urn
> In that state I came return.
>
> (29–32)

For Vaughan's poem, the goal of adult life is to elide itself. These words could well have concluded Wordsworth's Ode after stanza VIII, but they do not, and nothing like them does.

The dangers of Vaughan's religious system appear clearly in a lesser-known work, "Childe-hood," which is more obviously a part of the cultural polemic in which the Cambridge Platonists were immersed, the struggle with Puritanism—Gnostics and Montanists, once more face to face. It begins much like "The Retreate":

> I cannot reach it; and my striving eye
> Dazzles at it, as at eternity.
>   Were now that Chronicle alive,
> Those white designs which children drive,
> And the thoughts of each harmless hour,
> With their content too in my pow'r,
> Quickly would I make my path even,
> And by meer playing go to Heaven.
>
> (357; 1–8)

As Leah Sinanoglou Marcus has demonstrated so splendidly, "meer playing" was not an innocent diversion in the England of the seventeenth century. Earlier poets than Vaughan—Herbert, Herrick, and Crashaw—had taken the Puritan charge of childishness as a mark of honor, developing an aesthetic theology of play to counterpoint puritan earnestness, while simultaneously celebrating the innocence of an earlier England, imagined free of doctrinal wrangling.[26] Marcus gives us in Vaughan a deeply conservative Anglican whose poetic career was centered in the Interregnum, and who looks back upon his childhood and its creeds as a lost Eden (153–55). In the midst of the nightmare of history, Vaughan fixes his attention on earliest experience:

> How do I study now, and scan
> Thee, more than ere I studied man,
> And onely see through a long night
> Thy edges and thy bordering light!
> O for thy Center and mid-day!
> For sure that is the *narrow way*.
>
> (39–44)

For Vaughan the anathematic doctrine of Puritanism has usurped the world of Christian effort, the straight and narrow way, leaving as the soul's only recourse withdrawal and nostalgic meditation upon innocence. The doctrine seems adequate for the salvation of the self, but only at the price of renouncing life in historical time. For Wordsworth, the contrast between Vaughan's position and the stance of Milton after the Restoration would have been only too obvious. Stripped of a role in his country's affairs, blind, and impoverished, Milton did not retire to lament the passing of the golden age of the Saints: he went on to publish *Paradise Lost, Paradise Regained*, and *Samson Agonistes*.

Over a century and a half of commentary has had one salutary effect upon the reading of Wordsworth's Ode: it has moved the major crux and major turn of the poem from the conclusion of stanza IV to the conclusion of stanza VIII. If like Bloom we have become fairly secure of the fit between the quasi-personal experience of I–IV and the myth of V–VIII (perhaps more secure than we should be), we still have difficulties with the rhetorical turn from the death of custom to the outburst of joy which begins stanza IX:

> O joy that in our embers
> Is something that doth live
> That nature yet remembers
> What was so fugitive.
>
> (130–34)

Discussion of this passage and the remainder of the poem must begin from two frequently neglected accounts of the Ode by Stuart M. Sperry, Jr., and Kenneth R. Johnston, which reflect upon the role memory plays in the poem.[27]

For Sperry the Ode's most paradoxical quality is that its ultimate affirmations "spring not from any force of memory (in its active, conventional sense) but out of that very consciousness of obliteration with which the poem begins" (43–44). "At the risk of forcing paradox to its limit," Sperry adds, "one might say that the type of recollection celebrated in the 'Intimations Ode' is more the memory of a memory than a memory" (45). Johnston's readjustment and extension of Sperry's argument insists that the paradox be pushed further to acknowledge that Wordsworth is finding strength in "a memory of forgetting" (60): "a recollection that one has forgotten is something, even if one cannot remember *what* one has forgotten, and ultimately, after much pain, confusion, and regret, Wordsworth comes round to asserting that this 'something,' this memory of a process of loss, is the fulcrum which enables him to lift the freezing weight of custom . . . off his soul and celebrate" (62).

The Sperry/Johnston reading of the function of memory in the Ode is fundamentally correct. What is fascinating is the problem such a reading creates for a positive valuation of Wordsworth's central myth. Although Sperry proclaims the "extraordinary relevance of the doctrine" (43) to Wordsworth's original dilemma, he gives us a poem that accomplishes no more with the myth than it could have accomplished without it. Johnston's near dismissal of the myth is more forthright: "If the Ode is the radically humanist poem it seems to be, the myth must be a metaphor, nothing more. . . . The genius of the poem is its deriving gain from the felt reality of the loss (as Sperry has shown), and not from an outside source" (63–64). My own proposal for the role of the myth in the Ode offers a more sweeping solution to the problem which their readings and others, including those by Trilling, Bloom, Manning, and Christensen, have uncovered. The expression of joy which begins stanza IX is not created by the mythic exploration of the human condition which immediately precedes it. Within the logic which governs the poem, this—its genuine prayer of praise—has always been available. What the poet has required all along is not so much an ontology of the soul as a phenomenology of the memory, some way of rereading loss as gain without denying the profound emotional upheaval created by those feelings of loss. Such a phenomenology has to be strong enough to stand up to the possibility of the myth of pre-existence, which with all its dire consequences is only suspended rather than denied, but not so powerful as to trivialize the emotional waverings which have called it forth.

Wordsworth is most concerned in stanza IX to avoid the cosmic hyperbole of his preceding stanza. Stanza IX sees the child not as a "Seer blest" but as a fellow participant in a process of loss. Adult memory is figured as a dying fire in which "something" lives which has always been dying, through which nature can recall its "fugitive" emotions and perceptions. Despite the catalogue of lights which has pervaded the poem, the fire is a new figure. It simultaneously internalizes the source of the light and binds together childhood and adulthood, which were divided in the opening stanzas and juxtaposed antinomously in the myth. Even if the child's memory is conceived as the fire, and the adult's as its embers, the two are one, and their workings are identical. Given the terms of the poetic dialogue we have been tracing, it is crucial that Wordsworth's consolatory movement has settled upon an internally located figure as its final source of illumination. Coleridge had claimed that the soul must provide its own source of light, and Wordsworth is here providing that light through the power of memory to recall strength through the feeling of loss.

The stanza's claim that "The thought of our past years in me doth breed / Perpetual benedictions" (134–35) rings strangely, when we recollect that the originating occasion of the poem had in fact been a "thought of our past years" which had bred despair, and that the memorabilia of that past, the idealized spring landscape with its lambs and shepherd-boys, mother and child, had not only proved powerless to offer relief but had intensified the sense of loss. Again, though, Wordsworth declines easy consolation: if he will not offer the memory as anything more substantial than embers, he will not praise the readily apparent virtues of childhood. His benedictions are

> not indeed
> For that which is most worthy to be blest
> Delight and liberty the simple creed

Of childhood whether fluttering or at rest
With new-born hope for ever in his breast.
(135–39)

Instead, he will "raise / The song of thanks and praise" (140–41) for

those blank misgivings of a Creature
Moving about in worlds not realized
High instincts before which our mortal nature
Did tremble like a guilty thing surprized
. . . for those first affections
Those shadowy recollections.
(142–47)

In bringing forward for praise these attributes of childhood, Wordsworth's syntax is ambiguous. It is unclear whether his catalogue is additive or appositional, whether we should distinguish among "blank misgivings," "High instincts," "first affections," and "shadowy recollections" or collapse them into one another as manifestions of one phenomenenon. They jointly differ from the slightly earlier list—"Delight," "liberty," "creed," and "hope"—in that they are so fully experiential, so inseparable from the child's perceptual transactions with his surroundings. They are part of the actual experience of childhood rather than its hypothetical essence. Further, the first and last of the transactions, "blank misgivings" and "shadowy recollections," are clearly experiences of loss. The "High instincts" are compromised by the echo of the response of Hamlet's father's ghost to the crowing of the cock: "it started like a guilty thing / Upon a fearful summons."[28] Understood as an expression of appositional relationships, the syntax itself conjoins loss and gain, with the powers of childhood, its "high instincts" and "first affections," becoming the other side of its sense of displacement and loss.

Although the psychological phenomena which Wordsworth praises are partially derived from his myth of origins, without which "those blank misgivings of a Creature / Moving about in worlds not realized" and "Those shadowy recollections" would not be fully readable, the entire list is equally applicable to the psychological situation with

which the poem began in 1802, when the adult poet was perplexed
by similar phenomena. Adult and child are enlightened and dis-
turbed by the same faculty, so that

> Those shadowy recollections
> Which be they what they may
> Are yet the fountain-light of all our day
> Are yet the master light of all our seeing
> Uphold us cherish us and make
> Our noisy years seem moments in the being
> Of the eternal silence truths that wake
> To perish never
> Which neither listlessness nor mad endeavour
> Nor man nor Boy,
> Nor all that is at enmity with joy
> Can utterly abolish or destroy.
>
> (147–58)

The affective reversal of the poem's response to light could hardly be
more complete. For eight stanzas it has lamented, with variations,
the displacement of the celestial light by the light of common day.
Now it understands "the fountain-light of all our day" (not just its
dawn) and the "master light of all our seeing" (not just the child's)
to be "Those shadowy recollections" which are the glowing embers
of memory. All that has divided child and man has been united
through this faculty, the source of whose contents—"be they what
they may"—is not nearly so important as the fact of their existence.
With this dismissing gesture the Ode places its great myth in its
proper perspective. The myth is reduced to a speculative instrument
which has helped to uncover a truth more fundamental than the teleological certitudes it announced, which need no longer be credited,
and even if credited lose their destructive force. The memory does
not destroy human time—the desire of stanzas V–VIII—but has the
power to suspend it temporarily, to "make / Our noisy years *seem*
moments in the being of the eternal silence" (emphasis added). If
human development and aging are not unmitigated goods, they have
lost the destructive power with which they were earlier endowed.
The truths retained in the memory are imperishable, with an endur-

ance that none of our prevalent human failings, "neither listlessness nor mad endeavour / . . . Nor all that is at enmity with joy / Can utterly abolish or destroy." The poem has discovered its foundation for security in a faculty which is failing, and which has always been failing.

Stanza IX ends with a description of the act of memory:

> Hence in a season of calm weather
> Though inland far we be
> Our souls have sight of that immortal sea
> Which brought us hither
> Can in a moment travel thither
> And see the children sport upon the shore
> And hear the mighty waters rolling evermore.
>
> (159–65)

Memory acts constructively here rather than reconstructively, creating a scene of arrival to which the poem has not previously borne witness. Although memory is conceived as a voluntary power, the activity described also glosses the opening stanzas of the Ode. Its initiating, involuntary memory, then understood as a debilitating feeling of pure loss, has brought the poet to his current understanding. Even painful memory can be redemptive. To repeat Johnston's formulation, the "genius of the poem lies in its deriving gain from the felt reality of loss" (64).

Readers who have been fully attentive to the paradoxical nature of Wordsworth's emotional claims in the Ode have struggled to find some intertextual warrant for them, whether poetic, psychological, or religious. Most frequently their offerings have been anachronistic. For example, Johnston brings forward a poem by Jorge Luis Borges which explores a similar paradox: "Having known Latin and forgotten it / Remains a possession." As Johnston remarks, "both 'having known' and 'having . . . forgotten' are present possessions. Borges reinforces the ambiguity with an image of the inextricable unity of remembering and forgetting: 'forgetting is memory's dim cellar, one of its forms, / the other secret face of the coin' " (60). As Johnston goes on to reflect, even Cleanth Brooks had not pushed the Ode's paradoxism so far: "His Wordsworth may sound a bit like Donne,

but a Wordsworth who joys in the recollection of a forgetting sounds
more like Oscar Wilde—or Borges" (61).

For the past half-century intertextual commentary on the myth of
the Ode has gravitated toward the works and thought of Freud.
Lionel Trilling's powerful Freudian reading of the Ode, which first
appeared in 1941, has retained enough vitality to become newly controversial. Its anachronistic premises have been called into question
by Helen Vendler, who has offered one of the few recent global readings of the poem, and Vendler's argument has since been answered
by Jeffrey Robinson.[29] The biases of my study have been apparent in
its reliance on the readings of Bloom, Christensen, and Manning,
who take their warrants from Trilling even in disagreement. Fry calls
in the testimony of Otto Rank and Carl Jung as well. Psychodynamic
readings of the poem have had the enormous advantage of taking it
seriously as a human document, in all its confusions and perplexities.
Further, the very dialectical nature of the Ode, its questionings and
answerings, its seeking the source of present pains in past joys, finding those past joys to have themselves been pains, and then discovering the process of exploring pain to have been therapeutically
redemptive, reminds us inevitably of the talking cure.

Still, Freud's was not the first phenomenology of the memory, and
we might do well to seek analogues for Wordsworth's claims somewhat earlier in civilization's exploration of the psyche. While it is
more dubious as a Wordsworthian source than as a Borgesian source,
St. Augustine's *Confessions* is the locus classicus for the paradox of
memory that Wordsworth is exploring.[30] Although the story of Augustine's conversion to Christianity and baptism by Ambrose in 387
is too well known to need lengthy recapitulation, some discussion of
the religion to which he adhered from 373 until 382, Manichaeism,
will be useful, because it reveals the same set of problems—greatly
intensified—encountered in the theology of Origen. For our purposes the most important element of Manichaeism was its insistence
that the soul exists before and survives the flesh. The soul is light
which is buried in the darkness of the flesh during life on earth, and
its particles of light yearn to be free. Samuel N. C. Lieu cites the
following lines from an extant Coptic Manichaean psalm, which
sound like a gloss for stanza VI of Wordsworth's Ode:

The strangers with whom I mixed, me they knew not;
they tasted my sweetness, they desired to keep me with them.
I am life to them, but they were death to me.[31]

The Christology which proceeds from these understandings is pre-
dictably heterodox. The Christ of the Manichaeans

> was not a degraded, suffering saviour but a gnostic redeemer who
> imparted special wisdom to those who had been initiated into the
> faith. . . . He never experienced human birth as the notions of
> physical conception and birth filled the Manichaeans with horror
> and the Christian doctrine of the virgin birth was regarded as
> equally obscene. . . . The suffering, death, and resurrection of
> this Jesus were in appearance only as they had no salvific value but
> were an *exemplum* of the suffering and eventual deliverance of
> the human soul and a prefiguration of Mani's own martyrdom. The
> pain suffered by the imprisoned Light Particles in the whole of the
> visible universe, on the other hand, was real and immanent. (Lieu
> 126–27)

It is against this background of absolute gnostic dualism, with its
devotion to the soul and unmitigated enmity with the flesh, that we
must read Augustine's analysis of the memory, fully aware of the
dangers inherent in his addressing at all the faculty which since Plato
had been considered the doorway to gnosis.

Augustine's analysis begins at the conclusion of his narrative
proper. Memory becomes a second creation, containing the whole of
the first, simultaneously accessible in all its sensory, emotional, and
intellectual aspects. As Augustine works his way through the capacious lands of memory, moving up the ladder of perfection reaching
from memories of sensation to memories of "the reasons and innu-
merable laws of numbers and dimensions, none of which any bodily
sense impresses,"[32] it seems that a slight and inevitable movement
will take him to the theory of Platonic reminiscence, a doctrine
which he had silently rejected two years after his baptism and
replaced with his characteristic teaching of individual divine illumination.[33] Instead, the paradoxical fact that the memory can remember oblivion moves him to consider the relationship between

remembering and forgetting. "When the memory itself loses some-thing," he asks, "as happens when we forget and try to remember, pray, where do we look for it, unless in the memory itself? And in it, if one thing is presented in place of another, we reject it until the thing we are looking for turns up. When it does turn up, we say: 'This is it.' We would not say that unless we recognized it, and we would not recognize it unless we remembered it. Yet we certainly had forgotten it" (*Confessions* 288). Perhaps, he offers, forgetting is only partial. The thing disappears, but its absence is felt. If some-thing is "entirely wiped out of mind, then we do not remember even when reminded. And, if we even remember that we have forgotten it, then we have not yet completely forgotten" (288).

The consequence of this paradox for Augustine's search for the knowledge of God is clear. All men, he holds, seek the happy life. Some are happy in reality, some in the anticipation of hope, and some in neither way. "Still, unless this third kind of people possessed it, in some way, they would not desire to be happy; that they have such a desire is most certain. Somehow or other they came to know it, and so they possess it in some kind or other of knowledge" (289). If this knowledge is in the memory, as Augustine decides it must be, "then we were at one time happy, either all individually, or all in that man who was the first to sin, in whom also we all died, from whom we are all born amidst unhappiness" (289–90). The unhappiness of life becomes a token of a happiness once experienced in and felt through the flesh by the individual or by Adam. It provides the reminder that something is missing, and the proof that something better existed, which can again be experienced in life. The human life lived in time has been worth living, because its experience has been a source of knowledge, and its travails have been worth Augustine's telling. The concluding three books of the *Confessions* constitute a rapt commen-tary on the creation, as it is recorded in Genesis, with glowing praise for the God who could and did make this world. Augustine could not have found a more fitting way to express his repudiation of the Manichaeism of his early manhood, which had wholly rejected the creation, the creator, and the barbarous story of the creation alike.

I have adduced Augustine's text to demonstrate that the gnostic tendencies of Wordsworth's myth and the gnostic beliefs of Augus-tine's youth pose nearly identical problems for a positive valuation of human experience, and that the paradoxes of memory through which they redeem the faculty from its gnostic allegiances, which antedate not only Mani but Plato, are harmonious. We know very little about Wordsworth's theological and philosophical reading, but we know a great deal about his reading of Milton, whose conception of original sin and the fall of man is closely allied to Augustine's.[34] Indeed, one of Augustine's major contributions to Christian doctrine, echoed by Milton throughout *Paradise Lost*, was to differentiate the severity of Adam's sin, which led to the fall of man, from the greater sin which led to the defection of the rebel angels.[35] It makes an enormous difference for the perception of human existence whether man's Fall was from angelic and heavenly or from human and terrestrial bliss. When Wordsworth rescues the despised flesh from its Origenist entrapment, he does so largely through a secularized version of the fortunate fall, a paradox with which he was well acquainted. His recourse to it would have been as much a matter of cultural habit as of religious belief.

By the conclusion of stanza IX Wordsworth is able to turn once more to the scene he had created in 1802 in stanzas III and IV, deriving from that earlier landscape a strikingly different emotional response:

> Then sing ye Birds sing sing a joyous song
> And let the young lambs bound
> As to the tabor's sound!
> We in thought will join your throng
> Ye that pipe and ye that play
> Ye that through your hearts to day
> Feel the gladness of the May.
>
> (166–72)

Because Wordsworth takes up the original scene as it had existed before his disrupting "thought of grief" (22), he diminishes once more the role played in the poem by the acute cycle of depression—recovery—depression traced in stanzas III and IV. The first three lines of stanza X simultaneously echo and revise the parallel lines of stanza III. In the earlier section the creatures had constituted the occasional backdrop for the scene of the poet's emotional waverings

("*Now while* the Birds thus sing a joyous song / And *while* the young lambs bound / As to the tabor's sound" (19–21) [emphases added]). The "Then" which begins the direct address to the birds and lambs obliquely takes temporal priority over the earlier "Now," but it also specifies causality. As a consequence of the discoveries made in the poem the creatures may, in the recreated "now" of the new address, go about their creaturely business without calling forth once more the poet's lamentations.

Most noticeably missing in the revised scene is anything more than a faint reminder of the pastoral fantasy which Wordsworth had developed in stanzas III and IV as attempted compensation for the loss of the celestial light: we have no "Child of joy" (33), no "happy Shepherd boy" (35), no "jubilee" (38) or "festival" (39), no "coronal" (40), and no "Babe" leaping "up in his Mother's arm" (49). This earlier elaborate catalogue is collapsed into a "throng," composed of

> Ye that pipe and ye that play
> Ye that through your hearts today
> Feel the gladness of the May.
> (170–72)

No more is claimed for the implied children of this stanza than what they are, happy children at play, from whom the poet is necessarily distant. The throng is "your throng," not his. His identification is with another group: "We in thought." The phrase which identifies the "We" teeters between adjectival and adverbial functions: "We [who are] in thought" are to be distinguished by that quality from those children at play who are not; yet it is only "in thought" that "We" may "join" their "throng" at all.

Wordsworth does not attempt to diminish the power of the of the "visionary gleam" he had regretted losing. He makes no efforts to convert it into a misapprehension, as he had done with the force of poetic vision in "Resolution and Independence." This time he faces his loss for what it has been:

> What though it be past the hour
> Of splendour in the grass, of glory in the flower,
>   We will grieve not, rather find

> Strength in what remains behind;
> In the soothing thoughts that spring
>   Out of human suffering;
>   In the faith that looks through death;
> In years that bring the philosophic mind.
>   (173–80)

Wordsworth's description of the time of vision could not be stronger or more moving. The synecdochic vividness of "splendour in the grass" and "glory in the flower" is at least as compelling as the language of loss in stanzas I and II. Nor could his strategy of consolation be much plainer. The poem opens two possibilities for confronting the undeniable fact of the loss of a treasured time. The poem had explored the response of grief in its opening stanzas, building upon this foundation its mythic edifice of loss. The second possibility is finding "Strength in what remains behind," just as the memory of a forgetting has remained after the memory has itself has faded to where its existence can be discerned only through a vague feeling of deprivation. The same formulation, through which gain may be found in loss, without any claim that it is caused by or derives from loss, appears in the consolation to be found in "soothing thoughts that spring / Out of human suffering." We are not dealing here with a necessary causal relationship but with a psychological possibility that in and after suffering there is some overflow, some excess, from which soothing thoughts may spring.

Perhaps the best gloss for stanza X of the Ode is Book XII of *Paradise Lost*. Adam has been taken to the top of the mountain by Michael, who has unfolded for him the future of mankind, all determined by and through his and Eve's primal disobedience. Michael's story begins with the murder of Abel and ends with the passion of Christ, with some less savory stretches between. After the purpose of the atonement is revealed to him, Adam responds:

> O goodness infinite, goodness immense,
> That all this good of evil shall produce,
> And evil turn to good, more wonderful
> Than that by which creation first brought forth
> Light out of darkness! full of doubt I stand,

Whether I should repent me now of sin
By me done and occasioned, or rejoice
Much more that much more good thereof shall spring—
To God more glory, more good-will to men
From God.

                                    (12.469–78)

If this is in truth heroic argument, Wordsworth's is no less. The Ode
manages its reconciliations without a revelation on the mount, outside the boundaries of the Eden it has defined, and in the face of a
teleological myth which has threatened to undermine the very foundations of life on earth. It grounds its security in loss, which is surely
guaranteed, and faith, which is based not in the gnostic wisdom of a
divine vision but in the mind that lives in time: "In the faith that
looks through death; / In years that bring the philosophic mind."
Even here, where the poem seems most compatible with doctrinaire
consolations, its lines cut both ways. To see *through* death is either to
see by way and because of death, or to see beyond death, or perhaps
both at once. The comfort to be found in "*years* that bring the philosophic mind" (emphasis added) is offered in the face of the central
myth, which had recoiled in horror at the effects of a solar day and
had depicted maturation as the destructive agency bringing about
the *un*making of the philosopher. A poem which trembled at the
passing of hours has found the strength to embrace years.

   In keeping with its Augustinian and Miltonic affinities, the Ode
closes with a hymn to the creation, precariously counterbalancing the
intense paradisiacal longings with which it had begun:

And Oh! ye fountains meadows fields & groves
   Think not of any severing of our loves
Yet in my heart of hearts I feel your might.
                                    (181–83)

Wordsworth's concluding turn has been held suspect by many of his
most reflective readers. The petition that aspects of nature entertain
no thoughts of separation has seemed a dubious reversal, because all
along it has been the poet who has harbored these thoughts. The

claim that the "might" of the creation is felt in the poet's "heart of hearts" is equally oblique. The poem had begun with a failure of seeing, which could not be recompensed by feeling. Its myth translated the loss of vision into a larger problematic, by attributing the perception of the celestial light to the soul and its fading into earthly light to the soul's immersion in the concerns of the flesh and the world. The loss of the soul was recuperated by steadfast internalization, by the adoption of a mentalist perspective through which memory could retain the soul's vision even in its loss. With the abrupt emergence of the *heart* in the concluding stanza, the site of power—the paradise within—seems to have shifted once more, unless through some tortured periphrasis we are to read the "heart of hearts" as the residence of "the philosphic mind." At the risk of multiplying confusions, the poem does all it can to disperse the experiential sources of redeeming experience. When we recall the faculty warfare of Coleridge's contributions to this dialogue, with seeing pitted so firmly against feeling, outward beauty against inward joy, and imaginative strength against intellective activity, perhaps Wordsworth's strategy becomes more comprehensible. His perplexing shifts transgress boundaries, demonstrating that binomial taxonomies of human experience can only exacerbate divisions of the self.

The poem's claim of a renewed response to the material creation receives an even stronger statement:

> I only have relinquished one delight
> To live beneath your more habitual sway.
> (184–85)

"One delight": all the Ode's phrasings of its lost experience—"celestial light," "the visionary gleam," "the glory and the dream," "splendour in the grass"—are finally subsumed in this phrase. One delight must be one among many. The trace of regret which keeps the poem honest is transferred from the object lost to the last verb which describes the process of loss: "relinquished." Relinquishment is a voluntary act, but it carries connotations of compulsion. One relinquishes a sword, or a throne, or an entitlement only because the consequences of retaining them are worse than surrendering them. Even the adverb "only" jars against the connotative force of the verb. The purpose of this relinquishment is to "live beneath" the "more habitual sway" of natural things. Wordsworth turns necessity into choice, claiming an option which the poem has not illustrated. Or perhaps it has. One may not be able to choose to retain the celestial light, but he may choose to continue living under its sway by rejecting every human feeling that is not consonant with it. Indeed, the entire mythic movement of the Ode has displayed the potentially destructive human consequences of unwavering fealty to the light. The poem's choice is the "habitual sway" of the natural order, of *time* instead of "a time." By embracing habit, Manning has pointed out, Wordsworth accommodates "himself to the two conflicting demands upon him, the sense of an imperious immortality brooding over him like a master over a slave, and the 'custom' of ordinary adult existence."[36] The poem's final emphasis is on the latter demand.

The Ode has one remaining rhetorical task. It has claimed that memory can revivify the very experience which it has itself brought into question, and it has faced again the spring landscape which had set into motion its feelings of loss. The declaration of continuing response and love, though, must be demonstrated as compellingly as the earlier sense of deprivation. This demonstration is the burden of the next movement of the stanza:

> I love the brooks which down their channels fre[t?]
> > Even more than when I tripped lightly as the[y?]
> > The Innocent brightness of a new-born day
> > > Is lovely yet
> The clouds that gather round the setting [sun]
> Do take a sober colouring from an eye
> That hath kept watch o'er man's mortality:
> Another race hath been, and other palms are w[on?].
>
> > > > (186–93)

The poem offers here a reading, or rereading, of two objects of nature, the brook and the sun, both of which have figured importantly in its development.

The "brook," the more oblique of the two images, circles back to the "stream" (1), the last specific object cited in the opening catalogue of common sights which had lost their celestial splendor. Its voice was also heard in the poem's shortlived burst of recovered enthusiasm in stanza III: "The cataracts blow their trumpets from the steep" (25). And of course its earthly destination was implied in the memory/vision of children at play by the shores of "that immortal sea / Which brought us hither" (161–62). Memory's ability to hear the sea's "mighty waters rolling evermore" (165) had itself echoed the earlier trumpet-call of the waterfalls. What the final image of the brook does is reconnect the two disparate auditory images, linking the sounds of origin and destiny. It also insists on the importance of the unspectacular middle of the journey, which had lacked the prestige of beginnings and endings and from which "The glory and the freshness of a dream" (5) had vanished. If the cataracts are origins in a physical sense, and the sea is at once terminal physically and original symbolically, the brooks are medial. They "fret" down their channels, gnawing at the banks which, as they restrict their flow, also give them shape and direction. The verb echoes the lines from stanza VII about the four-year-old child, "Fretted by sallies of his Mother's kisses" (88) which similarly induct him into the world of human emotion and give his life shape and direction. The same tension exists between contained and container—water and channel, spirit and flesh—but now the tension is benign rather than destructive. The poet loves the brooks "Even more than when I tripped lightly as the[y]" (187).

Wordsworth's second image of newfound perception works even more strongly with earlier and more problematical sections of the poem. A tribute to the "setting sun" had been absent from the catalogue of lights of stanza II, where the only reference to direct sunlight had been a description of sunrise: "The sunshine is a glorious birth" (16). Given the logic of that personification, sunset could then have been at best a glorious death, too painful an analogue to the "glory" that has passed "away . . . from the earth" (18) even to be entertained. The poem echoes in its final stanza its earlier perception, "The innocent brightness of a new-born day / Is lovely yet," making even more manifest the personification of the earlier figure. The setting sun is now surrounded by clouds, echoing those "clouds of glory" (64) surrounding "our life's star"(59) at its rising in this life, which of course had been hypothesized as its setting in another. The clouds now "take a sober colouring from an eye / That hath kept watch o'er man's mortality." The eye, which had been bereft of a quality of light at the beginning of the poem, is now its origin, adding a "colouring" to the scene. Because adulthood has its proper vision, the child can no longer be the sole "eye among the blind" (111). Because the newly created coloration is called "sober," those earlier lamentations for a vanished light had implictly lacked that quality, which can, after all, only be supplied by thought. Further, the eye which has continued to live in time ("hath kept watch") has been able to keep "watch o'er mans mortality," which had been invisible to the child. In Wordsworth's interpretation of the sunset, mortality itself becomes not defeat but victory: "Another race hath been, and other palms are w[on]." Wordsworth's images tend, like all figures drawn from the natural world, to naturalize his consolation. But his meanings here are humanly imposed rather than inevitable. Nothing in the phenomenon of the sunset insists that it be interpreted as a sign of victory. To the contrary, Coleridge's Verse Letter and "Dejection" offer readings of the figure which are more "natural"—that is to say, which have a broader cultural warrant.

Manning's meditation upon Wordsworth's reading of his sunset figure is superb:

> The Christian resonance accords with the language of transcendence running throughout the poem: it strengthens, for example, the echoes . . . of I Corinthians 9:24–25: "Know ye not that they which run in a race run all, but one receiveth the prize? So run, that ye may obtain. And every man that striveth for the mastery is temperate in all things. Now they *do it* to obtain a corruptible crown; but we an incorruptible."
>
> I would argue nonetheless that the indirectness of the reference to Scripture is as important to the success of the poem as the reference itself. . . . It is noteworthy that although the ode is replete with declarations of the "truths that wake, / To perish never," such assertions are absent from the final stanza. If the concluding movement of elegy is consolation, then it is the restraint of

Wordsworth's final affirmations that is remarkable. . . . The poem exploits the resonances of Christian faith without committing itself to belief, to the conviction that would lessen its human uncertainty.[37]

In addition, behind this strongly Christian resonance is a strong pagan resonance. The "race" takes the Ode back to its generic origins in the victory songs of Pindar. However, the victory is not just an individual human accomplishment of individual salvation. "Race" tugs both ways, as agonistic contest and as a term for the human species, and it was precisely the role of the human race that had been most dangerously threatened by the Ode's central myth.

What Wordsworth's two figures, based upon the journeys of the brook and the sun, have most in common is that their work is accomplished in time. And they can only be valued through time and experience. They do not result from instantaneous apprehension or from visionary insight. They are made things, human things, whose very commonplaceness is a tribute to the experience of the species. What Wordsworth offers at the end of the Ode is not a gnosis but a technos, a way of story-making through reading nature allegorically for evidences that life is worth living. That evidence, the poem goes on to suggest, is not finally provided and proved by the eye, or even the mind, but by the heart, the organ which must live in time, keeping time:

> Thanks to the human heart by which we live
> Thanks to its tenderness its joys and fears
> To me the meanest flower that blows can give
> Thoughts that do often lie too deep for tears.
>
> (194–97)

The operative term in the Ode's closing figure is its verb, "can give." Human response is not automatic: the perceiver may choose to read the blooming flower as a pathetic emblem of his own brief, fragile life, or he may choose to read it as an example of endurance, fortitude, and regeneration. The flower exists only as a potential for a humanly imposed meaning. Its situation is similar to that of the leech-gatherer in "Resolution and Independence," initially envisioned as a victim but reperceived as a hero, except that the earlier figure had helped in his speech to articulate his own revised meaning. The choice is between tears and "Thoughts too . . . deep for tears." Wordsworth chooses the latter, and he has demonstrated through the Ode how the choice may be made in the face of some of the darkest conjectures that human thought has entertained.

Agreeing with Trilling that the Ode is ultimately a victory song, Vendler holds that the power of adulthood it holds forth is not "a new way of feeling." She offers instead:

> If it is truer to say, as I believe it is, that the Ode represents the acquisition of the power of metaphor; that to rest in either splendour of sense or in blank misgivings is not to be a poet; that to join the external world of sense-experience with the interior world of moral consciousness is to become an adult; that to express that juncture in metaphor is to become a poet—then all of Wordsworth's great poetry is the result of the humanizing of sense and the symbolizing of interior experience described by the Ode. (Vendler 84)

Much of my own reading of the conclusion of the Ode accords with Vendler's. It also sees the powers of adulthood demonstrated as well as proclaimed, and demonstrated precisely through the poem's management of its figures. Our difference, which is finally more telling than our similarity, is that my reading cannot rely upon the truth of metaphor.

Charting the intertextual dialogue between Wordsworth and Coleridge demonstrates above all else that metaphor is not sufficient. There is nothing naturally curative or restorative in linguistic arts of analogy, and tracing the relationships between outward sense and inward consciousness can be debilitating, either to the writer or his audiences, as the Ode of 1802, the Verse Letter, "The Leech-Gatherer," "Resolution and Independence," "Dejection," and the Ode of 1804 have all in their various ways shown. Metaphor is no more a redeeming gnosis than imagination, which until recently has been romanticism's savior for all occasions. To deny art—genuine art—its ability to wound is to strip it of its power. What is discovered in the dialogue I have traced is art's responsibility to the larger claims of human life.

In exploring reasons for what she calls Trilling's incapacity to deal with lyric utterance, Vendler cites a sentence from his *On Teaching Modern Literature*: "My own interests . . . lead me to see literary situations as cultural situations, and cultural situations as great elaborate fights about moral issues" (85). Perhaps, she suggests, "he was uneasy with the lyric because it turns inward, away from polemic, away from any explicit concern with those 'great elaborate fights' and away equally from the broad literary effects employed by epic, novel, and satire. . . . One feels that Trilling could never be quite happy with a work that presents itself, as the Ode does, as a history of past and present feeling" (85). Ironically, Vendler's description fits the Ode of 1802 much more closely than the Ode of 1804. She minimizes the completed work's powerful (if messy) engagement with centuries of cultural polemics on the nature of art, the nature of the artist, the nature of society, the nature of truth, and the nature of the soul— virtually everything that distinguishes the poem and its companions in the cycle as central documents of our culture.

9

Conclusion

*A*NY conclusion to a study of intertextual genetics can only be artificial: so long as anyone is moved to write by, about, or against a text, its intertextual life continues. But critical discourses must come to an end, and we might as well call that ending a conclusion, however inconclusive it will be. Let me just sketch a few possibilities for continuing study of this textual cycle and close with some reflections on the relationship of this study to a recent intertextual engagement of Wordsworth's Ode in one of the most highly visible current directions in romantic studies.

Poems cease neither to exercise nor be subject to intertextual forces because they have been completed. Somehow they must make their way into a writer's canon, and each publication or republication of a work creates the possibility, sometimes even the necessity, for a revisionary recontextualization. Canons alter individual poems just as surely as individual poems constitute canons. To choose the most obvious example, the Wordsworth who republished the Ode in his first collected edition of 1815 was not the Wordsworth who had first published it in his *Poems, in Two Volumes* of 1807. In 1814 he had brought out the first major long poem of his maturity, *The Excursion*. Indeed, becoming the author of *The Excursion* had in a sense authorized his collection of his shorter works. We should not be surprised that the Ode is contextualized differently in 1807 and 1815: it remains the concluding poem in each edition, but its epigraphs are changed, its title is altered, and it points to different relationships with its author, with literary tradition, and with the contents of the editions.[1]

More intriguing from the vantage point of this study is the way in which the initial book publication of each of the three poems erases the compositional links scholars have been able to trace among them. Both "Resolution and Independence" and the Ode are first published in the 1807 *Poems*. All indications are that Wordsworth was nervous about putting together this gathering of his shorter pieces. Compared to his aggressive advertisement (1798) and prefaces (1800 and 1802) to *Lyrical Ballads*, his canceled advertisement to the *Poems, in Two Volumes* is remarkably defensive:

> The short Poems, of which these Volumes consist, were chiefly composed to refresh my mind during the progress of a work of length and labour, in which I have for some time been engaged; and to furnish me with employment when I had not resolution to apply myself to that work, or hope that I should proceed with it successfully. Having already, in the Volumes entitled Lyrical Ballads, offered to the World a considerable collection of short poems, I did not wish to add these to the number, till after the completion and publication of my larger work; but, as I cannot even guess when this will be, and as several of the Poems have been circulated in manuscript, I thought it better to send them forth at once. They were composed with much pleasure to my own mind, & I build upon that remembrance to hope that they may afford profitable pleasure to many readers. (*P2V* 541)

We do not know whether Wordsworth dropped this advertisement on economic or diplomatic grounds (see Curtis *P2V* 26–27). If the latter, his move was understandable, because nothing could have been gained by his doing half a negative reviewer's work for him. Few could have resisted the comic temptations presented by an author who does not want to be considered a writer of "short poems," even though he has not published and is not yet ready to bring forth a long work.

Wordsworth's worries about poetic length are undoubtedly genuine, but they probably mask anxieties about responses to his subject matter as well. Of the hundred and fifteen poems included in *Poems, in Two Volumes* only seven exceed a hundred lines in length. Fifty-one are sonnets. Among the poems of middle length, two ("The Kitten and the Falling Leaves" and "The Blind Highland Boy") are—or at least begin as—poems for children; three ("The Horn of Egremont Castle," "Rob Roy's Grave," and "Song, at the Feast of Brougham Castle") are relatively undistinguished exercises in antiquarianism, which would never be one of Wordsworth's happier poetic modes. None of the five would have seemed likely to enhance his reputation as a poet of major themes, and none has.

Wordsworth's pre-emptive defense against charges of poetic minority was to group his poems under larger headings, thereby claiming a coherence and continuity for his efforts. He attempted to turn his works into a work. This strategy would continue, with further elaboration, in the collections he published over the remainder of his life. When Wordsworth began work in June 1806 on assembling his projected collection of shorter poems, he was thinking of a single volume (*P2V* 11–12). Curtis has reconstructed from surviving papers part of the plan for this volume, and among his most interesting revelations is that one of its major divisions was to be called *Resolution and Independence with other Poems* (*P2V* 13). As the planned single volume swelled to two, that category disappeared, and *Poems, in Two Volumes* was intended to be composed of poems distributed into seven categories:

VOLUME I: *The Orchard Pathway* [2]
              Poems Composed during a Tour, Chiefly on Foot
              Sonnets
                 Part the First. Miscellaneous Sonnets
                 Part the Second. Sonnets Dedicated to Liberty
VOLUME II: *Poems Written during a Tour in Scotland*
              Moods of My Own Mind
              The Blind Highland Boy; with Other Poems

Only two of these groupings are self-explanatory. The works in *Sonnets Dedicated to Liberty* constitute a fairly conventional sonnet sequence, united thematically and ordered chronologically. The works in *Poems Composed during a Tour of Scotland* form an itinerary sequence, a form to which Wordsworth would return in later years. The other groupings are idiosyncratic. The first two sections refer to places or circumstances of poetic origin. *The Orchard Pathway* was to be headed by a six-line motto:

> ORCHARD PATHWAY, to and fro,
> Ever with thee, did I go,
> Weaving Verses, a huge store!
> These, and many hundreds more,
> And, in memory of the same,
> This little lot shall bear *Thy Name!*
>   (P2V 63)

Wordsworth's lines here have the tone of *Home at Grasmere*, identifying a set of poems homebodyish in their origins. The following group is conceived as excursionary: "Resolution and Independence" was published as the final poem in *Poems Composed During a Tour, Chiefly on Foot*. The division contained only four other poems, "Beggars," "To a Sky-Lark," "With how sad steps, O Moon, thou climb'st the sky," and "Alice Fell." Not only were these poems not composed during any tour, there are no compelling compositional links among them. The category is no more than a fictive convenience.

The published version of the Ode is isolated both from "Resolution and Independence" and from other productions of the spring of 1802, many of which find their way into the section called *Moods of My Own Mind*. The 1807 table of contents lists the Ode as the last work of the last section of the second volume, *The Blind Highland Boy; with Other Poems*. (The thought of the Ode as some "other poem" subordinant to "The Blind Highland Boy" takes some getting used to.) But in fact the Ode is almost free standing as the final poem in the volumes. At Wordsworth's instructions, it was given a separate title page, bearing only the title "Ode," with the Virgilian epigraph, *Paulo majora canamus*, on the verso (P2V 269–270). Wordsworth's valuation of the poem is clear: it is his summative statement at this point in his career, singing of higher things than the rest of the volume and perhaps gesturing to higher things to come in the future.

Within Wordsworth's design for his volume, the Ode loses all its resonance with "Resolution and Independence." The associations which it does pick up are important for its subsequent recontextualizations in 1815 and thereafter. In *The Blind Highland Boy; with Other Poems*, it is immediately preceded by "Lines Composed at Grasmere, during a walk one Evening after a stormy day, the Author having just read in a Newspaper that the dissolution of Mr. Fox was hourly expected," and "Elegiac Stanzas, Suggested by a Picture of Peele Castle, in a Storm, painted by Sir George Beaumont." Our habit of thinking of the Ode as an elegy begins with this association, intensified in 1815 and after, when the Ode is retitled and again placed last in the collection, following the final category of poems, *Epitaphs and Elegiac Pieces*. Continuing scholarly efforts to read the Ode through the conventions of elegy, a form to which it is only marginally related, testify to the effectiveness of Wordsworth's much-disputed critical classification and arrangement of his poems.

The initial book publication of "Dejection" was delayed ten years behind that of Wordsworth's companion poems. It appeared in 1817 in *Sibylline Leaves*, where it plays a disproportionately small role in Coleridge's presentation of his poetical works. In Coleridge's volume three individual works are distinguished (as Wordsworth's Ode had been) by fly-titles: "The Rime of the Ancient Mariner," which leads off the volume proper; "Fire, Famine, and Slaughter. A War Eclogue"; and "The Three Graves." These longer poems are interspersed among shorter works organized into four categories: *Poems Occasioned by Political Events or Feelings connected with them*, *Love-Poems*, *Meditative Poems in Blank Verse*, and *Odes and Miscellaneous Poems*. "Dejection" is the first poem in the final category.

Coleridge's taxonomy of his works seems at first more straightforward than Wordsworth's, with two thematic and two formal categories. It is not. Only four of the twenty entries in *Odes and Miscellaneous Poems* are actually entitled odes, and two of his odes appear outside the category, their political content apparently taking precedence over their genre. "The Picture, Or the Lover's Resolution," so closely associated with "Dejection," is one of the *Love-Poems*, but "Dejection" itself is not. "Hymn before Sun-rise, in the Vale of Chamouny," the third of the triad of Coleridge's major works of 1802, is found as the first of the *Meditative Poems in Blank Verse.* The volume of poems presents Coleridge as a writer on canonical topics, war and love, and within poetic genres. It obscures all possible constructions of a literary life, as even within the generic categories themselves chronology is so thoroughly violated that avoiding it must have formed part of Coleridge's intent. *Sibylline Leaves* brings Coleridge forward not as a poet with a continuous work—the clear intention of Wordsworth's editorial labors when he gathered his shorter works in 1807 and 1815—but as a writer who has collected his productions in verse. The collection is oddly posthumous, so far as Coleridge the poet is concerned: only one substantial work in it, his magnificent response to Wordsworth's reading of the poem on his own mind, was composed or first published after the *Morning Post* version of "Dejection."[3]

It is intriguing that in *Sibylline Leaves* Coleridge does not follow his own advice about structuring his volume. In the fifth of his Bristol lectures, 11 November 1813, he had claimed that the "only nomenclature of criticism should be the classification of the faculties of the mind, how they are placed, how they are subordinate, whether they do or do not appeal to the worthy feelings of our nature." James Engell and Walter Jackson Bate cite this statement, noting that Wordsworth's principles of classification of his own poems in 1815 were "undoubtedly influenced" by Coleridge (*BL* 1:22, n. 3). That Coleridge makes so little effort to unify and codify his poetic canon reinforces my belief that a major strategy of *Sibylline Leaves* is to marginalize Coleridge the poet. By the time he published the collection, Coleridge had cast his lot with prose composition. The *Biographia Literaria*, originally thought of as an introduction to a volume of poems, was published a year before the poems themselves. One of the major burdens of the *Biographia* is to explain and to justify, if only to himself, Coleridge's ceasing to be a poet.

"Dejection" is almost hidden within the *Biographia*, where only two of its lines are quoted, excerpted, or adapted (*BL* 2:159). Generations of scholars have not been wrong, though, in using the poem as a heuristic explanatory device for Coleridge's subsequent writings. Entire sections of the *Biographia* are little more than "Dejection" writ large. Consider Coleridge on his precocious schoolboy philosophizing, from which he was temporarily rescued by the poetry of Bowles:

> Well were it for me perhaps, had I never relapsed into the same mental disease; if I had continued to pluck the flower and reap the harvest from the cultivated surface, instead of delving in the unwholesome quicksilver mines of metaphysic depths. But in after time I have sought a refuge from bodily pain and mismanaged sensibility in abstruse researches, which exercised the strength and subtlety of the understanding without awakening the feelings of the heart; still there was a long and blessed interval, during which my natural faculties were allowed to expand, and my natural tendencies to develope themselves; my fancy, and the love of nature, and the sense of beauty in forms and sounds. (*BL* 1:17)

Some of the largest topics of the *Biographia*—the irritability of genius, the intellectual bankruptcy of associationist philosophy, the shaping power of the imagination, the difficulty and rarity of genuine poetry, and the greatness of Wordsworth—find their clearest source in the early texts of "Dejection." The poem lies behind much of Coleridge's later career. While it is common to find in it premonitions and early sketches of later philosophical positions, it is equally or more appropriate to view the later philosophy as an explication, elaboration, and revision of this work. "Dejection" is one of those rare writings which shapes a life.

The influence of the Ode on Wordsworth is simultaneously more complex and, at our own historical moment, more controversial. For Jerome J. McGann the poem is the work by Wordsworth which best represents the romantic ideology, which is marked among other characteristics by its sharp valorization of the internal over the external, of consciousness over historical and social experience. Of the Ode in particular, he says, "The poem annihilates its history, biographical and socio-historical alike, and replaces these particulars with a record of pure consciousness."[4] McGann tries to be fair with Wordsworth, acknowledging his struggle with the great social and moral issues engendered by the French Revolution and its aftermath:

Wordsworth went on to struggle further with those problems and to arrive at what he believed was a solution. What he actually discovered was no more than his own desperate need for a solution. The reality of that need mirrored a cultural one that was much greater and more widespread. Wordsworth transformed both of these realities into illusions. The process began with the displacement of the problem inwardly, but when he went on to conceptualize his need, as we observe in the ode, the pity of Wordsworth's situation approaches tragic proportions. Indeed, it is a very emblem of the tragedy of his epoch, for in that conceptualization Wordsworth imprisoned his true voice of feeling within the bastille of his consciousness. Wordsworth made a solitude and called it peace. . . . From Wordsworth's vantage, an ideology is born out of things which (literally) *cannot* be spoken of. So the "Immortality Ode" is crucial for us because it speaks about ideology from the point of view and in the context of its origins. If Wordsworth's poetry elides history, we observe in this "escapist" or "reactionary" move its own self-revelation. It is a rare, original, and comprehensive record of the birth and character of a particular ideology—in this case one that has been incorporated into our academic programs. The idea that poetry, or even consciousness, can set one free of the ruins of history and culture is the grand illusion of every Romantic poet. This idea continues as one of the most important shibboleths of our culture, especially—and naturally—at its higher levels. (McGann 91)

Marjorie Levinson has recently extended and deepened McGann's basic understanding of the ideological tendencies of the Ode, with elaborate attention to the political implications of its figuration. "Tenet by tenet, phrase by phrase, image by image," Levinson argues, "Wordsworth deconstructs the Enlightenment's 'vision splendid.' To each of the *philosophes'* idols—freedom, individuality, joy, progress, Reason, illumination, Nature—Wordsworth opposes a bleak other: imprisonment, uniformity, sadness, accomodation, degeneration, memory, darkness, mind. To suggest that our greatest power, clearest amplitude, was in a past we can barely recall, much less recover, is to set a regressive ideal for mankind."[5]
My presentation of the Ode has had silent but uneasy relations with those of McGann and Levinson. We are in reasonably firm

agreement about the stylistic characteristics of the poem, especially
the uncharacteristic abstractness of its four opening stanzas and the
character of the literary resonances which underpin them. Even
Levinson's stipulation of an occasion for the poem—the conclusion of
negotiations for the Peace of Amiens—and her conjecture that the
artificial pastoral of stanzas I–IV screens memories of French Revolutionary festivals, are useful expansions of the intertextual resonances of the poem.[6] My own reading of the potentially destructive
consequences of the central myth is both more thoroughgoing and
darker than either of theirs. But we differ finally, and irreconcilably,
on the ultimate tendency of the poem.

For Levinson as well as McGann the Ode sets at nought the value
of historical time:

> Wordsworth celebrates the sort of truths that no amount of "list-
> lessness, nor mad endeavour"—one might say, no attempts at im-
> plementation—can destroy. History is exposed in the Ode as an
> unworthy object of human interest and involvement, its challenges
> are nugatory. "Another race hath been, and other palms are won";
> there are victories, the narrator's Pauline allusion suggests, far
> greater than those once anticipated from the French Revolution.
> Rather than grieve over these mundane losses, the reader is ex-
> horted to set his sights on other and spiritual palms. The heroism
> that Wordsworth ultimately defines is the capacity to live in the
> absence of a "consecrating dream," a "dream of human life"—by
> the end of the poem exposed as a belle dame sans merci.
>
> In place of that dream or "gleam," the narrator recommends the
> "soothing thoughts that spring / Out of human suffering." By this
> substitutive reemphasis, Wordsworth rejects the hectic, hopeful
> fellowship promoted by the Revolution. He derives the authentic
> human community from a common pathos, from a shared knowl-
> edge of irremediable human defect and deficiency. The object of
> Wordsworth's Ode is, like Gray's, "to teach [us we] are men."
> (Levinson 99).

Both Levinson's and McGann's evaluations of the Ode take the inhuman myth at its physical center as its final resolution, and they are
blind to or incurious about the Ode's recovery of human time as

meaningful. Perhaps I am blind as well to their distinctions, but I fail to see that genuine historical engagement can be built on anything other than a full acceptance of the value of lived experience. The green world of pastoral, to which Levinson here accords odd privilege, depends upon the obliteration rather than the acceptance of human time, whether its manifestations are found in the the erotic lyrics of the Renaissance, the festivals of Revolutionary France, or the streets of Haight-Ashbury. If Wordsworth's opening pastoral offers an implicit critique of pseudo-historical ritual theater—that "hectic, hopeful fellowship promoted by the Revolution"—that critique should not be taken as a repudiation of history. Such a procedure only displaces one nostalgia by another equally pernicious.

In offering historical readings of the Ode, McGann and Levinson remain surprisingly new-critical in their expectations of the poem, which is apparently supposed to answer all questions within its own borders. Nearly two centuries of reading experience provide adequate historical evidence that the Ode is not equal to this task. I have offered a rhetorical analysis of the poem which I think is correct and satisfying, but the fact that its understanding of the poem is uncommon leads me to acknowledge that the poem embodies and calls forth anxieties it cannot fully contain. To many readers the pulls of pastoral and myth remain too strong for Wordsworth's resolution to be effective. That phenomenon may say as much about our weaknesses as readers as about the Ode's possible weaknesses as a poem. Genuinely historical criticism would judge a work's tendencies historically, considering not just what it seems in itself to be but what it leads to. Here we are on certain ground.

As Wordsworth was completing the Ode in the early spring of 1804, he was simultaneously embarking on his massive expansion of *The Prelude*, which is the single most important literary decision of his life. Our own literary culture's chronic overprivileging of the childhood materials of *The Prelude*, which were composed much earlier, has undervalued the significance of this decision. Wordsworth chose finally to present not an internal life story, a story of isolated mystical moments, but a life lived in social, historical time. Far from emptying history of meaning, the Ode reveals the problems inherent in a poetry which elides the concerns of adult life, depending

on a bipolar oscillation between a splendid then and diminished now.
In completing the Ode Wordsworth discovers the dangers in his poetic project of the spring of 1802, that brilliant exploration of the
interplay between isolated moments of experience at which he was
better than any poet who ever lived. His immediate engagement
of the most significant historical experience of his early adulthood
marks the exact moment of his poetic maturity. Acknowledging this
achievement might also mark the maturity of our own historical
criticism.[7]

Notes

CHAPTER ONE. INTRODUCTION

1. As Peter J. Manning remarks in one of the finest recent essays on the Ode, Wordsworth himself also began the process of "encasing" his text with "glosses on his work" which retrospectively create "simulacra of its meaning." "Who," Manning asks, "now can read the poem without an intervening consciousness" of the poet's letters, notes, and reminiscences about the poem? "Wordsworth's Intimations Ode and Its Epigraphs," *Journal of English and Germanic Philology* 82 (1983), 526.

2. Geoffrey H. Hartman, "'Timely Utterance' Once More," *Rhetoric and Form: Deconstruction at Yale*, ed. Robert Con Davis and Ronald Schleifer (Norman: U of Oklahoma P, 1985), 37. See also Manning, who points out in the essay cited above that Lionel Trilling began his famous essay on the Immortality Ode by remarking that poems live in their "simulacra," those "false or partial appearances" generated through cultural response, as well as in themselves; see Trilling, *The Liberal Imagination* (New York: Viking, 1950), 129.

3. See Karl Kroeber's and Max F. Schulz's relevant sections in *The English Romantic Poets: A Review of Research and Criticism*, ed. Frank Jordan (New York: Modern Language Association of America, 1985), 299–303, 311–312, 404–407. Their reviews are unfailingly generous and should not be held accountable for the inference I have drawn.

4. Clifford H. Siskin, *The Historicity of Romantic Discourse* (New York and Oxford: Oxford UP, 1988), 39.

5. For a superb unpacking of the accumulated lore surrounding *Lyrical Ballads*, see Kenneth R. Johnston, "The Triumphs of Failure: Wordsworth's *Lyrical Ballads* of 1798," in *The Age of William Wordsworth: Critical Essays on the Romantic Tradition*, ed. Johnston and Gene W. Ruoff (New Brunswick, NJ: Rutgers UP, 1987), 133–159.

6. Jonathan Arac, *Critical Genealogies: Historical Situations for Postmodern Literary Studies* (New York: Columbia UP, 1987), 55.

7. Morris Dickstein, "The Price of Experience: Blake's Reading of Freud," *The Literary Freud: Mechanisms of Defense and the Poetic Will*, ed. Joseph H. Smith (New Haven and London: Yale UP, 1980), 67–68.

8. That most of my examples are taken from studies of Wordsworth reflects the relative proportions of my work, my own scholarly origins, the special circumstance created by the brevity of Coleridge's poetic career, and my perception, which may be in error, that the state of scholarship and critical commentary on Coleridge is relatively less advanced.

9. Arac, 49–50, 56.

10. James Butler, ed., *"The Ruined Cottage" and "The Pedlar"* (Ithaca: Cornell UP, 1979).

11. Jonathan Wordsworth, *The Wordsworth Circle* 10 (1979), 244.

12. M. H. Abrams, gen. ed., *The Norton Anthology of English Literature*, 5th ed., 2 vols. (New York: W. W. Norton, 1986), 2:2491.

13. On the cultural underpinnings of the second genetic tale "of pathologically interrupted male development" (176), see Siskin, esp. 164–78. As always, generalizations immediately bring counter-examples to mind. The work of Peter Manning is especially to be noted for its sensitivity to textual change and freedom from common preconceptions about the pattern of Wordsworth's revisions: see his essay on the Ode, cited above, "Wordsworth, Margaret, and The Pedlar," *Studies in Romanticism* 15 (1976), 195–220, and "'My former thoughts returned': Wordsworth's *'Resolution and Independence*,'" *TWC* 9 (1978), 398–405.

14. Alan Grob, *The Philosophic Mind: A Study of Wordsworth's Poetry and Thought, 1797–1805* (Columbus: Ohio State UP, 1973).

15. See Arthur Beatty, *William Wordsworth: His Doctrine and Art in Their Historical Relations*, 2nd ed. (Madison: U of Wisconsin P, 1922); Melvin M. Rader, *Presiding Ideas in Wordsworth's Poetry* (1931; rpt. New York: Gordian P, 1968), and *Wordsworth: A Philosophical Approach* (Oxford: Clarendon P, 1967); Newton P. Stallknecht, *Strange Seas of Thought: Studies in William Wordsworth's Philosophy of Man and Nature* (Bloomington: Indiana UP, 1958). John A. Hodgson, *Wordsworth's Philosophical Poetry, 1797–1814* (Lincoln: U of Nebraska P, 1980), takes advantage of more recent textual information than was available to Grob.

16. William Heath, *Wordsworth and Coleridge: A Study of Their Literary Relations in 1801–1802* (Oxford: Clarendon P, 1970).

17. On this issue I am pleased with the concurrence of Jonathan Wordsworth, *The Borders of Vision* (Oxford: Clarendon P, 1982), esp. 155–61.

18. Thomas McFarland, "The Symbiosis of Wordsworth and Coleridge," *SIR* 11 (1972), 264. McFarland later incorporated this essay into into *Romanticism and the Forms of Ruin* (Princeton: Princeton UP, 1981). In his recent work McFarland has addressed the theories of Harold Bloom, offering his own countertheory of influence; see *Originality and Imagination* (Baltimore: Johns Hopkins UP, 1985).

19. George Dekker, *Coleridge and the Literature of Sensibility* (New York: Barnes & Noble, 1978).

20. Wordsworth, *Borders of Vision*, esp. 149–73.

21. Lucy Newlyn, *Coleridge, Wordsworth, and the Language of Allusion* (Oxford: Clarendon P, 1986).

22. Paul Magnuson, *Coleridge and Wordsworth: A Lyrical Dialogue* (Princeton: Princeton UP, 1988), ix.

23. Jared R. Curtis, *Wordsworth's Experiments with Tradition: The Lyric Poems of 1802* (Ithaca: Cornell UP, 1971); Stephen Parrish, *The Art of "Lyrical Ballads"* (Cambridge: Harvard UP, 1973); Paul Fry, *The Poet's Calling in the English Ode* (New Haven: Yale UP, 1980); Jeffrey C. Robinson, *Radical Literary Education: A Classroom Experiment with Wordsworth's "Ode"* (Madison: U of Wisconsin P, 1987); Stuart Curran, *Poetic Form and British Romanticism* (New York: Oxford UP, 1986).

CHAPTER TWO. WORDSWORTH'S ODE OF 1802

1. Magnuson, "The Genesis of Wordsworth's 'Ode,'" *TWC* 12 (1981), 23–24. Magnuson's essay and my own "'Fields of Sheep': The Obscurities of the Ode, I–IV," *TWC* 12 (1981), 45–51, join the work of Curtis in *Wordsworth's Experiments with Tradition* and *Poems, in Two Volumes, and Other Poems, 1800–1807* (Ithaca: Cornell UP, 1983), as attempts to talk rigorously about the Ode as a text of 1802. Magnuson's work has helped to confirm many of my hypotheses and has suggested others. I retrace some of Magnuson's steps in this chapter, but I am also interested in the Ode's relationship to the traditions of English poetry. Magnuson's essay is incorporated into *Lyrical Dialogue*, 273–88. For photocopies and facing-page transcriptions of the two extant versions of the Verse Letter, see Stephen Maxfield Parrish, ed., *Coleridge's Dejection: The Earliest Manuscripts and the Earliest Printings* (Ithaca: Cornell UP, 1988), 73–97, 106–31.

2. The revision is found in the Longman MS. in the British Library; see *P2V*, 376–77; 41.

3. Hartman, "'Timely Utterance' Once More," 18–26.

4. Magnuson makes a similar point about the role of childhood in the Ode of 1802; see "Genesis," 24.

5. See, of course, Trilling's argument in his classic essay, "The Immortality Ode," 129–59.

6. Abrams, "Structure and Style in the Greater Romantic Lyric," in *From Sensibility to Romanticism*, ed. F. W. Hilles and Harold Bloom (New York: Oxford UP, 1965), 527–60.

7. Wordsworth's hesitation at presenting general truths without qualifying them rhetorically or embedding them in particular situations which implicitly condition them has received increasing commentary. For a provocative treatment of this tendency in English Romanticism generally see L. J. Swingle, *The Obstinate Questionings of English Romanticism* (Baton Rouge and London: Louisiana State UP, 1987), esp. 13–78.

8. Manning, "Wordsworth's Intimations Ode," esp. 538–40, argues persuasively that Wordsworth's attaching the lines from the poem on the rainbow to the Ode has distorted critical responses to it.

9. My texts for "To a Butterfly," "To a Cuckoo," and "Extempore" are the versions found in "Sara Hutchinson's Poets" (Dove Cottage MS. 39). All are printed by Curtis in *WET*, 158, 161–62, 163, from which my citations are taken.

10. Parrish, *The Art of "Lyrical Ballads"*, discusses the continuities of such poems with the dramatic ballads of 1798; see 135–37. While Parrish rightly insists as well on differences between these and the earlier ballad experiments, they are far closer in technique and spirit to them than to the contemporaneous lyrics I am discussing.

11. Magnuson, "Genesis," 30.

12. *The Complete Poems of Thomas Gray*, ed. H. W. Starr and J. R. Hendrickson (Oxford: Clarendon P, 1966), 7; 11–20.

13. For a concise account of Wordsworth's adaptations of Chaucer, see *CMY*, 132–35, n. 31.

14. *PW* 4:218; 21–30. In this and following citations I have restored earlier manuscript readings; parenthetical citations give line numbers.

15. The relationship between Wordsworth's translations of Chaucer and "Resolution and Independence" is discussed by Anthony E. M. Conran, "The Dialectic of Experience: A Study of Wordsworth's *Resolution and Independence*," *PMLA* 75 (1960), 66–74.

16. Abbie Findlay Potts, "The Spenserian and Miltonic Influences in Wordsworth's *Ode* and *Rainbow*," *Studies in Philology* 29 (1932), 607. See also Samuel E. Schulman, "The Spenser of the Intimations Ode," *TWC* 12 (1981), 31–35.

17. Parrish devotes an excellent chapter to Wordsworth's pastoralism in *The Art of "Lyrical Ballads"*, 149–87. If I see Wordsworth working against pastoral convention more frequently than with it, the cause may lie in my narrower construction of the tradition. The same is true of my apparent disagreement with Curran, *Poetic Form and British Romanticism* , 85–127, and "Wordsworth and the Forms of Poetry," in *The Age of William Wordsworth* ed. Johnston and Ruoff, 115–32. Curran sees renewal of pastoral as the guiding objective of Wordsworth's poetic endeavor, and the case which he presents is persuasively argued. I am looking at the matter from another direction. Assuming that Wordsworth succeeded in his earlier experiments in stripping pastoral of its artificial props and returning it to its elemental dignity, I am asking why, at this stage in his career, he is engaging conventions he had largely cast off.

18. Ruoff, "1800 and the Future of the Novel: William Wordsworth, Maria Edgeworth, and the Vagaries of Literary History," in *The Age of William Wordsworth*, ed. Johnston and Ruoff, 298–305.

19. *The Complete Poems of Ben Jonson*, ed. William B. Hunter, Jr. (New York: New York UP, 1963), 136.

20. David V. Erdman and Stephen M. Parrish, "Who Wrote the Mad Monk? A Debate," *Bulletin of the New York Public Library* 64 (1960), 209. Subsequent citations of the poem are from the version presented in this article.

21. Frederick L. Beaty, "Mrs. Radcliffe's Fading Gleam," *Philological Quarterly* 42 (1963), 126.

22. James H. Averill, *Wordsworth and Human Suffering* (Ithaca: Cornell UP, 1980).

23. Geoffrey Hartman, *Wordsworth's Poetry, 1787–1814* (New Haven: Yale UP, 1964), 307.

24. Potts, 613.

25. *John Milton, Complete Poems and Major Prose*, ed. Merritt Y. Hughes (Indianapolis: Odyssey P, 1957), 439; 11.282–85.

26. There have been many such readings, but the outstanding philosophical treatment of the poem is Alan Grob's in the final chapter of *The Philosophic Mind*, 232–75.

CHAPTER THREE. COLERIDGE'S VERSE LETTER
TO SARA HUTCHINSON

1. Norman Fruman, *Coleridge, the Damaged Archangel* (New York: Braziller, 1971), 511–12, n. 14.

2. Dekker, 30.

3. In his long essay in the *Quarterly Review* of 1834, H. N. Coleridge

called "Dejection" "one of the most characteristic and beautiful" of Coleridge's lyric poems. He also contrasted it favorably with "France: An Ode" and "Ode on the Departing Year" as being "poetry throughout, as *opposed* to oratory." See *Coleridge: The Critical Heritage*, ed. J. R. de J. Jackson (New York: Barnes and Noble, 1970), 634, 646–47. Barbara Garlitz has traced the cultural impact of Wordsworth's Ode in a fascinating essay, "The Immortality Ode: Its Cultural Progeny," *SEL* 6 (1966), 639–49.

4. On the backgrounds of the poem in Coleridge's relationship with Sara Hutchinson see George Whalley, *Coleridge and Sara Hutchinson and the Asra Poems* (Toronto: U of Toronto P, 1955); on the psychosexual implications of the Verse Letter see Beverly Fields, *Reality's Dark Dream: Dejection in Coleridge* (Kent, Ohio: Kent State UP, 1967), esp. 119–64, and Fruman, esp. 421–34; on Coleridge's philosophy of nature, see Thomas McFarland, *Coleridge and the Pantheist Tradition* (Oxford: Clarendon P, 1969), and Dekker, 101–76; on the "Dejection" cycle as a symptom of a religious crisis see Marshall Suther, *The Dark Night of Samuel Taylor Coleridge* (New York: Columbia UP, 1960); on Coleridge's thoughts about love see Anthony John Harding, *Coleridge and the Idea of Love* (London and New York: Cambridge UP, 1974), esp. 6–78; and on the relations of the poem to the literature of sensibility, see the fine chapter in Dekker, 58–100.

5. McFarland, "The Symbiosis of Wordsworth and Coleridge," 263–303.

6. Wordsworth and Coleridge began their brief joint work on "The Rime of the Ancient Mariner" 12 November 1797; Coleridge finished the poem by 23 March 1798. Wordsworth probably began *Peter Bell* on 20 April 1798. See Reed, *CEY*, 210, 228, 233.

7. Coleridge's allusion to *Peter Bell* has been widely recognized. Fields, 129–30, remarks the allusion to the "Rime." See also Newlyn, 67–68.

8. Magnuson, *Lyrical Dialogue*, 281.

9. Jay Arnold Levine, "The Status of the Verse Epistle before Pope," *SP* 59 (1962), 658–84.

10. *The Poems of Alexander Pope*, ed. Geoffrey Tillotson, 2nd ed., 2 vols. (London: Methuen and New Haven: Yale UP, 1954), 2:2; 49–50.

11. Fry, esp. 1–14.

12. See Curran, *Poetic Form and British Romanticism*, 72–73, for a different response to "Departing Year" and "France" as political odes.

13. Tillotson provides a succinct account of the backgrounds of the story of Eloisa and Abelard as well as Pope's modifications of the version of Hughes; see *The Poems of Alexander Pope*, 2:275–93.

14. See Magnuson, *Lyrical Dialogue*, 290.

15. Longinus, *On Sublimity*, tr. D. A. Russell (Oxford: Clarendon P, 1964), 14–15.

16. Howard Jacobson, Ovid's *Heroides* (Princeton: Princeton UP, 1974), discusses the degree to which *Heroides* 15 has become a major source of biographical information about Sappho. He mentions in passing a notion once held that Ovid's "epistle was a translation of an actual poem of Sappho's" (278).

17. Dekker, 47–54.

18. References to the text of "A Soliloquy of the full Moon" are to Whalley's transcription of DC. MS 41 in *Coleridge and Sara Hutchinson*, 5–7. Newlyn, 67–68, comments on the Verse Letter's echo of the "Soliloquy."

19. Fields, 128, gives a full reading of the erotic suggestions of Coleridge's text at this point.

20. Dekker, 75–78, discusses Coleridge's admiration of and correspondence with Mary Robinson; Curran, *Poetic Form and British Romanticism*, discusses Robinson's *Sappho to Phaon. in a Series of Legitimate Sonnets* in *Poetic Form and British Romanticism*, 31.

21. I follow the text of *Heroides* 15 in Ovid, *Heroides and Amores*, ed. and tr. Grant Showerman (Cambridge and London: Harvard UP, 1921), 180–97.

22. In a chapter on the dramatic structure of the *Heroides*, Jacobson, 363–70, discusses the relationship between the point in time at which a heroine is shown as writing and the known outcome of her story.

23. Jacobson's work on the *Heroides* is almost throughout a defense of Ovid's art against widespread critical dismissal of the work. For an overview of adverse critical opinion on "Eloisa to Abelard," coupled with a defense of the work, see Henry Pettit, "Pope's *Eloisa to Abelard*: An Interpretation" (1953), rept. in *Essential Articles for the Study of Alexander Pope*, ed. Maynard Mack (Hamden, CT: Archon Books, 1964), 297–309. For a sustained defense of Coleridge's Verse Letter see David Pirie, "A Letter to [Asra]," in *Bicentenary Wordsworth Studies in Memory of John Alban Finch*, ed. Jonathan Wordsworth (Ithaca and London: Cornell UP, 1970), 294–339.

24. See Newlyn, 71–75, for an account of echoes of Wordsworth's and Coleridge's early work found in this passage.

25. My analysis of the parasitic imagery of this passage parallels in many details the discussion in Newlyn, 75–78.

26. *Barron Field's Memoirs of Wordsworth*, ed. Geoffrey Little (Sydney: Sydney UP, 1975), 100. Field does not date his recollection; however, his greatest intimacy with Wordsworth began in 1827, when he and Horatio

Smith visited Wordsworth and Southey in the Lake District. What Field recalls sounds like something Wordsworth might have said after Coleridge's death.

27. *Prose Works of William Wordsworth*, ed. Alexander B. Grosart, 3 vols. (London: Edward Moxon, 1876), 3:427.

28. Reed discusses the dating of work on *Home at Grasmere*, including the Prospectus section, in an appendix of *CMY*, 656—86. His more recent belief, that the Prospectus was probably composed before 4 April 1802, is summarized by Beth Darlington in *HG*, 21—22.

29. Stephen F. Fogle, "The Design of Coleridge's 'Dejection,'" *SP* 48 (1951), 49—55.

30. Robinson, *Radical Literary Education*, devotes the final section of his book to Hazlitt's erotic/political critique of the Ode (153—85).

31. William Keach, "Obstinate Questionings: The Immortality Ode and *Alastor*," *TWC* 12 (1981), 39. Citations from "Alastor" are from *Shelley's Poetry and Prose*, ed. Donald H. Reiman and Sharon B. Powers (New York: W. W. Norton, 1977), 70—87, as given by Keach.

CHAPTER FOUR. WORDSWORTH'S "THE LEECH-GATHERER"

1. In "Wordsworth's Two Replies to Coleridge's 'Dejection: An Ode,'" *PMLA* 86 (1971), 982—89, Milton Teichman reviews the history of joint commentary on the relationships between Wordsworth's and Coleridge's poems. The connection seems to have been noticed first by George McLean Harper, *William Wordsworth: His Life, Works, and Influence*, 2 vols., 3rd ed. (New York: Scribners, 1929), 2:383. It received its first full treatment from G. W. Meyer, "'Resolution and Independence': Wordsworth's Answer to Coleridge's 'Dejection: An Ode,'" *Tulane Studies in English* 2 (1950), 49—74. The most specific treatments of the relationship between Coleridge's Verse Letter and Wordsworth's poems on the leech gatherer are in Dekker, 66—77, Magnuson, *Lyrical Dialogue*, 309—17, and Newlyn, 117—37.

2. Conran, 68—69, notes that the particular variant of rhyme royal used by Wordsworth is also used in Milton's Nativity Ode and Chatterton's "Excelente Balade of Charitie."

3. My discussion of the relations between "The Leech-Gatherer" and Wordsworth's earlier canon is indebted throughout to the excellent analysis in Parrish, *The Art of "Lyrical Ballads*," 213—21.

4. I follow the text of the poem in DC MS. 41, as given by Curtis, *P2V*, 78—79; 1—4.

5. In "Wordsworth on Language: Toward a Radical Poetics for English

Romanticism," *TWC* 3 (1972), 204–11, I use "The Sailor's Mother" and Coleridge's strictures in the *Biographia Literaria* as the basis for an extended comparison of the two writers' views on poetic language.

6. Texts for the first two poems are from a letter from Wordsworth and Dorothy to Coleridge, 16 April 1802; texts for the last two are from DC. MS 41; all texts are given in Curtis, *WET*, 171–75.

7. For an interesting discussion of this little-known poem, see Jonathan Wordsworth, *Borders of Vision*, 162–65.

8. Schulman, "The Spenserian Enchantments of Wordsworth's 'Resolution and Independence,' " *Modern Philology* 79 (1981), 24–44. Citations of Thomson are from *The Castle of Indolence and Other Poems*, ed. Alan Dugald McKillop (Lawrence: U of Kansas P, 1961); parenthetical citations give canto and stanza numbers.

9. Dekker, 60–66.

10. *Letters of Charles Lamb*, ed. E. V. Lucas, 3 vols. (London: Dent and Methuen, 1935), 1:193.

11. *The Life and Works of Robert Burns*, ed. James Currie, 4 vols. (Edinburgh: Macredie, Skelley, and Muckersy, 1815), 1:229, 230. Further citations of Currie are given parenthetically. The edition cited is a reprinting of Currie, *The Works of Robert Burns, with an Account of His Life, and a Criticism on His Writings* (Liverpool, 1800).

12. The standard work on the relationship between the two poets remains an article by Russell Noyes, "Wordsworth and Burns," *PMLA* 59 (1944), 813–32, which traces thoroughly Wordsworth's reflections of his readings of Burns in the published poetry and prose. For a larger view of the impact of Burns on the writers of the romantic period see Raymond Bentman, "The Romantic Poets and Critics on Robert Burns," *Texas Studies in Language and Literature* 6 (1964–65), 104–18. Wordsworth's use of Burns in the poems on the leech-gatherer has been given detailed consideration only by Dekker, 66–75, and Newlyn, 123–24.

13. *The Complete Works of William Hazlitt*, ed. P. P. Howe, 21 vols. (London: J. M. Dent, 1930), 5:131.

14. Citations are from the facsimile reprint of Robert Burns, *Poems, Chiefly in the Scottish Dialect*, published as *Poems, 1786 and 1787* (Menston, UK: Scolar P, 1971), 158. Subsequent parenthetical citations give page numbers only.

15. Newlyn, 125, n. 16, notes the appositeness of a "something given" to Coleridge's Verse Letter.

16. See Grob, *The Philosophic Mind*, 217–29.

17. The indebtedness of the leech-gatherer poems to "A Narrow

Girdle" is discussed by Manning, "'My former thoughts returned,'" 398–400.

18. Parrish, 214.

CHAPTER FIVE. WORDSWORTH'S "RESOLUTION AND INDEPENDENCE"

1. Curtis, *WET*, 97–113.

2. Cf. Newlyn, 129–37, for a wholly different understanding of the figurative power of Wordsworth's additions in "Resolution and Independence."

3. Theresa M. Kelley, "Proteus and Romantic Allegory," *ELH* 49 (1982), 644.

4. The fullest study of the ontological restraints Wordsworth places on the faculty of imagination remains my "Religious Implications of Wordsworth's Imagination," *SIR* 12 (1973), 670–92.

5. The Spenser passage is cited by Schulman, "Spenserian Enchantments," 41–42. My citations from *The Faerie Queen* are from *The Works of Edmund Spenser*, ed. Edwin Greenlaw, Charles Good, and Frederick Padelford, 10 vols. (Baltimore: Johns Hopkins UP, 1932–57), 2.12.7. Subsequent parenthetical citations give book, canto, and stanza numbers.

6. On Wordsworth's consistent refusal to present the imagination as a moral faculty, or to build ethical extensions of its revelations, see again my "Religious Implications of Wordsworth's Imagination," esp. 679–82.

7. Conran, 68.

8. Dream-vision analogues are offered by Conran, 72.

9. The relevance of the "spring elegy" is stressed by Heath, 123–27.

10. Radical protestant confessional literature is cited by Richard E. Brantley, *Wordsworth's "Natural Methodism"* (New Haven, Yale UP, 1975), 127–32.

11. Both Parrish, 213–21, and Curtis, *WET*, 97–113, see Wordsworth's achievement in "Resolution and Independence" as having grown out of his ballad experiments.

12. Burns, *Poems, 1786 and 1787*, 88. Subsequent parenthetical citations give page numbers.

CHAPTER SIX. COLERIDGE'S "DEJECTION," 4 OCTOBER 1802

1. For a splendid example of how revealing study of both the textual evolution and recontextualizations of Coleridge's poems can be, see Magnuson, "'The Eolian Harp' in Context," *SIR* 24 (1985), 3–20.

2. Apparently the translation was completed more in wish than deed, or so the most recent biographer to review the episode concludes; see

Oswald Doughty, *Perturbed Spirit: The Life and Personality of Samuel Taylor Coleridge* (Rutherford, NJ: Fairleigh Dickinson UP, 1981), 209.

3. Citations of "The Picture" are from *The Morning Post*, 6 September 1802, page 3, column 1; citations of "Chamouny" are from *The Morning Post*, 11 September 1802, page 3, columns 2–3.

4. Michael J. Kelly, "Coleridge's 'Picture, or the Lover's Resolution': Its Relationship to 'Dejection' and the Sources in the *Notebooks*," *Costerus* 5 (1972), 75–96, offers an alternative account composed from the materials I have been addressing. Kelly cites the received text of "The Picture" throughout rather than the shorter and less elaborately arch *Morning Post* text, which, in the historical context he is exploring, is the significant version. Kelly's use of notebook sources concentrates on the impact of the walking tour of 1–9 August upon the topical details of the poem. His critical conclusions about "The Picture" seem forced by the need to bring it into line with Coleridge's later dicta about poetry: "'The Picture,' as its very title suggests, is a poem about the bringing together of disjointed images, emotions, and experiences into a meaningful wholeness. The poem is like a picture; it has vivid pictorial qualities, and the narrator, by being very precise in all his descriptions, requires that we examine it with the same care that we would a picture. When we do, we find that Coleridge has, in the guise of 'The Picture's' 'Gentle lunatic,' salvaged much of his former self from the wreck of 'Dejection' (92). My understanding of "The Picture" is closer to that of Max F. Schulz, *The Poetic Voices of Coleridge* (Detroit: Wayne State UP, 1963), 137–39, who is more attentive to the twists and turns of the narrator's self-disclosures.

5. The writings of Gessner were widely available in England through a series of translations, reviews, and excepts in magazines beginning in 1760 and continuing well past 1802, the date of a three-volume edition in English of his life and works. Gessner's impact in England may be traced through John Boening, ed., *The Reception of Classical German Literature in England, 1760–1860: A Documentary History from Contemporary Periodicals*, 10 vols. (New York and London: Garland, 1977), 4:348–413. An essay from the *Universal Magazine* (1795) favorably contrasts the purity of his pastoral vision to that of Theocritus: "The shepherds of Gessner are beings of a rank superior to human nature: to all the simplicity of the infancy of the world, they unite the most delicate sentiments of the cultivated man. . . . The pastoral world of Gessner, is situate under a most happy climate, described in glowing colours; the sun of gold and the moon of silver shine with the liveliest lustre; and the inhabitants are worthy of so happy an abode. Their love is as pure as ether. . . ." (Boening 4:389). For

further consideration of Coleridge's use of Gessner in "The Picture," see Schulz, 137–39, and Garold N. Davis, *German Thought and Culture in England, 1700–1770* (Chapel Hill: U of North Carolina P, 1969), 105–6.

6. Gessner, *Samtliche Schriften* (Zurich: Orell Fussli, 1972), Band 2, Tiel 3, 123.

7. In Gessner, 123, the speaker's repudiation of love and dedication to a life of melancholy and earnest contemplation are forgotten in a similar turn, when the speaker discovers in the sand of the banks of his secluded river a tiny footprint.

8. The strongest and most interesting reading of the poem is in Reeve Parker, *Coleridge's Meditative Art* (Ithaca: Cornell UP, 1975), 144–72. Parker makes copious use both of the letter to Sotheby and of a later letter to an unknown correspondent in 1819 (*STCL* 4:974–75), which describes retrospectively the poem's meditative procedures through contrast to those of Milton, Thomson, and the Psalms. I will touch only obliquely on the issue of Coleridge's plagiarism, which has preoccupied commentary since De Quincey's revelations in 1834. On this topic consult Adrien Bonjour, *Coleridge's "Hymn before Sunrise"* (Lausanne: La Concorde, 1942), and Fruman, 26–30.

9. See Dekker, 107–8, for a discussion of Coleridge's sources for the wind harp.

10. Given the mass of Coleridge's canon and my own limited command of it, this statement depends on the authority of professional Coleridge-watchers. The letter to Sotheby is the earliest evidence cited for the distinction in Wilma L. Kennedy, *The English Heritage of Coleridge of Bristol, 1798: The Basis in Eighteenth Century English Thought for His Distinction Between Imagination and Fancy* (New Haven: Yale UP, 1947), vii. McFarland does not make such a claim for the passage, perhaps because he is intent on seeing the distinction as something always implicit in Coleridge's thinking (and, indeed, to a limited extent in Western thought since Plato). However, the letter to Sotheby of 10 September 1802 is the earliest document that I find brought forward in *Coleridge and the Pantheist Tradition* in which the two faculties are clearly discriminated. The letter to Sotheby is also cited as the first instance of Coleridge's distinction between the faculties in Patricia Mavis Jenkins, *Coleridge's Literary Theory: The Chronology of Its Development, 1790–1818* (Smithtown, NY: Exposition P, 1984), 28–29.

11. An exception to this rule is the analysis of Parker, 149–51, which should be read in creative tension with my own. We are interested in different things within the letter, and our constructions of it and "Chamouny" are not at all the same.

12. For earlier examples of his work in something approaching this

genre, see two translations apparently composed as metrical exercises in 1799: "Hexameters: Paraphrase of Psalm XLVI" (*CPW* 1:326) and "Hymn to the Earth: Hexameters," adapted from F. L. Stolberg's "Hymne an die Erde" (*CPW* 1:327–29).

13. Fry, 7–8. The best-informed treatment of the relationships between the hymn and ode as literary forms is in Curran, 56–84. Curran disagrees with the distinction drawn by Fry, which I cite and follow heuristically, and Curran's reading of the dynamics of "Chamouny" differs from mine.

14. Parker, 160.

15. Erdman, "The Otway Connection," in *Coleridge's Imagination: Essays in Memory of Pete Laver*, ed. Richard Gravil, Lucy Newlyn, and Nicholas Roe (Cambridge: Cambridge UP, 1985), 154.

16. There is of course a long history of readings of the relevance of the ballad fragment to Coleridge's poem. For recent interesting speculations see Cyrus Hamlin, "The Hermeneutics of Form: Reading the Romantic Ode," *Boundary* 2, 7:3 (Spring 1979), 13–14, and Fry, 164–65.

17. Fry, 180, remarks that Coleridge could not call his poem "an 'Ode to' or even an 'Ode on' dejection, because clearly his affliction was not a quality to be openly invoked, nor was it something a celebratory poem could finally be 'on' or about."

18. Eugenia Logan, *A Concordance to the Poetry of Samuel Taylor Coleridge* (Gloucester, MA: Peter Smith, 1967).

19. Lane Cooper, *A Concordance to the Poems of William Wordsworth* (London: Smith, Elder, and Co., 1911), 204.

20. Cf. A. Harris Fairbanks, "The Form of Coleridge's Dejection Ode," *PMLA* 90 (1975), 882, who remarks that these added lines tend "both to direct our expectations toward some emotional release coincident with the outbreak of the storm and to limit our expectations. The poem does not raise the question of whether or not the speaker will regain his lost joy, but only the question of whether or not his grief will gain release, perhaps the only sort of progression that would be plausible in this span of time."

21. Luther Tyler, "Losing 'A Letter': The Contexts of Coleridge's 'Dejection,'" *ELH* 52 (1985), 420.

CHAPTER SEVEN. TIME PASSES

1. As late as 24 January–7 February 1804 Wordsworth described his autobiographical poem as "a Poem on my own earlier life which will take five books or parts to complete, three of which are nearly finished" (*EY* 436).

2. Mary Moorman, *William Wordsworth: A Biography*, 2 vols. (Oxford: Oxford UP, 1957–65), 1:553–68.

3. Robinson, pursuing the hypothesis that Wordsworth's lament for the lost gleam of childhood at the beginning of the Ode is a displacement of other anxieties, offers another way of approaching the relationship between the Ode and the political sonnets; see "The Immortality Ode: Lionel Trilling and Helen Vendler," *TWC* 12 (1981), 66–67.

4. James K. Chandler, *Wordsworth's Second Nature: A Study of the Poetry and Politics* (Chicago: U of Chicago P, 1984), 93, makes a similar point about the absence of explicit politics from *LB*, but his study does not directly engage the political sonnets of 1802–4.

5. Christopher Wordsworth, *Memoirs of William Wordsworth*, 2 vols. (London: E. Moxon, 1851), 1:207.

6. *Journals of Dorothy Wordsworth*, ed. William Knight, 2 vols. (London: Macmillan, 1897), 1:170–71.

CHAPTER EIGHT. WORDSWORTH'S ODE OF 1804

1. Abraham Cowley, *Poems*, ed. A. R. Waller (Cambridge: Cambridge UP, 1905), 170.

2. My genetic understanding of Wordsworth's suppression of erotic elements coincides with conclusions arrived at by Robinson through a cultural critique; see *Radical Literary Education*, 159–78.

3. For sharply dissimilar ways of approaching the cruxes of stanzas I–IV see Hartman, "Timely Utterance," 37–49, and my "'Fields of Sheep,'" 45–51.

4. Manning, "Wordsworth's Intimations Ode," 531.

5. Harper, 2:449.

6. John D. Rea, "Coleridge's Intimations of Immortality from Proclus," *MP* 26 (1928–29), 206. I have given the text of 1 November 1796 of Coleridge's sonnet: *STCL*, 1:246.

7. Newlyn, 142–43, bases her argument on an "allusion" to "To H. C." in a letter from Coleridge to Thomas Poole, 14 October 1803 (*STCL* 2:1014). Coleridge says, "Hartley is what he always was—a strange strange Boy—'*exquisitely wild*'!" With considerable justification Newlyn takes the phrase as establishing an earlier date than 1804 for the composition of Wordsworth's poem on Hartley. Given the habits of mutual quotation of the Wordsworth-Coleridge circle, it is also possible that Wordsworth's lines, "O happy Vision blessed Child, / That art so exquisitely wild" (MS. M), employ a household commonplace about young Hartley, a formulaic tag which Coleridge emphasizes in his letter.

8. For discussion of Wordsworth's possible reaction to Wedgwood's edu-

cational proposals, see Erdman, "Coleridge, Wordsworth, and the Wedgwood Fund," *BNYPL* 60 (1956), 425–43; 487–507. On the relations between Wordsworth's educational polemic and French educational theories and programs, see Chandler, 93–119.

9. Carl Woodring, *Wordsworth* (Boston: Houghton, 1965), 92. See also Cleanth Brooks, "Wordsworth and the Paradox of the Imagination," *The Well Wrought Urn*, rev. ed. (London: Dennis Dobson, 1968), 113.

10. *Prelude*, 21, n. 8; 78, n. 8.

11. Cf. Helen Vendler, "Lionel Trilling and the Immortality Ode," *Salmagundi* 41 (Spring 1978), 66–86. Vendler provides an impressive reading of stanza VII as a satiric tableau of socialization. Vendler accedes almost wholly to the satire, though, identifying the child depicted with the model child of *The Prelude*: "The voice cries out in protest: the child is socialized by male approval into all those rôles and dramas and dialogues, says the voice, 'as if his whole vocation / Were endless imitation.' We know that in Wordsworth's lexicon the opposite of imitation is creation, and the true human vocation is not to be imitative, but rather to be 'a sensitive being, a *creative* soul'" (75). Vendler may know this, but Wordsworth did not: her reading evades the import of the bonding passage from *The Prelude*, which had been adduced by Trilling in the essay she is confuting.

12. Helen Darbishire, ed., *Poems in Two Volumes* (Oxford: Clarendon P, 1952), 453, n. 103.

13. William Shakespeare, *As You Like It*, 2.7.139–140.

14. Cf. Vendler's comment on the invocation of stanza VII: "If it is true that all odes address a Divinity, then the Divinity of this Ode is Reciprocity—a mutual Divinity which consists of the child receptive to the Eternal Mind and Immortality brooding over the child" (75).

15. Coleridge did not think so: see his objection, *BL*, 2:140–141.

16. My local readings of Stanza VIII are deeply indebted to Jerome Christensen's more thoroughgoing deconstructive analysis in "'Thoughts That Do Often Lie Too Deep for Tears': Toward a Radical Concept of Lyrical Drama," *TWC* 12 (1981), 52–64. See also Manning, "Wordsworth's Intimations Ode," 526–40, and Fry, 138–55. Although Manning is primarily concerned with textual encrustations that lie beyond the scope of my study, much that he says about the problematics of the myth is germane to my reading. Fry, 152, sees clearly the dark side of the Ode's myth, and remarks that the "conclusion seems inescapable that Wordsworth's Intimations are best forgotten."

17. Bloom, *The Visionary Company*, rev. ed. (Ithaca: Cornell UP, 1971), 171–72. Vendler objects to the three-part division of the Ode as it is proposed by Trilling and (implicitly) Bloom, preferring what she calls "a

powerfully plotted succession of . . . 'wounds' and 'cures'" (79). "As I see the Ode," she says, "Wordsworth implies, as much by the prior position of the one 'answer' to the other as by any other means, that the acquisition of the philosophic mind depends upon our participation [in the social rituals of adult life]. . . . the poem affirms (by its own schema of Child, Boy, Youth, and Man) that those stages are inescapable" (78).

18. Johannes Quasten, *Patrology*, 3 vols. (Westminster, MD: Newman P), 2:2.

19. McFarland, *Coleridge and the Pantheist Tradition*, 317.

20. Origen, *De Principiis* 1.6, in *The Ante-Nicene Fathers*, ed. Alexander Roberts and James Donaldson, 10 vols. (Grand Rapids: Eerdmans, 1956), 4:261.

21. Quasten, 2:87.

22. Quasten, 2:39.

23. Charles Joseph Hefele, *A History of the Councils of the Church*, 5 vols. (Edinburgh: T. and T. Clark, 1893–96), 4:225.

24. See Stallknecht, 267–73; and Rader, *Wordsworth: A Philosophical Approach*, 71–80.

25. My citations are from Vaughan, *Poetry and Selected Prose*, ed. L. C. Martin (London: Oxford UP, 1963), 249–50; 1–6. Subsequent parenthetical citations give line numbers.

26. Leah Sinanoglou Marcus, *Childhood and Cultural Despair: A Theme and Variations in Seventeenth Century Literature* (Pittsburgh: U of Pittsburgh P, 1978), 94–152.

27. Stuart M. Sperry, Jr., "From 'Tintern Abbey' to the 'Intimations Ode': Wordsworth and the Function of Memory," *TWC* 1 (1970), 40–49; Johnston, "Recollecting Forgetting: Forcing Paradox to the Limit in the 'Intimations Ode,'" *TWC* 2 (1971), 59–64. My dissertation, "Wordsworth's Categorization and Arrangement of his Shorter Poems," U of Wisconsin, 1970, 264–66, reached conclusions almost identical to those of Sperry and Johnston on the nature and function of memory in the Ode. Cf. Vendler, 81, who argues that the phenomena praised at the beginning of stanza IX, "Fallings from us, vanishings," etc., are not integrally related to the recollections of "glory, dream, freshness, light, and gleam," but embody "Wordsworth's *second* account of the psychological conditions he recalls from childhood."

28. Shakespeare, *Hamlet*, 1.1.148–49; on the allusion to *Hamlet* see Christensen, 57, and Manning, "Wordsworth's Intimations Ode," 530.

29. See Trilling; Vendler; and Robinson, "The Immortality Ode," 64–70, much of which is incorporated into *Radical Literary Education*.

30. The most sensitive and appreciative study of Augustine's impor-

tance to the romantics is Abrams, *Natural Supernaturalism: Tradition and Revolution in Romantic Literature* (New York: W. W. Norton and Co., 1971), esp. 83–87.

31. Samuel N. C. Lieu, *Manichaeism in the Later Roman Empire and Medieval China: A Historical Survey* (Manchester: Manchester UP, 1985), 127.

32. Saint Augustine, *Confessions*, trans. Vernon J. Bourke (Washington: Catholic U of America P, 1953), 279.

33. See Augustine, *The Teacher*, trans. Robert P. Russell (Washington: Catholic U of America P, 1968), 52–55.

34. According to Joseph E. Duncan, *Milton's Earthly Paradise: A Historical Study of Eden* (Minneapolis: U of Minnesota P, 1972), 52, "St. Augustine provided succeeding centuries with the most penetrating and influential Christian interpretation of the thought of his time. During the sixteenth and seventeenth centuries he was claimed by both Catholics and Protestants. . . . For seminal discussions of the original condition of man, the nature of the Fall, and the pattern of Christian history, Milton and most of his readers would have looked to St. Augustine as a recognized authority." See also J. M. Evans, *Paradise Lost and the Genesis Tradition* (Oxford: Clarendon P, 1968), 92–99, on the sway of the Augustinian synthesis of the doctrine of the Fall: "All the various and conflicting elements of four centuries of patristic thought were thus fused in a reading of the story which was to be the basis of Fall speculations for the next thirteen centuries and more" (99).

35. On the Augustinian origin of Milton's depiction of the consequences of the falls of Satan and Adam, see C. A. Patrides, *Milton and the Christian Tradition* (Oxford: Clarendon P, 1966), 119–20. In a classic essay, Arthur O. Lovejoy, "Milton and the Paradox of the Fortunate Fall," *ELH* 4 (1937), 161–79, cites Augustine and his mentor St. Ambrose as among the earliest promulgators of the doctrine of the fortunate fall (171–74).

36. Manning, "Wordsworth's Intimations Ode," 534.

37. Manning, 538.

CHAPTER NINE. CONCLUSION

1. For the most thoroughgoing analysis of Wordsworth's contextualizations of the Ode in 1807 and 1815, see Manning, "Wordsworth's Intimations Ode," 539–40.

2. As Curtis points out, *The Orchard Pathway* did not appear as the heading of the introductory section of the work: *P2V*, 26–28. The separate title page for this section, with verses, may like the advertisement have fallen victim to printers' economies.

3. For an alternative understanding of Coleridge's designs in *Sibylline*

Leaves see Joseph A. Wittreich, Jr., "'The Work of Man's Redemption': Prophecy and Apocalypse in Romantic Poetry," *The Age of William Wordsworth*, ed. Johnston and Ruoff, 47–49.

4. Jerome J. McGann, *The Romantic Ideology: A Critical Investigation* (Chicago: U of Chicago P, 1983), 90.

5. Marjorie Levinson, *Wordsworth's Great Period Poems: Four Essays* (Cambridge: Cambridge UP, 1986), 95.

6. Levinson's arguments have been the subject of heated (and frequently unedifying) dispute at a number of scholarly meetings. My major major problem with her construction of the early stanzas of the poem is that it neglects the Ode's engagement with erotic as opposed to political pastoral, or perhaps fails to see that to the extent that the political is engaged, it is through the erotic. She cites Hazlitt's political elaborations of Wordsworth's Ode (83–84) but ignores his equally compelling erotic elaborations, on which see Robinson, *Radical Literary Education*, 159–164.

7. My concluding point echoes Arac, 54, in calling for increasing acknowledgement of the social rather than psychological materials of *The Prelude*.

Index